THE THEFT
OF A DECADE

THE THEFT OF A DECADE

How *the* Baby Boomers Stole *the* Millennials' Economic Future

JOSEPH C. STERNBERG

PUBLICAFFAIRS
New York

PublicAffairs
Hachette Book Group
1290 Avenue of the Americas, New York, NY 10104
www.publicaffairsbooks.com
@Public_Affairs

Printed in the United States of America
First Edition: May 2019

Published by PublicAffairs, an imprint of Perseus Books, LLC, a subsidiary of Hachette Book Group, Inc. The PublicAffairs name and logo is a trademark of the Hachette Book Group.

The Hachette Speakers Bureau provides a wide range of authors for speaking events. To find out more, go to www.hachettespeakersbureau.com or call (866) 376-6591.

The publisher is not responsible for websites (or their content) that are not owned by the publisher.

Print book interior design by Jeff Williams.

The Library of Congress has cataloged the hardcover edition as follows:

Names: Sternberg, Joseph C., author.
Title: The theft of a decade : baby boomers, millennials, and the distortion
    of our economy / Joseph Sternberg.
Description: First edition. | New York : PublicAffairs, [2019] | Includes
    bibliographical references and index.
Identifiers: LCCN 2018053192 (print) | LCCN 2018055305 (ebook) | ISBN
    9781541742383 (ebook) | ISBN 9781541742369 (hardcover)
Subjects: LCSH: Generation Y—United States—Social conditions. | Generation Y—
    United States—Economic conditions. | United States—Economic
conditions—1945– | United States—Social conditions—1945-
Classification: LCC HQ796 (ebook) | LCC HQ796 .S82684 2019 (print) | DDC
305.2—dc23
LC record available at https://lccn.loc.gov/2018053192

ISBNs: 978-1-5417-4236-9 (hardcover), 978-1-5417-4238-3 (ebook)

LSC-C

10 9 8 7 6 5 4 3 2 1

Contents

Taking a Bite Out of the Big Avocado of Life

THIS IS A BOOK ABOUT AVOCADOES.

A curious global debate erupted in 2017. Amid years' worth of complaints that young adults couldn't afford to climb onto the first rung of the property ladder, Australian businessman Tim Gurner told a television interviewer the solution was easy: eat a simpler breakfast. "When I was trying to buy my first home, I wasn't buying smashed avocado for $19 and four coffees at $4 each," he said on Australia's *60 Minutes*.[1] (In US dollars, around $15 per avocado and $3 per coffee.) Gurner—who was being featured on television in the first place because he's a fabulously wealthy property magnate in his mid-thirties who built his business from scratch—bemoaned the lack of a work ethic in younger would-be homebuyers who wanted to buy first houses in nice neighborhoods without sacrificing much in the way of fancy breakfast foods to save for a down payment.*

---

* Gurner wasn't the first person to highlight the avocado-youth-housing nexus. Credit for that goes to another Australian, Bernard Salt, who suggested in a tongue-in-cheek column in the *Australian Magazine* in October 2016 that young people could save more quickly for a home if they ate out less often (Bernard Salt, "Moralisers, We Need You!," *Australian Magazine*, October 15, 2016). Salt had previously coined the phrase "Goat's Cheese Curtain" to describe the boundary between trendy, hipster-infested inner cities where goat's cheese is a menu staple and the normal rest of the country. Why Australians have a particular fixation on the dining habits of the young remains a mystery.

1

The reaction was swift and furious. "Millennials have enough problems as it is. Must they give up avocado toast, too?" a *New York Times* article asked. That story went on to estimate that if young adults cut back their annual restaurant expenses to what their parents currently spend on eating out, it would still take 113 years for a young person to save up a 20 percent down payment on the median American home.[2] Presumably young people in the United Kingdom are slightly better off, because in that country an angry columnist calculated she'd need to forego avocado toast for only 100 years to save her down payment. And because that was in the left-wing *Guardian* newspaper, the writer also needed to point out sternly that "brunch has become a convenient scapegoat for structural inequality."[3] The *Los Angeles Times* figured that a young person would need to pass up on daily $19 avocado toast—and not spend money on any other breakfast, either—for around 15 years to save up a down payment on the median house in Los Angeles County.[4] Britain's *Independent* newspaper captured some of the irate social media reaction from Millennials who had taken to Twitter—where else—to vent about Gurner's suggestion: "'Stop buying avocado toast' is 2017's 'let them eat cake,'" said one. "I was gonna put a down payment on a house last year but then I spent $44,000 on avocado toast," tweeted another.[5]

Then came the reaction to the reaction. "Avocado toast, expensive hobbies, car payments and the other splurges hurt our finances in huge ways," personal-finance columnist Holly Johnson wrote in the *Indianapolis Star*. Johnson did some math of her own: "For example, ditch spending $20 on lunch and coffee on weekdays and you've got $100 per week and $400 per month to save. That's $4,800 [per year] to save for a home or throw towards those nagging student loans."[6] That theme reappeared in Britain in November, when a real estate agency concluded that if young couples stopped spending on coffee, gym memberships, vacations, eating out, new cellphones, and lottery tickets (really?!) for five years, they could in fact save enough for a down payment.[7] And maybe young people were putting a little too much emphasis on avocado after all.

A survey released only a few months after Gurner's firestorm found that one-third of British young adults rated the prospect of buying an unripe avocado by accident to be among their biggest worries.[8] Within roughly a week of Gurner's now-infamous interview, an Australian coffee shop invented the "avolatte"—a latte served in an avocado skin, combining in one bizarre product the two expensive vices that allegedly prevent the modern young adult from saving.[9] Just one month before Gurner gave his interview, an all-avocado restaurant had opened in Brooklyn, New York's bastion of the hip and the young.[10]

∞∞∞∞

The whole avocado thing neatly encapsulates the way we think and talk about Millennials. Gurner didn't literally mean that one could save for a down payment simply by giving the Starbucks or the vegan café a pass in the morning, even if we do all spend more than we realize on fancy coffee each year. But he *was* pretty direct in claiming today's young people are lazy. The bigger point of his avocado riff was his account of his intense work ethic when he was just starting out, working what sounds like eighteen-hour days to build a property empire. He argued that today's twenty-somethings have lost that element of get-up-and-go. They're not trying as hard as their elders did to get ahead in the world, and shouldn't be surprised when they don't enjoy material payoffs as a result.

This impression of youth work ethic is unfair to Millennials. But it's a pervasive attitude that seems intuitive to a lot of older adults and even many younger ones. And one reason so many older adults believe younger adults are spoiled is because in a way we are.* The material well-being of people in their late teens, twenties, and thirties today is better than for any generation in history at this point in their life cycle. More of us, who were born starting around 1980, have survived to an age where we can contemplate spreading avocado on toast. In the developed world, we've licked the childhood

---

* I'm a Millennial myself, having been born in 1982.

diseases—polio, measles, whooping cough, smallpox—that used to terrify the parents of the Baby Boom generation as they sent their children out to the playground or the public swimming pool. Almost every aspect of daily life is easier now than it was even twenty years ago, from doing homework (Google), to communication (iPhone), to entertainment (Netflix), even to hailing a taxi (Uber) or finding a mate (Tinder). Millennials are the first American generation in at least three not to grow up against the backdrop of a major war threatening its young men with mass conscription just as they enter adulthood.*

Much of this is the legacy of the Baby Boomers. The way we talk about the Boomers is just as skewed as the way we discuss their Millennial young adult children. Boomers get a bad rap, sometimes deservedly so, for their selfishness and frivolity, their spendthrift tendencies and their apparent fear of aging, their failure to think about the future. One author has even called them "a generation of sociopaths."[11] But the One Big Thing they've done right is to create a world for their children that is in many important ways more secure and more prosperous than the one they inherited, or than any previous generation could have imagined. The Boomers reduced or eliminated many of the threats that used to imperil young people— by curing diseases, installing airbags in cars, inventing new weapons to fight wars at lower risk to troops, and so much more. And other benefits are in store, too. The avocado uproar obscured what to an economist was one of Tim Gurner's more interesting observations: Baby Boomers will eventually pass to their children an enormous inheritance windfall in the form of the Boomers' own houses. Why aren't their kids a little more grateful?

The paradox for Millennials is that while daily life is now safer and more comfortable than ever before, long-term security feels much more elusive than it was for our parents, even as those parents didn't always have such an easy time either. We can have that

---

* For all that the wars in Afghanistan and Iraq—and more recently Syria—have dominated the news and our politics, to an extraordinary degree they have *not* impinged on the daily lives of the vast majority of young Americans.

avocado toast, or vegan granola, or a tall skinny chai latte, on our way to work. But that work is more likely to be a contract position with fewer benefits than our parents had. We can live among the bright lights, constant stimulation, and modern conveniences of the big city. But good luck affording our first house or apartment. We can stash away some spare change—perhaps from eating less avocado toast—in an online bank account whose balance we can check on our smartphones, but how much will we need for a comfortable retirement, and will we ever be able to save up *that* much spare change? We can inherit substantial property wealth from our parents' estates, but considering our parents' average life expectancies, we're unlikely to get our hands on that money when we really need it to buy a house, invest for our retirement, or put our own kids through college one day.

So both sides were right in the Great Avocado Battle of 2017. Millennials *are* spoiled in ways that baffle both our elders and ourselves. But we also are suffering economically, in ways that will have profound consequences. That paradox can, and should, be framed in a more controversial way: How is it that the Baby Boomers who are bequeathing their children such a comfortable today have also managed to steal those children's tomorrows out from under them? That's the story of this book.

Millennial Madness

First, though, a simple question with a surprisingly complex answer: What the heck is a "Millennial," anyway? There are scads of books and articles debating how to market to us in stores and online, and how to manage us in the workplace; what we like to watch on TV and at the movies, and where we like to live; and what we think about the society around us, and how we vote. We're variously described either as America's next "greatest generation" in waiting or as a bunch of pathetic snowflakes who will never make anything of ourselves or our country. Millennials ourselves seem unsure about whether we face the prospect of a difficult life or whether we're the luckiest generation in history. And we don't know whether we're victims of social and economic forces beyond our control or whether we're victims of our own bad decisions.

The one thing all these assessments have in common is that they never manage to agree with each other over what a "Millennial" is.* The contrast with the Baby Boom is instructive. That generation arose in a definable historical and social moment—between the end of World War II and the introduction of the birth control pill—and also was the product of an identifiable demographic phenomenon. For about twenty years after the war, for reasons that still aren't fully understood, America's fertility rate shot upward. At the height of the Baby Boom, the average American woman could expect to have three children over her lifetime—compared to an average of two in the generation before and the decades since.[12] The demographic expansion ran from 1946 until 1964 before dropping off, and those years have become the most widely accepted parameters for what constitutes a Baby Boomer.

Millennials don't have a clearly defined starting point of that sort.† We're more famous for a *midpoint*: the year 2000. The term "Millennial" traces back to pop historians William Strauss and Neil Howe, who coined it in the late 1980s to describe the preschoolers of that era—kids who would graduate high school in 2000. Millennials featured prominently in their 1991 book, *Generations: The History of America's Future, 1584–2069*, partly because at the time Millennials were the next big new thing and partly because Millennials would also make a good test case for Strauss and Howe's controversial theory that generations display identifiable common social traits and that different types of generational characteristics repeat in predictable cycles.[13]

Not that they were exactly prophetic. They did expect that Millennials would experience an economic crisis at some point in our

---

* They don't even always agree on what to call us. "Generation Y" sometimes shows up to describe Millennials, since we followed Gen X.

† Throughout this book, I'll include notes on the birth years researchers use to define different generations in their work.

early adulthood, as part of the authors' broader theory that such crises recur at predictable intervals.* Some of Strauss and Howe's predictions for what the Millennials would be like when we reached adulthood seem quaint now. Millennial "youth culture," they said, "will be more clean-cut and homogeneous" than anything since the 1930s, and teen sex would become more responsible both in the wealthy suburbs and in the inner cities.[14†] Their work and many similar theories over the years feed off of a general tendency to overstate the significance of "generations." To think about a generation as a world-historical force implies that its members share common experiences and, as a result, a common worldview that's different from the experiences and outlooks of their elders or their children. Strauss and Howe took things one step further by suggesting that generations were shaped not only by common experiences but by some innate natural cycle. But people and societies are much more complex than that, as the Boomers themselves demonstrate. Baby Boomers encompassed flower-power hippies, Vietnam War recruits and draftees, and even the yuppies of the early 1980s. Their young musical tastes ranged from Motown to disco to punk rock, depending on exactly when they were born, where they grew up, and their own individual preferences.

The alternative to talking about "generations" is the far more modest idea of a birth cohort, which emphasizes that often the only thing many members of a so-called generation share with each other is their age.[15] That is certainly true of American Millennials, who show the same remarkable diversity of ethnic and cultural backgrounds, religious views, economic status, and political views as every previous generation (or birth cohort) has—or more so.

---

* Although there's less to this cyclicality than their book made out: Major crises in the Anglo-Saxon world recur at eighty-five-year intervals, they note, except for one that occurred at a remove of eighty-seven years from the prior crisis, and another at ninety-nine years. And all five of the crises they describe exhibited substantially similar generational characteristics among their protagonists, except for the one—20 percent of the sample—that didn't. (William Strauss and Neil Howe, *Generations: The History of America's Future, 1584–2069* [New York: William Morrow, 1991], 86–92.)

† This is at odds with actual experience, which shows growing differences in social mores across socioeconomic and urban-rural divides.

Still, there is an identifiable Millennial cohort or generation simply as a matter of numbers.* Approximately sixty-two million Millennials were born in the United States between 1981 and 1996, the cutoffs the Pew Research Center has adopted for our cohort. That's more than the fifty-five million members of Generation X born between 1965 and 1980, but well off the seventy-six million births during the Baby Boom.[16] The Millennial birth boom coincides with the period when the largest number of Boomers were in their late twenties through their early forties. But the Millennial cohort is at best an echo of the Baby Boom. Boomer women didn't replicate their mothers' higher fertility rates. There are a lot of Millennials primarily because there are a lot of Boomers, not because each Boomer had a larger-than-usual number of children.

The number of Millennials born in the United States tells only part of the story, however. There were around seventy-one million Millennials living here as of 2018, compared to seventy-four million Boomers, and within a year Millennials will outnumber Boomers.[17]† Some studies, defining Millennials using slightly different birth years, estimate that we had overtaken Boomers even earlier.[18]‡ That's because we're a generation of immigrants. Some 15 percent of Millennials now residing in the United States were born somewhere else.§ That's not quite as high as the foreign-born proportion was for young adults in the middle of the large waves of immigration that crested in the 1910s, but it's close.[19] And in addition to those Millennials who are immigrants ourselves, many of us are the children of immigrants. Around 25 percent of Millennials speak a language other than English at home, compared to 10 percent of Boomers.[20]¶

---

* For simplicity, I'll use these terms interchangeably throughout the book.

† Using Pew's birth-year demarcations.

‡ This study defines Millennials as born 1981–1997.

§ Millennials born 1978–1993 and ages twenty to thirty-four in 2013.

¶ Boomers born 1946–1962; Millennials born 1981–1997. Note that some studies cited in this book will use nonstandard definitions for Boomers, too. Much government data, such as Census Bureau statistics, sort numbers based on the age of the respondent when the survey is taken, rather than cohort. For example, this survey focuses on data for individuals ages eighteen to thirty-four at the time the survey was performed.

Partly owing to that immigration trend and partly as a result of longer-running demographic transformations (including differences in birth rates among members of various ethnic groups who already were living in the United States), Millennials look very different from previous cohorts. As of 2015, around 56 percent of American Millennials were white, compared to 75 percent of Americans born before 1960.* Hispanic representation among Millennials has exploded, such that Hispanics now account for 21 percent of the Millennial population compared to 7 percent of Boomers when they were the same age in 1980.† The representation of Asians and African Americans among Millennials also has increased.[21] And that's only one factor that can make us tough to peg in a cultural sense. It's probably fair to say that Boomers shared more common cultural experiences with each other than had been the case for earlier generations. Their youth, which coincided with the proliferation of television, seemed to produce a single national culture to a degree that hadn't quite existed before. Millennials, in contrast, have come of age in an era of the internet, smartphones, video streaming, and a seemingly inexorable trend toward individualization in everything from music playlists on Spotify to targeted advertising on Google and Facebook.

The Crisis Generation

Yet there *is* something that binds Millennials together, even if it's not a character trait or clear-cut cultural tastes: an economic catastrophe. The one experience Millennial Americans all share is that our early adult years have been dominated by an economy that has failed us over and over again. The 2007–2008 global financial panic and ensuing Great Recession hit us at a particularly vulnerable moment in our economic lives, and since then we've had a decade stolen out from under us.

---

* Millennials born 1981–1997.

† Boomers born 1946–1962; Millennials born 1981–1997. These data compare ethnic composition in 1980 and 2015.

That crisis didn't match the 1929 stock market crash and Great Depression for sheer scale of economic destruction, but the events of 2007 and after were by far the most dire since the 1930s. And it has become a cruel joke for Millennials because at first it looked as if we'd escape the worst of the carnage. Take the housing market, whose downturn set the calamity in motion. Changes in house prices are hard to measure, since the housing market is both large and diverse, but by one plausible estimate, homes lost 33 percent of their value nationwide from the 2006 peak to the 2011 trough.[22] In the hardest-hit geographic areas, house prices fell far more. American households are estimated to have lost more than $7 trillion in housing equity during the crisis.[23] Millennials were mostly too young to have bought into the market—the biggest losers from this downturn were members of Gen X, who were most likely to have bought at the peak of the market and to own the least equity—and in theory a downward correction in prices could have given us a boost as we prepared to buy in the following years.

It was the same with the stock market, which started to swing wildly as the housing meltdown gathered pace. Between the stock market's peak in October 2007 and its trough in March 2009, the Dow Jones Industrial Average measuring the stock prices of America's bluest of blue-chip stocks lost 54 percent of its value. The S&P 500, a larger index of big companies, lost 57 percent between its peak and trough. And shares had a bumpy ride on the way down, with massive up-and-down swings from day to day for more than a year through the financial panic. This shouldn't have been a disaster for Millennials, since we were mostly too young to own shares at that point, and a down market might even have presented a buying opportunity.

But of course we didn't escape, because the crisis didn't stop there. Instead, these market gyrations triggered an economic disaster that has echoed for years. Wall Street couldn't cope. Banks had accumulated more and more securities whose value was tied to the mortgage market, as we'll see in greater detail in Chapter 4. When the housing market seized up, so did the banks. Three hundred twenty-two banks with assets totaling $641 billion failed between 2008 and 2010, compared to only a handful per year before the crisis period; bank bankruptcies would continue at a higher than usual rate until at least 2014.[24] And that was just the deposit-taking banks covered by the Federal Deposit Insurance Corporation. Investment banks, mortgage lenders, and insurers would suffer their own traumas. Some of Wall Street's most storied names—Bear Sterns, Lehman Brothers, Merrill Lynch—would disappear entirely or be absorbed by stronger rivals. So would newer upstarts that had nevertheless become household names in areas such as mortgage financing, Countrywide Financial being the largest. Fannie Mae and Freddie Mac—which, as we'll see, had played such an important role in the housing market before the crisis—were effectively nationalized.

This financial-and-housing pandemonium inevitably fed into the Main Street economy, as some businesses struggled to judge how quickly the economy might recover and others struggled to borrow from banks that were teetering on the edge. Gross domestic product (GDP), adjusted for inflation, shrank by around 4 percent from its 2007 peak to its 2009 trough.[25] Around 4.3 million individuals and 165,000 businesses filed for bankruptcy between 2009 and 2011, as the effects of the recession sank in, and personal bankruptcies in particular would remain elevated for several years after.[26] The overall unemployment rate shot up to 10.6 percent (not seasonally adjusted) at its peak in January 2010, a level not seen since early 1983.[27]

And when the economy did return to growth, it did so only very slowly. Annual GDP adjusted for inflation wouldn't recover to its precrisis level until mid-2011. That was years after the Great Recession officially ended in 2009, and a longer lag than the American economy had experienced after any previous recession during Millennials' lifetimes.[28] Even after recovering the ground lost in the recession, the economy hardly roared back to life. GDP growth averaged around 2 percent per year in the first five years of the recovery. This was unprecedented compared to previous recessions, when the economy had rebounded much more quickly, with growth rates topping 3 percent in the early years after the downturn.[29] One percentage point might sound undramatic, but it makes an enormous difference in an economy America's size—hundreds of billions of dollars in output that never happened. And because GDP growth compounds, the slow recovery put America on a permanently lower trajectory. Unemployment glided down only very slowly and was still around 6 percent five years after its peak. It wouldn't approach its prerecession low until late 2016.

This is definitely not what Millennials grew up expecting the economy to be like for us. Americans of all ages have been living with the aftermath of the Great Recession for so long that it can be easy to lose sight of the particular experiences of Millennials. So it's worth looking at the group of people born in 1982, the most millennial of Millennials who graduated from high school in spring 2000. This is a birth-year cohort I know well, since I'm part of it.

When we were in high school in the late 1990s, we could tell times were good. I grew up in Vermont, one of the poorer states in America on average, so it certainly didn't feel like a go-go era. But there was a sense that for people who worked hard enough, there would be opportunities. Those of us who were paying close attention might have noticed that America's transition away from a manufacturing-focused economy was accelerating (I will not claim to have understood this at the time myself), but we were young enough that we had time to prepare for other careers instead. The internet was coming into its own as an economic phenomenon. And in plenty of other ways that mattered, the economy was terrific. Such as the price of gas. When we Millennials started to get our driver's licenses in 1998, I could put more than half a tank of gas in my mom's emerald-green Plymouth Voyager minivan for $10 or less if I went to the right gas station. That didn't quite make up for having to drive an emerald-green Plymouth Voyager minivan all over town, but it helped.

Those of us who decided to skip college and go straight to work entered the labor force in spring 2000, when the late-'90s economy still was booming along. At that point, the unemployment rate was below 4 percent, a level not seen since the late 1960s.[30] These Millennials were more exposed to the labor market during the recession of the early 2000s, but in retrospect that downturn seems mild—a GDP contraction of 0.6 percent in inflation-adjusted terms and an unemployment high of around 6.5 percent that quickly started to fall again.[31] The rest of us went to college, graduating in 2004. By then the tech bubble had long since burst, and America had suffered the worst terror attack in its history on September 11, 2001. But while we may have felt some economic anxiety about our job prospects—to say nothing of the effects terrorism and the ensuing wars in Afghanistan and Iraq had on our general sense of security—it still felt as if things would work out for us in the end. The economy appeared to be rebounding from its post–dot-com and terrorism trough. It wasn't yet clear (as we'll see in coming chapters) that from that point forward America's postrecession recoveries would be "jobless," failing to re-create lost employment opportunities.

And sure enough, those of us older Millennials who had the good fortune to graduate earlier in the 2000s did enjoy a few reasonably good years. The 2004–2006 period was a boom. It felt as though most members of my graduating class from the College of William and Mary were landing on our feet in the working world. My first job was at a small quarterly magazine in Washington, DC, and although the pay was hardly glamorous (it took me months to save up the money to buy an Ikea dresser so I could store my clothes somewhere other than the floor), I got an above-inflation raise within the first year, and an even bigger pay bump when I moved into my second job. The only sour note was a property market that, especially in areas like DC, was so hot that it was clear ownership would have to wait for a few years. By late 2006, when I got a life-changing job offer to go work for the *Wall Street Journal* in Hong Kong, I'd managed to move far enough up the career-and-pay ladder to afford luxuries like occasional nights out, a growing collection of books, and a new set of pots and pans in the kitchen of my first solo apartment.

I was incredibly lucky, and so were the other Millennials born at the same time who followed roughly the same trajectory. Because by 2007—when we were just turning twenty-five and barely starting to hit some of our prime career-building years—the worst financial crisis since the Great Depression had started. We'd struggle to hold on for dear life as the crisis and ensuing Great Recession threatened our jobs and nascent prosperity. Those who were born just a few years after us would struggle to stay afloat at all. Millennials born after 1990—and many born in the years just before that—have only ever known one of the deepest recessions and the slowest post-recession recovery in American history during their working lives.

The Theft of a Decade

This book calls that phenomenon—the uniquely serious economic challenges Millennials have faced since 2008—the theft of a decade. It's important to be clear from the start about who stole what from whom, and how. The "how" is in some ways the easiest question to answer, although it will take the bulk of this book to dig into it in depth, and my conclusions may be challenging for both the political Right and the political Left.

Since 2008, Millennials have fallen victim to two separate but closely related economic problems. The first is a longer-term transformation in the American economy, and it isn't quite the transformation most people usually have in mind when this subject comes up.

We're used to thinking about America's economic evolution from a manufacturing powerhouse into a services titan. That change has preoccupied the Boomers for most of their own working lives. Going back to the 1970s, American factories already were starting to close, while those that remained had invested ever more heavily in automation. The "death of American manufacturing" is mired in controversy—by some measures manufacturing has declined steadily as a proportion of total GDP since the 1950s; by other measures it's holding more or less steady—but America still is very much an economy that produces physical things in addition to all those services.[32] And it's clear that the *nature* of American manufacturing has changed significantly, as has the nature of employment within manufacturing industries. This work has become progressively higher skilled and more productive, while many workers who couldn't keep up with the transformation (or, far more often, whose employers couldn't keep up) have struggled to navigate the new economy. Manufacturing's share of employment has fallen from above 30 percent in the 1950s to less than 10 percent now.[33]

Countless economists going back forty years or more have tried to dig into what's driving this transformation. Commonly cited culprits include technological advances, especially the computing revolution; foreign trade, especially with super-efficient industrial powerhouses such as Germany or Japan or low-wage behemoths such as China; US domestic tax policies and economic regulations; other policy failures such as deteriorating public education—you name it, someone has probably thought of it as an explanation for this switch. Yet it's important to note that while this particular transformation has been painful for many Americans, it's been good for many others. The broadening of the US economy to encompass more and more creative service industries has created unprecedented new career opportunities for Americans. It's safe to say that in twenty-first-century America, it is easier than it has been at any earlier time in human history for people to find their niches in the economy no matter what their precise mix of individual skills and interests.

But this book will argue that debates about the evolution of manufacturing and services have distracted from a much deeper transformation, which has also become especially problematic for Millennials. The way America thinks about investment—how we stimulate it, how we direct it, how we tax it, how we regulate it— has changed in important ways over the past thirty to forty years. We've developed a taste for quick but large returns at the expense of slower and steadier growth rooted in broad-based investment to make large numbers of workers and industries more productive.

We've focused more and more on the financial mechanics of the economy to create an appearance of economic growth, while missing the true significance of the fact that the American economy was becoming less well balanced—less productive than it could or should be in many areas, while new investment of both money and human energy was devoted to a relatively small number of industries, such as finance or tech.

This sounds like a theme that some economists and authors on the political Left have started to run with in recent years,* so I should be clear from the start that this is not an indictment of Wall Street, or "the finance industry," or "short-termism" among corporate managers, or excessive executive pay. The success of the American economy relies on our world-leading financial system, which does a better job than any of its competitors anywhere at funding innovation. One thing I've found striking as a journalist in Asia and Europe is how jealous foreign business leaders and politicians are—whether or not they admit it—of America's dense network of pension funds and institutional investors, investment banks, hedge funds, private equity, and venture capital. They recognize that these innovations have fueled what growth America has experienced over the past decade, and for many decades before that. Foreigners are in awe of the financial prowess we Americans so often disdain.

Rather, I'm going to argue that too often our *political* leaders have gotten in the way of the best parts of our financial web, and that this has gotten worse as Boomers of both political parties have progressively gained control of Washington. "Financialization," as critics describe the outsize role Wall Street plays in the American economy, didn't happen because cynical finance whizzes manipulated naïve politicians into letting the bankers get away with economic murder. Rather, Boomer politicians themselves understood

---

* To name just a couple, concerns about an out-of-control financial system form part of Steven Brill's explanation for American economic dysfunction in *Tailspin: The People and Forces Behind America's Fifty-Year Fall—and Those Fighting to Reverse It* (New York: Knopf, 2018). This also is the subject of journalist Rana Faroohar's *Makers and Takers: How Wall Street Destroyed Main Street* (New York: Crown Business, 2016).

the need to stimulate more investment on Main Street but chose problematic ways to do so. America's failure, which has become Millennials' acute crisis, is that politicians have steadily narrowed the range of investments that can be profitable for investors. The Boomers managed, mostly accidentally, to create an economy that rewards certain kinds of investment and punishes others. As we'll see, too often this has meant rewarding the kinds of financial activity that contributed to the 2007–2008 crisis and could yet cause another one and punishing financial activity that would invest in job creation and real economic growth on Main Street. Millennials as a cohort are paying the heaviest price yet for these decisions.

Our changing approach to investment has had a wide range of effects on the Millennials who emerged into this new economic universe. For example, the American economy has witnessed a growing wariness on the part of many companies to invest in industries or technologies that require substantial labor, and instead have shifted toward investments in labor replacement. This isn't new in economic history, but the scale and effects of these trends in the United States right now also aren't obviously inevitable and are leading our economy in new and often troubling directions. One consequence Millennials grapple with is a hollowing out of the job market, which can provide some work for very highly skilled individuals in the upper reaches of the economy and a lot of jobs in service industries at the bottom of the ladder, but which struggles to create jobs in the middle ranks in terms of skills and pay.

Another consequence of this transformation is that as companies invest less in their own workers, workers must invest in their own training and skills. Millennials have done so with sometimes reckless abandon. This is part of the explanation for our fetish for advanced education and the enormous debts we've taken on to go to school. And most spectacularly, especially in the 2004–2006 period, the American economy seemed to become a giant machine for diverting investment capital into housing—with dire consequences for Millennials that continue to this day, in the housing market and beyond.

This need not be a partisan issue. Many free-market conservative or classically liberal economists and commentators* are wary of many of the turns our economy has taken over the past generation—because too often these distortions have happened thanks to misguided policy decisions made in Washington, DC. One problem Millennials face in the labor market now is that for many years, Washington has leaned on the scales by using regulation to inadvertently make hiring workers in many potentially highly productive industries too expensive, while making investment capital cheaper than it otherwise would have been. The argument here isn't that the free market has failed, but that Washington has failed to let the free market work as it should. If there's a challenge for political conservatives in this, it's to recognize that for all the political successes Republicans have notched up since the 1980s, significant areas of the economy remained incompletely or improperly reformed.

Importantly, those failures feed directly into the second economic problem that has afflicted Millennials since the Great Recession: the Boomers who by then controlled Washington got the response to the financial crisis and its aftermath mostly wrong.

One of the surprises lurking throughout this book is the realization of just how little changed in the American economy after 2008. That's counterintuitive because the political battles that marked the aftermath of the crisis were so fierce—and continue to this day. President Barack Obama, elected by frightened and frustrated voters in the depth of the financial crisis, came into office with a left-wing, progressive vision of American governance that sparked passionate controversy. The fiscal-stimulus bill he and Democratic allies on Capitol Hill passed broke records for one-off spending legislation. The Affordable Care Act, also known as Obamacare, sought to remake a health care system that accounted for around one-sixth of annual economic output. He signed a sweeping overhaul of Wall Street regulations. Other policymakers took unprecedented steps—especially the Federal Reserve, which cut interest rates to levels they'd never been before and rolled out policies such

* I'm one of these, too.

as quantitative easing that most people have heard of but few fully understand. And then, eight years after the crisis, in 2016 Americans embarked on yet another big experiment—some might call it a huge gamble—with Donald J. Trump. We've never had a president like him, for better or for worse, and his administration alongside a Republican-controlled Congress for his first two years* refashioned America's tax code and overhauled economic regulations to an extent most Americans don't realize.

So in one sense it often feels like the decade since the crisis and Great Recession has been a period of nearly unprecedented experimentation in Washington, as politicians and policymakers have struggled to recover from an enormous financial panic and then put the economy back on track to generate growth and jobs. Yet as we'll see again and again throughout this book, the standard response from both political parties—now firmly under Boomer management—has been to double down on economic theories and policies leftover from when they were younger. This was clear in many of the Obama administration's labor policies, and it's apparent in a Trump trade policy that's straight out of the 1970s and '80s. It's true in some surprising ways of the Affordable Care Act† and also in some of Trump's ill-considered pronouncements on what he wishes the independent Federal Reserve would do with interest rates. The response to the crisis has been more of what didn't work before—more, in fact, of what created the conditions that led to the crisis in the first place. This fact is at the heart of much of what has gone wrong for Millennials entering the economy for the first time during that crucial decade.

And yes, it's all the Boomers' fault—even going back to the 1980s.

That's not always obvious. Although the first Boomer wasn't elected president until 1992, and Boomers didn't account for a

---

* Which are the last two years of the decade with which this book is concerned.

† Particularly in the way that the law emphasized pushing as many people as possible into health insurance provided by an employer—a way of providing coverage America has been struggling with for generations now.

majority of members of the House of Representatives until the 1998 midterm election, Boomers have played a decisive role in American life and our political process since they were much younger.[34] Ronald Reagan won the presidency in 1980 and 1984 with the support of large numbers of young voters—he effectively tied with Jimmy Carter for voters ages eighteen to thirty in 1980, and thumped Walter Mondale in that age bracket in 1984.[35] Those voters were Boomers, and their role in shaping what would prove to be such consequential election outcomes is evidence of the Boomer generation's political clout. Also in that era growing numbers of Boomers were climbing corporate ladders across the country and increasingly shaping business decisions, moving to Washington and state capitals and serving as the policy aides and junior staffers who influence so much of what happened in government, becoming journalists, teachers, and community leaders, and taking on many other influential roles. They may not have been fully in charge in an obvious sense until Bill Clinton moved into the White House in January 1993, but their political and policy perspectives started exercising a pull in American public life well before that.

They got a lot wrong in their day—a lot—and Millennials continue to pay the price for those mistakes. But one needs to have a certain respect, and even sympathy, for the Boomers. They didn't always have such a great run in the economy of their day. The industrial and investment transformations that started in earnest in the 1970s hit the Boomers just as they were launching their careers—the same point in the lifespan at which the Great Recession clobbered Millennials. The Boomers have spent most of their political lives—not to mention most of their careers—trying to manage the fallout from those transformations. Nowadays we tend to associate Boomers with a long-bygone era of suburbia, *Leave It to Beaver*, and the lifetime factory job. But that was their *youth*, and the main adult beneficiaries of that economy were the Boomers' own parents. By the time the Boomers were young adults, America was suffering through bouts of stagflation, urban riots, gas lines, and President Jimmy Carter's infamous "malaise" speech.

That doesn't let the Boomers off the hook for their bad decisions over the past generation, but it offers some important context. Many of their worst economic policy mistakes in the years since are best understood as failed attempts to grapple with the changes they were forced to live through. Their economic sin, and it's a big one, has been to fail to recognize soon enough that their fixes weren't truly working as hoped, and their insistence after the Great Recession on doubling down on what they thought they knew, instead of admitting that America needed to go back to the drawing board.

Meanwhile, if we're not going to go quite so hard on the Boomers—calling them a "generation of sociopaths" is probably a bit much—we also shouldn't go quite so easy on Millennials. Or more precisely, it's important to understand that not all Millennials are the same, and some have suffered differently or worse in the postcrisis economy than others have.

My husband and I enjoy sometimes watching the reality competition show *The Amazing Race*, in which teams of two rush around the world running or driving through exotic locales as they scurry to complete challenges that often resemble a scavenger hunt. One thing the show hammers home (and the source of much of the dramatic tension in each episode) is that not everyone has a very good sense of direction. Some contestants seem to be natural navigators, able to quickly decipher maps and orient themselves in foreign cities. Others, well, aren't. And more often than not, the team that misses a crucial exit on the highway or makes a wrong turn while hurrying through a Vietnamese fish market or a German castle ends up losing the game.

A similar divide is emerging among Millennials as we struggle to navigate an economy that has gone haywire over the past decade. Some of us are what I'd call navigator Millennials. Those Millennials have managed to intuit the tips and tricks they need to keep their bearings and figure out how to launch careers, pay off school debts, and maybe even buy a house despite all the challenges bad Boomer decisions have thrown at them. Often, of course, their families or communities have helped. This can take the form of direct financial aid to pay for college or put a down payment on a home. But probably more important is what sociologists think of as "social capital." That encompasses the skills their parents teach them, anything from character traits such as perseverance to coaching on navigating a collaborative white-collar office job to how to pick a good credit-card deal. It includes the expertise of the guidance counselors at better high schools in terms of gaming selective college-admissions processes. And don't forget the social connections these Millennials build up in their neighborhoods and schools, which help launch them into internships and jobs.

But others of us lack those advantages. It's not quite right to say these Millennials lack a natural sense of direction, but they're missing a map that would help them find their way through an education system, labor market, housing market, and society in general that all have been reshaped—or deformed—by the Great Recession. Sociologists have started tackling this problem of social capital and the fact that some people seem to be losing it. The reasons are many and complex, and that's not what this book is going to be about. But it's an important backdrop to much of the economic discussion that will follow here. One consequence of the ways in which our economy has evolved, and of the ways that this evolution has accelerated since the financial crisis, is that it is becoming harder and harder for Millennials to navigate without a map.

This can have significant implications for understanding what's going wrong for us. For example, don't automatically pity the Millennial who has graduated from college with a master's degree in English and $100,000 in debt. There are very few of us who labor under that sort of burden—fewer than 5 percent of all student-loan borrowers. And the vast majority of that small minority who do end up in that trap are navigator Millennials. They have a lot of debt today, but they also have an education with brand-name cachet, immense social capital, a lot of personal connections in the academic and working worlds, and many other advantages that give them the wherewithal to boost their earnings over time.

Rather, the crisis of student debt is among mapless Millennials—students who borrowed "only" $15,000 for a degree they thought would yield a higher-paying job but who either weren't able to complete the degree or discover they misjudged how the labor market would reward their education. Those Millennials don't have a wealth of parental experience in navigating a complex job market to tap, or a lot of tony connections from school to ease a path into a career. They've just got the debt and no clear avenue available for paying it off.

These mapless Millennials are some of the biggest victims of the Boomer theft of a decade.

Once Upon a Time . . .

There have been many disasters worse than the Great Recession. The Babylonian conquest of Jerusalem, the collapse of the western Roman Empire, the Black Death, and the World Wars of the twentieth century all come to mind. It pays to keep some perspective. Unlike so many of those natural or historical disasters, we're going to have a chance to try to fix our own disaster soon. Many of our ills over the past decade have resulted from political and policy choices, not impersonal forces of nature or history. That means that, as we Millennials reach the point in our lives where we're finally voting in larger numbers, holding political office, and shaping our economy from the grassroots up, we're going to have a chance to change course. And we'll be responsible to ourselves and our own children if we fail. We need to understand what has happened to us over the past decade so we can make better decisions over the coming decade.

Put a different way: we need to get our facts straight.

Millennials are in search of explanations for what has happened to us over the past decade, and we will reward politicians, parties, or movements that can offer a plausible story about the crisis, the recession, and the way forward. We're not offering our party loyalty; we're demanding answers.

We've already figured out what didn't, and doesn't, work: the big idea that the Boomers have followed for most of their political lives. This idea is an economic centrism that holds that one can meld the power of the state with the power of the market to deliver both prosperity and economic security. This centrism has taken many forms over much of the Boomers' lifetimes, among both Republicans and Democrats. It's the type of Republican neoconservatism that teaches one can use the insights of the markets to deliver better government services such as education or entitlements, and the Democratic "third way" espoused by Bill Clinton that would use the government to try to guide the market toward specific outcomes such as better wages or more investment in productive high-tech industries. Neither party has always been entirely comfortable with it, and some politicians—Ronald Reagan and Barack Obama, for example—have pulled further away from the center than others. But the Boomers in this sense mostly thought they could have it all: the security of a government looking out for them and the prosperity only a free market can provide. This idea is embedded in a lot of the bad Boomer decisions this book will highlight.

That system seemed to work for a while, but over the past decade Millennials have confronted its failings and then some. Those include many of the distortions we'll encounter throughout this book.

Our lingering uncertainty on what will truly work for us is why it's so important that we look back over the past decade and make a serious effort to understand what has happened to us, and to the economy. It's not about feeling sorry for ourselves, or cataloging all the mistakes Boomers made that have backfired to our detriment—although that's necessarily a big part of this story. Rather, my goal is to tell a story of the way the post-2008 decade was stolen from Millennials so that we can demand better of ourselves in the future. Even a decade on, we still don't fully understand where we are or how we got here. It's time for us to start figuring it out.

CHAPTER 1

The Young and the Workless

IT WAS THE BLOG POST HEARD 'ROUND THE WORLD, *THE* VIGNETTE THAT SEEMED to encapsulate everything everyone thinks is wrong with Millennials. "I Was Fired from My Job for Writing a Proposal for a More Flexible Dress Code," the headline read. In 2016, a Millennial wrote in to the popular workplace advice blog Ask a Manager, run by Alison Green:

> I was able to get a summer internship at a company that does work in the industry I want to work in after I graduate. Even though the division I was hired to work in doesn't deal with clients or customers, there still was a very strict dress code. I felt the dress code was overly strict but I wasn't going to say anything, until I noticed one of the workers always wore flat shoes that were made from a fabric other than leather, or running shoes, even though both of these things were contrary to the dress code. . . .
>
> I spoke with my manager about being allowed some leeway under the dress code and was told this was not possible, despite the other person being allowed to do it. I soon found out that many of the other interns felt the same way. . . . We decided to write a proposal stating why we should be allowed some leeway under the dress code. We accompanied the proposal with a petition, signed by all of the interns (except for one who declined to sign it) and gave it to our managers to consider. . . . It was mostly about the

footwear, but we also incorporated a request that we not have to wear suits and/or blazers in favor of a more casual, but still professional dress code.[1]

They were all fired the next day.

The intern was writing in surprise, or rather "shock," that this had happened despite her well-written, well-reasoned petition. Many of the blog's readers were shocked, too—at the intern's nerve organizing a petition against an office dress code. Soon this poor intern's question had ricocheted around the internet. It became yet another morality tale about snowflake-y Millennials failing to understand how the professional world works. The post seemed to speak to stereotypes about coddled Millennial coworkers who don't understand the importance of showing up in the office early and staying late, of paying dues by doing menial tasks, or of showing initiative rather than waiting for instructions—and who seem to require constant emotional validation.

But was that really what was going on here? Green herself thought not. Her initial reply to the intern was stern but fair. Of course the interns had been out of line. Yet as the blog post exploded across the internet, Green appended a reminder to readers of all ages atop the now infamous question:

> This situation is not about "young people today." The letter-writer's generation is far from the first to bridle at dress codes or misunderstand office culture or start out with little knowledge of how things work in offices. This is about being young and new to the work world, not about what generation they belong to. Most of us made plenty of mistakes when we first started work—I certainly did. So please go a little easier on this person.[2]

Green was right. Many commentators, particularly among the Boomer and Gen X cohorts, have developed a skewed view of that new species, the Millennial at work. The premise so often is that the young generation is different from the old in some fundamental way, that somehow Boomers (and Gen Xers) were just better equipped in their youth to enter the world of work. And this perception has serious implications for a discussion about the topic of this book: the theft of a decade of productive work opportunities from Millennials. What, a Boomer might ask, has my generation really "stolen" from a cohort whose biggest complaint seems to be a shortage of organic chai lattes in the office nap room? Maybe rather than being victims of a bad economy, Millennial workers have never had it so good.

Yet Millennials truly are entering the workforce under much tougher conditions than their Boomer parents faced. That's not to say the labor market ever worked perfectly for the Boomers— far from it, in fact. But rather than leaving the economy in better shape for their children than they found it themselves, Boomers made it worse. Millennials will probably have to live with the consequences of this aspect of the theft of a decade for many more decades to come.

Our Brave New Working World

If you're a Millennial in 2019, this really is the best of times to be in the job market. It's also the worst of times.

The good news is really, really good. Millennials have a lot of different kinds of jobs available that didn't exist fifty years ago—or ten. List-obsessed *U.S. News and World Report* has started publishing a list of the jobs Millennials* might find most desirable,† and the remarkable thing about it is how diverse it is.[3] The magazine's most highly recommended Millennial job is web developer, of course. But dental hygienist, mechanical engineer, and insurance sales (yes, really) also make the list. Many of these job roles have existed for

---

* Born 1983–1997.

† It's a slightly patronizing list because rather than directly asking Millennials what jobs they'd like to do, *U.S. News* surveyed Millennials about what they look for in a job and then developed a list of jobs that best match the characteristics Millennials say they seek. But this method does filter out Millennials' own biases about work to show that plenty of traditional jobs, in their modern form, can satisfy Millennial career goals.

decades or more, but not in their current form. Cartographer is on the list, but the magazine is careful to note that modern cartographers aren't drawing just any old maps. Millennial cartographers need to be able to manipulate satellite- and light-based imaging technologies to develop high-quality maps and surveys that will be useful to a range of high-tech industries. The category of "translator and interpreter" speaks (pun intended) to the advancing globalization of the economy and its workforce—a trend of which American Millennials are simultaneously products and beneficiaries.

This theme—"old" jobs transformed into new jobs to which Millennials are especially well suited—repeats when you look at other data. Financial consulting website SmartAssets looked at professions in America that have the highest concentrations of Millennial workers based on data from the US Bureau of Labor Statistics.* Top of the list of Millennial-heavy jobs is statistician, nearly 45 percent of whom are Millennials.[4] Little wonder, given the growth of "big data." Parsing the data a different way reveals what proportion of Millennial workers are in each occupation the government measures. I used my own Millennial data-analysis skills on the Current Population Survey for 2017 to do just that.[†5] Roughly 35 percent of Millennials are in management or professional (read: white-collar) jobs, such as marketing or accounting. And in some of these fields, Millennials already outnumber workers older than thirty-five—news reporting being a notable example that also speaks to Millennials' growing influence in politics. The 11 percent of Millennials in blue-collar or manual work are seeing the effects of economic and technological change, too: another field where Millennial workers outnumber older employees is installation of solar panels.

Those solar-panel-installing Millennials point to another quirk to bear in mind while analyzing these career data. A lot more economic transformation lurks beneath the numbers than meets the

---

* Born 1982–1991.

† I ran some calculations in an Excel spreadsheet and expanded the net to include Millennials born 1983–1997.

eye, because these days "conventional" jobs are anything but. A "lawyer" may actually be a specialist freelance lawyer reviewing records ahead of securities litigation, or an architect may specialize in a single type of retail store, or a marketer might develop social media thought-leadership strategies, or a human resources specialist could design highly technical advanced-training programs.

This kind of job specialization almost certainly intersects with Millennial attitudes toward work and careers in important ways. When we live in a world where seemingly anyone can find a job for their niche, why shouldn't we aim for personal satisfaction in addition to a paycheck? Millennials who have started to establish careers—an important caveat we'll revisit shortly—are more likely than our Baby Boomer parents or even our Gen X older cousins to say we expect a job that's fulfilling and fun. One representative study of more than ten thousand Millennials globally found that 57 percent ranked a "positive workplace culture" as "very important" when choosing a job—compared to 51 percent who considered financial rewards and benefits that significant.*[6] We prefer to work for employers we perceive as ethical, in jobs we view as contributing to society.

We also have what to older ears can sound like some peculiar ideas about our relationships with our bosses—because we don't want "bosses" in the traditional sense. We want mentors or coaches. That's probably the origin of the perception a lot of older workers seem to have that Millennials are bizarrely needy in the office, demanding frequent emotional validation from their supervisors and colleagues. Read between the lines of detailed Millennial surveys, and it becomes clear that what we're really after is training, and lots of it. A theme that emerges over and over in books such as *Not Everyone Gets a Trophy: How to Manage the Millennials* is that Millennials have a voracious appetite for new challenges and new know-how.[7] Much of the generational conflicts that make it into watercooler chatter and workplace blogs about "presumptuous" Millennials involves young adults aching to dive into the deep end in their companies, but not having been given enough context

---

* Born 1983–1994.

to know how to make a genuine difference. Boomers, rejoice! We don't want you to tell us how wonderful we are. We want you to tell us how to get better at our jobs.

And yet this rosy picture is only half of the story. For too many Millennials, the wide array of job opportunities that exists in theory is just that, a theory. The Bureau of Labor Statistics again offers some insight into what's going on, by looking at two key indicators: the unemployment rate and the labor-force participation rate. The unemployment rate shows the percentage of people who want to find a job but can't, and throughout the post-2008 decade the unemployment rate for young workers has been higher than for the population as a whole. In October 2009, when the overall unemployment rate reached its Great Recession peak of 10 percent, the unemployment rate for people ages twenty-five to thirty-four (born 1975–1984, so the youngest Gen Xers and oldest Millennials) was 10.6 percent, and the unemployment rate for the bulk of Millennials then in the workforce (ages twenty to twenty-four, with birth years from 1985 to 1989) was 15.8 percent. Only in mid-2018, a decade after the Great Recession, did the unemployment rate for those ages twenty-five to thirty-four approach parity with the unemployment rate for the overall labor force.

And that unemployment situation is actually worse than it looks, because fewer young adults are trying their luck with job hunting at all. The other key piece of data is the labor-force participation rate: the percentage of people of a given age who either are working or have made some effort to find work in the recent past, excluding those who are in school (or prison). The long-term trend since the mid-1980s has been a decline in labor participation for people ages twenty to twenty-four as college attendance has become more common, and an increase in the labor participation rate for people ages twenty-five to fifty-four as economic growth recovered from its 1970s malaise and more women entered the workforce. But since 2008, the gap between labor participation for the twenty to twenty-four set and the twenty-five to fifty-four cohort has expanded.

From a 6-percentage-point gap in the 1990s—when typically around 84 percent of older people were working compared to 78 percent of young twenty-somethings—the gap widened to nearer 8 percentage points in the 2000s. And since the Great Recession, the gap has expanded to 11 percentage points.[8]

Some portion of this trend is understandable, given that our economy is transforming into one that will require ever more skills. It makes sense that a growing proportion of young people will delay entering the working world so they can boost their skills first by obtaining a college degree or some other form of advanced training. But a *sudden* change like this is suspicious—a cliff edge on a graph that doesn't have a natural explanation. And in this case, we should suspect there's less to the education boom than meets the eye. There's growing evidence that more people are obtaining more education than they need for their jobs once they find work. It's likely that Millennials have gone to, stayed in, or gone back to school primarily because they couldn't find the kinds of jobs they wanted. And as we'll see in Chapter 3, they're paying an enormous cost to do so. This set of Millennials also has a rather different attitude toward workplace satisfaction than the fully employed Millennials in the surveys a few pages ago. Global temping firm ManpowerGroup surveyed a pool of Millennials that included thousands of its own temp-agency workers, a cohort who tend to be more precariously employed or underemployed relative to their level of education and skills. Those Millennials' top workplace hopes and dreams? Money and job security.[9]

Speaking of underemployment, there's another way in which the already dispiriting data about Millennial employment could mask an even bigger problem. Those numbers don't fully capture Millennials who are working for low or no pay in internships. No one knows exactly how many interns there are at any one moment—estimates for a typical summer intern season might range between one and two million. It's also impossible to say how many of those are unpaid, although some experts peg the proportion at around half.[10]

This is the one area of the labor market that most confuses and infuriates Millennials.* A first-order problem is separating the "good" internships from the "bad." The former category captures internships that are paid, that allow interns an opportunity to do some substantive work, and that have some realistic prospect of leading to full-time employment because the company uses the internship program as a means of spotting and nurturing talent. But there also are countless bad internships out there—unpaid, offering the "interns" little insight into the real work of the employer beyond fetching coffee and running off photocopies, and with no plausible path into a full-time role at the company. These aren't internships so much as they are unpaid, entry-level grunt work. Millennials often have felt compelled to do this sort of work anyway because it seems like the only path onto a career ladder, or because no other paid employment opportunities were available.

So the reality Millennials face as we enter our early middle age is that we've inherited a fabulous job market—so long as we have in-demand skills *and* can get a job *and* can get paid for it.

Polar Opposites

To get a handle on why the job market for Millennials is so complicated, it's important to step back and take a broader look at what's happened to the American job market overall during the past decade. The key fact about the Great Recession is that the pain of job losses wasn't evenly distributed. And the fact that not all jobs were equally at risk of being axed during the Great Recession has had a profound effect on Millennials, because it turns out the sort of jobs

---

* I have to confess to a certain amount of confusion on this myself. In 2010, a colleague at the *Wall Street Journal* and I wrote an op-ed about how we had benefited earlier in our careers from opportunities to take unpaid internships. Those "jobs" had given us a foot in the door in a competitive field, and had reduced the element of financial risk for employers in hiring us temporarily. I still believe that argument was correct as far as it went, but with the benefit of more experience and knowledge I'd wonder why it is that employers are now more reluctant to take risks on training *paid* entry-level employees than they used to be—a subject for Chapter 2.

we've been vying for as new entrants to the labor market were the most exposed, directly or indirectly, to the downturn.

The headline numbers are well known by now: from a low of 4.4 percent in May 2007, months before the recession started, the unemployment rate skyrocketed to 10 percent by October 2009.[11] But beyond that fact, much of what people think they know about the labor market turns out to be wrong. To start, the jobs that were most at risk were mid-skilled jobs—those in what used to be the fat middle of the job market. This is the heart of the working woes Millennials have faced over the past decade.

One way to measure this is to look at losses or gains in jobs relative to what those jobs pay, since wages typically track the general level of skill required for a given job. Jobs in the middle range of the labor market got creamed during the recession. Roughly 60 percent of net job losses between early 2008 and early 2010 were concentrated in mid-wage jobs paying between around $27,000 and around $40,000 (in constant 2011 dollars) per year.* A bit more than 21 percent of net job losses in the recession fell into the lower-pay grouping, and a bit less than 19 percent of net losses hit higher-paying jobs.[12] The share of mid-wage jobs as a proportion of total employment shrank between 2007 and 2013 as a consequence of the Great Recession.[13]

This phenomenon is an outgrowth of significant changes over the past generation in the kinds of skills the job market rewards and the kinds of tasks employers require people with those skills to do. Economists have studied this by dividing jobs between "routine" roles that mainly involve performing functions that are relatively mechanical or that require following specific rules (such as working on an assembly line, data entry, or some aspects of bookkeeping); nonroutine manual jobs such as truck driving or customer service in a retail shop; and nonroutine "cognitive" jobs such as marketing.[14]

---

* The study from which these data are taken, by the National Employment Law Project, classifies jobs based on hourly wages and defines mid-range jobs as those paying between $13.53 and $20.66 per hour in 2011 dollars. To arrive at a rough yearly estimate for a full-time employee, I multiplied those figures by 40 hours per week, and assumed 50 working weeks in a year.

Traditionally, routine jobs encompassed a wide range of clerical and blue-collar work that required some training or education but not a prohibitive amount—and jobs in which young workers especially might acquire skills that would allow them to move up the ladder over time. Those jobs have borne the brunt of recent recessions. By one estimate, nearly 12 percent of routine jobs disappeared during the Great Recession. All in all, those routine jobs accounted for 94 percent of the job losses during the recession.[15]

This isn't a new phenomenon, but it has been a surprise to economists. It's now clear that routine jobs in the *middle* of the skills-and-wage spectrum have accounted for well over 90 percent of job losses in recessions at least going back to the 1970s.[16] But it wasn't supposed to be like that. For decades, economists, commentators, and politicians had assumed that the lowest-skilled, lowest-paid jobs would be the most vulnerable to job losses both during recessions and in normal economic times—because the lowest-skilled jobs would be easiest for machines to take over. Thinking about jobs not in terms of the skills they require but rather in terms of whether they're routine or rote offers the answer. The demand for the highest level of skills speaks for itself. But at lower levels of skills, you end up in customer-service-oriented professions such as health care aide work, child care, or a lot of retail settings. Maybe some of those jobs could be replaced by robots one day in theory (robots already are taking on some of the functions of nurses, and not only in Japan), but consumers mostly want to deal with human beings.*[17] Sociologists have put their own spin on this by distinguishing between "caring" jobs and other forms of low-wage work to help explain which jobs exactly are vulnerable to technological change and which aren't.[18]

---

* Note how even in a "rote" role within the retail industry—cashiers—machines are only partially replacing human labor. At most supermarkets I've ever shopped in, in the United States or in Britain, the lines for registers staffed by human cashiers are generally as long as the lines for self-checkout machines. Clearly a nontrivial number of consumers are still prepared to sacrifice some time in exchange for interacting with a live person.

This approach helps to explain several important phenomena that have become crucial for Millennials. First, since the recession of the early 1990s, these lost routine jobs haven't come back during economic recoveries. Routine jobs kept disappearing even after the Great Recession formally ended: another 2.3 percent were lost in the two years after the American economy tipped back into positive growth in 2009.[19] And second, this form of "jobless recovery"—an economic rebound in which continuing losses of routine jobs prevent the total number of jobs created from rising appreciably—reached full flower just as Millennials started entering the workforce.

This trend has affected American workers of all ages. But it has affected different generations differently—and Millennial young adults are getting the shortest end of an already short stick. Age has something (although not everything) to do with both skill level and pay. Within a given profession, the youngest workers are typically the least skilled, and the oldest tend to be the most skilled—the best able to combine education with long personal experience in the field to accomplish nonroutine job tasks. Younger workers take up entry-level jobs with which to start building their skills, but many entry-level jobs often have a strong whiff of the routine or rote task about them.

The hollowing out of the middle of the market is pushing older mid-tier workers back down the ladder, cutting off the rungs young people traditionally used to ascend their own career ladders—and has pushed a lot of Millennials completely off of any career ladder at all. Younger workers would have a leg up if the only thing employers cared about was finding warm bodies to do low-skill jobs cheaply—since younger workers are generally less skilled but cheap. But what employers increasingly care about, even in "low-skilled" jobs, is finding workers who are able to perform nonroutine tasks well. Older workers, with more life and career experience, will often have an advantage. No wonder that when economists David Autor and David Dorn looked at the age distribution within hollowing-out professions, they found that for each percentage

point that a particular job role's share of total employment fell between 1980 and 2005, the average age of the people doing that job
increased 0.78 years. And this was after accounting for the fact that
the aging of the bulging Baby Boomer bracket was pushing the
labor force as a whole older and older.[20]

There's a benign explanation for part of that trend. Young adults
are savvy when it comes to sniffing out which fields are thriving and
which are dying. If it's becoming clear a particular industry is am-
bling off into the sunset, fewer new workers will want to start their
careers in it. But Autor and Dorn's research also yielded an omi-
nous discovery for Millennials: by studying geographic areas where
routine jobs had been the dominant form of employment, the
economists were able to estimate where workers of different ages
went when routine jobs started to disappear. They concluded that
most older workers (age thirty and above) who left mid-tier jobs
took lower-skilled, lower-paying positions instead. And while some
younger workers were able to shift upward into the high-paying,
high-skilled, nonroutine job echelon, twice as many younger workers tended to shift into low-skilled, low-paying employment, too—
a level of the job market where they now had to compete with older
workers with more job experience.[21]

One manifestation of this trend is a startling shift Millennials have experienced acutely: it increasingly pays to be old. One
study compared changes in median wages over time for men ages
twenty-five and thirty-four and between forty-five and fifty-four.*
Whereas older men tended to earn about 4 percent more than their
younger counterparts in 1950, older men earned 11 percent more
than younger men in 1970, and as of 2011 earned a whopping 41
percent more. The theory is that companies investing in technology
to replace workers find it relatively easier to replace younger workers
with machines, and younger workers then get pushed down the jobs

---

* Focusing on men makes it easier to compare changes over time since their
labor-force participation has been higher over the twentieth and twenty-first centuries, whereas women's labor participation only started to increase significantly in the
last quarter of the twentieth century.

ladder into lower-skilled, less productive jobs as a result.[22] Using the same Census and Bureau of Labor Statistics Data, I ran similar calculations for other years after the Great Recession and found that despite some improvement, older workers still get a bigger share of the pie: as of 2016, older workers still earned 35 percent more than younger workers.[23] These are remarkable, and depressing, findings considering the substantial efforts Millennials have made—and the expenses they've racked up—to make themselves more marketable to employers by improving their education and skills.

Another piece of indirect evidence for the claim that older, more experienced workers squeezed Millennials out of the job market is that companies during the Great Recession became more demanding about the prior job experience they expected job applicants to have. A major study of online job postings found that in metropolitan areas hit hardest by recessions, the number of job ads requiring a minimum level of prior experience increased, to 52 percent from 32 percent. Although most of that increase came from employers seeking between zero and three years of experience (to 24 percent from 13 percent), this still signals that employers felt they could expect applicants to walk in the door with some prior experience already.[24] That study didn't look specifically at the consequences of this transformation by age cohort, but one implication is that new job seekers were especially vulnerable to getting squeezed out by more experienced workers.

Declining job openings in general and increasing skill requirements led to another worrying trend that afflicted Millennials in the rapidly polarizing post–Great Recession labor market: we didn't change jobs as much as young adults usually do, because we weren't confident we'd end up keeping a new job if the employer downsized. Young workers are particularly prone to job hopping. It's how they figure out what they're interested in and what they're good at, how they start acquiring skills and work experience, and how they move up the salary ladder, given that the biggest wage jumps come from finding a new job rather than waiting for your current employer to give you a raise. That makes it a problem that the total number of people voluntarily quitting a job fell year-on-year in 2007, 2008, and 2009, and didn't return to its pre–Great Recession peak until 2016.[25]

Comparing this figure to what economists know about the different tendencies of different age groups to change jobs, by one count Millennial young adults account for two-thirds of the shortfall between actual job creation after the Great Recession and the jobs that would have been created if the economy had continued growing at the same pace as before. Put another way, Millennials between 2009 and 2013 missed out on some fifty-five million job opportunities they otherwise might have been able to hop between on their path to a stable career.[26]

All of these data points paint a picture of a jobs ladder that effectively collapsed for Millennials after 2008. That ladder is exactly what it sounds like—within a given profession, some jobs are better than others because they pay more, offer more stability, open more opportunities for promotion, or carry more prestige. Economists tend to assume that larger employers are "better" because data consistently show they pay more. And some studies comparing the size of the company to the age of its workers show how this job ladder relates to age. A recent analysis of Canadian companies and workers, for example, found that the median age (the point where half the company's workers are older and half are younger) for companies with 20–99 employees was 40.5 years, compared to a median age of 41.3 years for employees at companies with 100–499 workers and 42.6 years for the largest companies with 500 or more workers.* What's more, the youngest employees within large companies tended to be noticeably older than the youngest employees at smaller companies. The top age for the youngest 10 percent of the workers at smaller companies was 31.9 years, compared to 36 at the largest companies.[27]

---

* The researchers found that the median age of workers at the very smallest companies, with one to nineteen employees, was forty-two years, a fact they attributed to the higher likelihood that this group of companies would include sole proprietorships established by older entrepreneurs.

In some counterintuitive ways, this ladder traditionally worked reasonably well for younger workers even in recessions. Larger companies would hire more than small companies do when the economy was growing and the unemployment rate was low— because large companies could afford to poach relatively scarce workers from smaller firms. But during and immediately after recessions, small companies would do a disproportionate share of new hiring because when more people are unemployed, more people are willing to work for the lower wages smaller companies can afford to pay.

Yet after 2008, this youth-friendly trend reversed. The most complete study on this question to date found that hiring at firms of all sizes essentially froze during and in the immediate aftermath of the Great Recession—even at the smaller companies that had weathered previous recessions relatively well. And as a result, the rate at which employees left one job to jump directly to the next also plunged. It became harder for workers who were on the ladder to move upward, and it became harder for workers who weren't yet on the ladder—including Millennials—to jump on at all.[28]

These trends could hamper Millennials' earnings for decades. One of the most widely cited analyses in this vein found that when comparing white men (for simplicity's sake) who graduated from college between 1979 and 1989, those who graduated during the early-1980s recession still were paid less fifteen years later than cohorts who graduated during better times. In the first year of work, each 1-percentage-point increase in the national unemployment rate caused new-graduate wages to fall as much as 6 or 7 percent. And even fifteen years later, a 1-percentage-point increase in unemployment during the graduation year was holding down wages by around 2.5 percent.[29] Put another way, if you graduated when the unemployment rate was 7 percent, you'd expect to earn around 6 percent less in your first year of work than someone who graduated when the unemployment rate was 6 percent—$47,000 per year compared to a luckier, year-older graduate who started at $50,000. And a decade and a half later, you'd still be earning on average 2.5 percent less.

Another study, based on Canadian data, found that graduating into a typical recession—where the unemployment rate was 5 percentage points higher than normal—led to 9 percent lower earnings in the first year. Although those graduates eventually evened the score after ten years, they never made back the money they lost early in their careers. Someone who graduated into a recession would likely earn around 5 percent less in total over his lifetime than his luckier peers.[30] One of the big causes for this earnings lag that both studies flagged was a tendency to find work at smaller, less-well-paying companies, *and* a need to stay in those jobs for longer.

These polarization trends challenge a lot of the conventional wisdom about the working world that Boomers tried to pass on to their Millennial children. That wisdom was that as rapid technological change threatened to displace growing numbers of workers, the first workers to get the ax would be those with the lowest level of education and skills. The solution looked obvious: focus on obtaining more education and training to land a white-collar job that would be less prone to technological replacement. That did turn out to work for workers at the top of the skills ladder. But for everyone else, an alarming pattern would start to emerge later in the 1990s: mid-skill *white-collar* jobs were vulnerable to hollowing out, too. The software-and-telecommunications revolution of the 1990s made it possible for companies to "mechanize" many functions that previously had been performed by mid-skilled clerical workers, or to hire far-away outsourcing firms to do those jobs more cheaply. No one, it turns out, is safe from the polarization of the labor market.

Surrender, Dorothy

And what's remarkable is that we Millennials have been told for years that we shouldn't think this is all that remarkable. Instead, we've been told since we were in college to expect that fewer and fewer of us will genuinely be able to succeed.

Boomers and Gen Xers usually try to put a more positive spin on it, of course, but that's really the message. Richard Florida's 2002 book *The Rise of the Creative Class* was published just as the oldest Millennials were entering the work force or picking their college majors. Its first sentence said it all: "This book describes the emergence of a new social class." The creative class of the title, which Florida estimated comprised more than 30 percent of America's workforce at that time, derived its identity from its members' "roles as purveyors of creativity."[31] This highly skilled, highly creative class's attitudes to work, leisure, society, and so much more would reshape America's economy and its culture. And everyone else? Like any good upper crust, the creative class would feel a sense of *noblesse oblige* toward its inferiors: "To build true social cohesion," Florida warned, "the members of the Creative Class will need to offer those in other classes a tangible vision of ways to improve their own lives by becoming part of the Creative Economy or, at the very least, by reaping some of its rewards."

More recently, Erik Brynjolfsson and Andrew McAfee's influential 2014 book *The Second Machine Age* argued that the American economy inevitably will be characterized by a "bounty" of fabulous economic gains for workers and entrepreneurs with the right skills, but also a widening "spread" between those winners and the growing army of losers whose jobs will disappear under a tidal wave of technological change.[32] That book won approving reviews or front-cover blurbs from public figures many Millennials have grown up respecting, such as *New York Times* columnist Thomas Friedman, Netscape founder Marc Andreessen, and someone whose job title is "chief maverick" at *Wired* magazine. Millennials to the Right end of the political spectrum who distrust those figures could instead turn to books like *Average Is Over* by free-market blogger and professor Tyler Cowen, who in 2013 presented a similar argument about the future of work, with a somewhat more dystopian twist: "I imagine a world where, say, 10 to 15 percent of the citizenry is extremely wealthy and has fantastically comfortable and stimulating lives, the equivalent of current-day millionaires, albeit with better health care. Much of the rest of the country will have stagnant or maybe even falling wages in dollar terms but a lot more opportunities for cheap fun and also cheap education."[33] The one thing both Left and Right seem to be able to agree on is that there won't be any jobs for Millennials (and Gen Zers after us) in the vast middle of the skills and aptitude—and wages—spectrum.

If that sounds bad, there's a twist that makes it even worse: it also is starting to appear that after around 2000, the growth in the number of highly skilled cognitive jobs slowed significantly, too.[34] One startling trend to emerge from the Great Recession is that college graduates have become more vulnerable to economic downturns than they used to be. By one estimate, during the Great Recession each 1-percentage-point increase in the overall unemployment rate hit the unemployment and wages of recent college graduates two to three times harder than rising overall unemployment had hurt college graduates in past recessions.[35]

If future research bears out these conclusions, the implications for Millennials are dire. It would mean that the growing numbers of Millennials who have obtained expensive education and training to put themselves in the highest-skilled level of the job market will discover there aren't as many jobs in that top tier as they had expected. The same economists who noticed the drop-off in the creation of skilled jobs also have noticed that since 2000, a smaller proportion of people who graduate with bachelors' degrees are going on to work in the highest-skilled segment of the labor market, and it's taking longer for those new grads to find their way into those high-skilled jobs.[36] That leads to results like a Federal Reserve survey in 2014 that found that 28 percent of working young adults born between 1983 and 1995 reported feeling overqualified for their jobs.[37] This would be easier to attribute to youthful hubris if it weren't for hard data suggesting these Millennials may well have a point.

Given the magnitude of the crisis, Boomers' stock answer that everyone just needs to get used to this feels less and less satisfying. The key question that hovers over our jobs problem is, How much of this *is* inevitable? Technology will change the economy as well as jobs for Millennials—just as technology has transformed the economic lives of many previous generations. Yet it turns out that the type and magnitude of the transformation that has affected Millennials both before and after the Great Recession might not have been quite as inevitable as many pundits and wonks seem to think. Instead, this is where the Boomers have perpetrated their big heist of a decade.

CHAPTER 2

Not Our Parents' Job Market

ONE OF THE MOST IMPORTANT BOOKS TO APPEAR IN 2016 WAS A MEMOIR: *Hillbilly Elegy*, lawyer J. D. Vance's tale of growing up in a steel town in Ohio populated by families, including his, who had migrated from rural Appalachia in search of work. Vance (a Millennial, born in 1984) captured the social and economic values of a community so far removed from the mores of America's prosperous coasts that to some American readers it probably felt as if he were describing a foreign country. Indeed, Vance's memoir seemed, after the surprising outcome of the presidential election in November that year, to provide a big part of the explanation for why so many Americans had elected a president who so many other Americans took for granted was manifestly unfit for the job. Donald Trump's "Make America Great Again" message had spoken to the frustrations of Rust Belt workers in America's heartland left behind after the Great Recession.

That's all largely true, but incomplete. I'm not the first to point out that the social and economic problems Vance describes long predate the Lehman Brothers bankruptcy, the bailouts, Obamacare, or any of the other bruising policy and political debates that have emerged in the wake of the Great Recession. Vance was writing about his own Millennial childhood in what are now fondly remembered as the booming 1990s. Much of his memoir focuses on the culture of his community, but the bits of economics that seep into Vance's boyhood recollections reveal an economy that already was badly misfiring even before the 2008 catastrophe.

This is a crucial point to remember for anyone who wants to understand what has gone so badly wrong for Millennials since 2008. An oddity of so many arguments about Baby Boomers versus Millennials today is that people forget that the Boomers didn't have things so great, either. Maybe people don't notice how tough life was for Boomer adults because life for Boomer *children* was so great. The American notion of what a Baby Boomer is often looks like something out of *Leave It to Beaver* or *The Brady Bunch*—prosperous and secure and generally happy even if sometimes unconventional. But grownup Boomers are the generation of the movie *Wall Street*, with its greedy corporate raiders slashing jobs left and right—Baby Boomers' jobs. The Boomers are the generation that started their careers in the middle of the oil crises and stagflation of the 1970s, and who lived through the deep recession of the early 1980s. The Boomers are the ones who had to pick up the pieces of their careers when the local steel mills or factories closed.

The reality is that America hasn't gotten the economy right for decades. And this puts a new spin on what has happened to Millennials since 2008. Boomers didn't inherit a great job market and break it, so much as they inherited a tough job market and made it a lot worse. That happened for a specific reason: because the Boomers never fully understood what had happened to *them*, they expended most of their political energy during and after the Great Recession doubling down on policy choices that in reality had already failed in important ways. Millennials have spent the past decade paying for those bad decisions.

Things Fell Apart

Most Boomers would have to admit that the labor market failed them in some important ways. Boomers grew up during an era of unprecedented economic growth and job security in America. The mid-twentieth century of their childhoods was, in retrospect, the high-water mark for a particular model of employment that had never been seen before in human history and is unlikely ever to appear again: a world of near-lifetime employment at large industrial powerhouses promising generous economic security.

These were good jobs up and down the career ladder, jobs that lifted millions of breadwinners and their families solidly into the middle class. The economy was thriving, and it's not only Boomer nostalgia that feeds a sense that workers got more of a "fair share" of prosperity back then. The percentage of economic output paid to workers as compensation during the 1950s and '60s hovered above 64 percent; that proportion, called the labor share, has been declining for most of the time since then.[1]

So it's easy to understand the Boomers' surprise when the labor market fell apart right as they were entering their first jobs. At the time, it seemed as if the problem was primarily the downsizing revolution that had started in manufacturing in the 1970s amid recessions, oil shocks, rampant inflation, and the political upheaval of the Watergate era. Suddenly, "employment for life" just didn't exist anymore. The US Bureau for Labor Statistics started measuring "worker displacement" in 1984 to count the number of workers who had been with a company for at least three years but then had lost their job for reasons beyond their control, such as downsizing, offshoring, or a corporate relocation to somewhere else in the United States. Over the next twenty years, that category would encompass at least thirty million workers.[2]

Workers were alarmed. But economists didn't worry to the same degree at first. There wasn't consistently less employment overall. Although the unemployment rate did trend higher throughout the 1970s and '80s than it had been for stretches of the 1950s and '60s, that change could be partly explained by the fact that, counterintuitively, the labor participation rate kept climbing throughout the downsizing era. With more people competing for jobs, the unemployment rate might be a bit higher while people job-hunted.[3] The total number of hours worked, another important measure of the health of the labor market, also kept rising.[4] It appeared that people who were laid off from jobs at large companies were simply getting hired by smaller firms, or starting their own businesses.

Maybe, it seemed possible to believe, the "downsizing crisis" was a case of perception versus reality. The economic transformation that began in the 1970s had involved a change in the nature of employment, but not necessarily the amount of employment. And although labor's share of GDP kept falling throughout the 1970s— it would dip below the 64 percent average of the Boomers' youth in 1974—maybe it had been a little on the high side before after all.[5]

If they were honest, Boomers realized an economic transformation was overdue. Several unusual factors had contributed to the stable-employment system the Boomers grew up with. The United States had been the only real industrial powerhouse in the world, as Japan and Western Europe rebuilt from two devastating World Wars and the Communist countries walled themselves off from the rest of the world. The domestic US economy had been relentlessly expanding, thanks to the demographic bubble created by the Baby Boom itself and lifestyle trends such as the move to new suburbs.

But, as became obvious by the 1970s, America had developed a productivity problem—as in, there wasn't enough productivity. Underlying the stable employment boom of the mid-twentieth century was the fact that more people were working more hours. And each year they were producing more than they had the year before for the same amount of work time—churning out 103 widgets per hour on the assembly line instead of 100 widgets per hour. One common and simple measure of labor productivity, output per hour worked (excluding farming and adjusted for inflation), grew on average 2.7 percent per year in the 1950s and 2.5 percent in the 1960s.*[6]

---

* "Productivity" is a concept that's easy to explain but devilishly hard for economists to measure. I'm using here one productivity measure—output per hour worked— that is cruder than some others. Economists also often consider measures of labor and capital productivity separately (how much more output does one additional hour of labor produce, versus one additional dollar's worth of machinery?), and then can also estimate "total-factor productivity," which includes non–capital and labor factors such as the quality of roads around a factory that might influence how efficiently the owners can ship the factory's products to customers. Those measures can be useful in some contexts, but for purposes of this discussion I think they tend to provide a false sense of precision regarding what economists do and don't know about what drives changes in productivity.

There's no mystery as to what created this productivity boom. It was investment, which boomed in the mid-twentieth century. Gross fixed investment (including replacing old equipment and excluding housing, as I will with all the investment data in this chapter) grew an average of 3.6 percent per year in the 1950s and 6.5 percent in the 1960s.[7] This accounted for the phenomenal productivity surge that built the houses the Boomers grew up in—literally. The investment boom and its upward push on employment and wages made it possible for millions upon millions of families with Baby Boomer children to move into new houses in new suburbs across America, that they'd travel to and from in new cars and fill with new appliances.

There are a couple things to note about this boom. The fact that both labor hours and labor productivity were growing at the same time suggests companies on the whole were investing in certain kinds of technologies—technologies that would *complement* labor instead of substituting for it. And it turns out that this investment-and-productivity boom explains most of what went right for the Boomers' parents during their careers. Employers had new incentives to boost wages, improve working conditions, and extend lifetime employment guarantees (often with company pension plans as an inducement for workers to stay until retirement) in order to retain their now more valuable workers. Other factors, such as labor regulations that began to appear in earnest during the Great Depression and especially increasing unionization, played a role in employment stability. But those were possible primarily thanks to this productivity boost. Unions especially derived their power not as much from the political muscle of their leadership as from the hard-to-replace skills of their membership. Employees gained power in the marketplace (via their unions) by "selling" a commodity employers knew was particularly valuable: the workers' skilled labor, which wouldn't be easy to replace.[*][8]

_____

* This point was colorfully made by my columnist colleague Holman W. Jenkins Jr. when he pointed out that fan frustration with replacement referees hired by the National Football League during the 2012 lockout of unionized refs reminded the league that the professional refs provided significant value.

The other fact about this boom—a fact that would take on greater and greater significance as the Boomers aged—concerns consumption. Economists have long debated the relationship between consumption and investment. Does the investment in more productive capacity ultimately create the labor productivity and wage growth that fuels domestic consumption?* Or does growth in demand stimulate investment in productivity to meet that demand?† In the 1960s America of the Boomers' youth, the reality was generally the former. Although that is remembered as a heyday of new consumerism and the labor share of GDP was relatively high, personal consumption as a proportion of annual economic output hovered around 60 percent for most of the 1950s, '60s, and '70s, before it started drifting steadily upward in the 1980s.[9] That change would have significant implications for Millennials, as we'll see.

The Boomers' problem was that the mid-century investment-and-productivity boom started to lose steam in the 1970s and '80s. Recall that average annual growth in output per hour worked had been 2.5 percent in the 1960s. In the 1970s, it was only 1.4 percent, while the growth rate in number of hours worked started to slow.[10] This helped trigger the job market upheavals that would traumatize Boomers in their own young adulthood, even as the American economy struggled to reorganize itself to operate more productively in the face of stiffening global competition from Western Europe and Japan.

Initially, it seemed the problem was primarily in manufacturing. Examples abounded of American industries caught flat-footed by new competition. One prominent case was steel. Giant American steelmakers had resisted the introduction of high-tech new systems such as oxygen furnaces in favor of continued reliance on increasingly outdated open-hearth technologies.[11] Tens of thousands

---

* This is the underlying meaning of the often quoted but not often fully understood Say's Law, formulated by French economist Jean-Baptiste Say, which is typically paraphrased as "supply creates its own demand."

† This interpretation was a cornerstone of the work of British economist John Maynard Keynes, whose views came to dominate much of the economics and political establishment over the twentieth century.

of layoffs of American steelworkers ensued from the 1970s to the 1990s under pressure from imports, and some of America's most famous steel titans would be bankrupt by the early 2000s. Another was cars, where everyone could see that by the 1980s consumers were flocking to Hondas and Toyotas to avoid American car models that were too heavy and fuel-inefficient and generally badly engineered. It raised the question of how productive American workers had been even in the golden age of the 1950s and '60s: Had high prices arising from less global competition masked poor quality or lagging skills in the productivity numbers?*

Boomers in Charge

By the 1980s, as Boomers were starting to work—and, crucially, vote—in large numbers, there already was a growing consensus that America needed to find ways to boost productivity again, and fast. The problem for Millennials is that politicians (elected by Boomers in the 1980s, and then Boomers themselves from the 1990s onward) have consistently gone about trying to boost productivity in ways that distort the economy rather than stimulating investments that would enhance the value of workers up and down the career ladder.

It's not that the Boomers didn't have good instincts about what was going wrong. There was a widespread understanding starting at least in the 1970s that the United States needed to gin up more investment. Fixed investment in the 1970s would grow an average of 5.4 percent per year, with a distinctly downward trend over the course of the decade.[12] Why, and what to do about it, would become a political preoccupation for the Boomers for the next thirty years.

---

* Conservative writer William Safire captured this notion in a 1982 column, when he wrote that as a result of the deep recession then under way, "Workers who priced themselves and their industries out of the world market are getting laid off, and after they quit hollering for tariff protection, they'll come back to produce better products at less cost." (William Safire, "The Recession Speaks," *New York Times*, December 13, 1982.)

Ronald Reagan's presidency, although he wasn't a Boomer himself, would represent the Boomers' first big shot as adult voters at grappling with the problems of the economy they had inherited—and notably, younger Boomer voters supported Reagan in numbers that proved important to his victories. It became the era of the supply-side revolution, which held that suffocating regulation, high taxes, and rampant inflation were stifling investment, and with it productivity and opportunities for good jobs and rising standards of living. The greatest early popularizer of supply-side economics (and one of my forebears at the *Wall Street Journal* editorial page) was Jude Wanniski, whose modestly titled 1978 book *The Way the World Works* set out the supply-side diagnosis and prescription for the 1970s stagflation. A big problem, Wanniski and other supply-siders thought, was the tax code.[13] Reagan's signature policy would become tax cutting. Nowadays people remember that he reduced the top rate on the wealthiest taxpayers to less than 39 percent from 70 percent when he was elected. But encouraging more capital investment was the real preoccupation of supply-side economists in the 1980s. They thought the most important elements of Reagan's tax reforms were the effective cuts to capital gains taxes.[14]

Supply-siders also worried that economic regulations were sapping the investment incentives (and the cost of complying with regulations was sapping the financial capital) of American businesses. Here, too, they were barking up the right tree. Economic research in the decades since has found that the level of regulation does weigh on both investment and productivity growth—and has noted that the 1970s decline in productivity was accompanied by a major boom in regulations.[15] The problem was that the supply-siders never succeeded as well in their quest to restrain regulations as they did at cutting taxes. Although many people think of the late 1970s and the '80s as an era of laissez-faire, the total amount of federal government regulation (as measured, roughly but plausibly, by the number of pages in the federal code books) fell for only one year in that era, 1985.[16] Instead, supply-siders settled for reorienting regulations. By the end of the 1980s, most New Deal–era rules setting prices and regulating business practices in specific industries had been cleared away, to be replaced by an enormous web of new rules focused on environmental protection, occupational safety, and other "lifestyle" issues.[17] Some of these rules were obviously beneficial—the improvement to America's environment is one of the great successes of recent generations—but such regulations quickly got mired in questions about whether they really represented the best (most effective and most affordable) way to achieve their goals without weighing too heavily on jobs and economic growth.

This was a problematic mix of policies from the perspective of job creation. The supply-side revolution was dramatically cheapening capital investment, and especially financial capital, but allowing intrusive regulations to continue discouraging investment in many industries. An early warning sign was that fixed investment didn't exactly recover to its mid-century levels. Despite a bumper year in 1983 as the economy roared back from its recessionary malaise, fixed investment grew by an average of only 4.1 percent per year between 1983 and 1990—higher than the doldrums of the late 1970s and early '80s, to be sure, but far off America's mid-century investment peak. Output per hour worked grew a relatively sluggish 1.9 percent per year during this span.[18]

Instead, falling borrowing costs, as America emerged from the stagflationary 1970s and the high interest rates of the early 1980s, and low taxation on capital created a new boom in financial engineering: leveraged buy-outs, mergers and acquisitions, and other Gordon Gekko–like techniques. The basic principle was that companies would use cheap credit to borrow heavily against their assets and expected future revenue and then use the money either to buy other companies or to buy back the company's own stock. Interest payments on the debt would then become tax-deductible, reducing the company's effective tax burden under America's relatively high corporate tax rates. Meanwhile, the capital gains that arose as stock prices themselves rose would be taxed at the much lower capital gains rate—a particular benefit for executives who started to receive a growing share of their compensation in the form of stocks and stock options.

Not all of the 1980s financial boom was phony in this way, as evidenced by the fact that productivity did increase relative to the 1970s. That would be enough to create a real economy boom for a few years. Unemployment plummeted to 5 percent in 1989 from a high of 10.8 percent in 1982, the labor participation rate hit what at the time was a record high of nearly 67 percent, and in absolute numbers more Americans were at work than at any time in history. But it would leave the economy on a shaky foundation over the longer term. And crucially, the way America financed the investments it did make was changing. The clue is that this time around, the uptick in investment happened alongside a steady growth in personal consumption—which by 1990 had climbed above 64 percent of GDP.[19] This was possible because at the same time the supply-siders had cut tax rates to stimulate investment, they had not managed to trim government spending. Much of that spending was devoted to welfare payments intended to boost household consumption, and in an era of growing deficits, a lot of it was funded by debt. A dangerous imbalance had been born: tax laws and economic regulations were discouraging productive investments and encouraging more financial activity designed to exploit quirks in the tax code, and Americans were investing less of their own resources and relying more heavily on debt to support both consumption and what investments they were making.

Boomer Rules

And the notable thing about America's first Baby Boomer president, Bill Clinton, is how little things actually changed after he entered the White House in January 1993.

Under Treasury Secretary Robert Rubin and his eponymous "Rubinomics" program, which would come to dominate the 1990s, Washington would continue its effort to stimulate more business investment, only in a different way. Reagan-era supply-siders hadn't cared too much that the 1980s saw an enormous expansion in the federal budget deficit to a high of 6.3 percent of economic output in 1983, and in the debt to 37.3 percent of output by 1989. But maybe, some economists speculated, mounting concern about Washington's ability to pay its debts was holding back the economy—stifling productive capital investment by causing investors to demand higher rates of return (interest rates) than they otherwise would. The core of Rubinomics was to cut government spending a little bit and raise taxes a fair bit, especially on wealthier taxpayers, to restore confidence in America's ability to manage its finances. Interest rates would then fall, and the general boost in consumer and business sentiment would fuel an investment-and-jobs boom using the cheap financial capital. "Responsible" fiscal policy following a tax increase in 1993 allowed the Federal Reserve, now led by Alan Greenspan, to keep the federal funds rate, the key interest rate set by the Fed at its meetings eight times a year, at around 5 percent for years at a time, a virtually unprecedented level of stability. The economy boomed.

But Washington was still focused on maintaining unusually low interest rates as the best (and maybe only) way to stimulate productive investment. The Clinton era saw the same divergence between high taxes on corporate profits and personal incomes (the fruits of productive investment and hard work) versus low taxes on capital gains that were more prone to unproductive gamesmanship. The only difference was that the gap widened a little after a 1997 tax reform pushed by a Republican Congress cut the top capital gains tax rate to 20 percent, while the top corporate income rate stayed at 35 percent. And if anything, the regulatory thicket that discouraged productive investment compared to financial engineering got *worse* in the 1990s, despite the Clinton administration's "Reinventing Government" gimmick. Labor regulations such as the new Family and Medical Leave Act and new standards on indoor air quality— plus an expansion of the scope of earlier labor rules to encompass more small companies—raised the cost of employing human beings, indirectly discouraging capital investments that would require more workers to pay off.

The 1990s did see an investment and productivity boom that at the time led many people to conclude the Clinton-era policy mix worked. Fixed investment grew an average of 8 percent per year during the eight years of Clinton's presidency.[20] Output per hour worked increased 2.2 percent per year on average—to the chagrin of many Republicans, who had been convinced Clinton's policies would be a flop.

But there wasn't quite as much to this new-look investment-and-productivity boom as met the eye. It was all about one kind of investment in one kind of technology: the computer. Computers had been around—and used in offices and factories—for a couple decades, but suddenly, thanks to new innovations, they were cheaper to buy, and the software was more intuitive to use than ever before. Almost overnight, companies raced to adopt the machines. By the time Clinton was preparing to leave office in late 2000, information technology and software accounted for 33 percent of private fixed investment in the United States, up from 27 percent when he entered the White House.[21] It seemed to be just what the economy needed. The unemployment rate kept falling, to a low of 3.8 percent in 2000, and the participation rate topped out above 67 percent at around the same time.[22] And workers seemed to benefit more from this boom than they had from the boom of the 1980s: the labor share of GDP rose slightly to 62.5 percent during Bill Clinton's eight years in office, compared to 61.6 percent during Reagan's two terms.[23]

Even here, though, Washington's interventions to help this boom along would do more harm than good over the longer term. The main thrust was to change *financial* regulations to make it easier for tech companies to obtain cheap financing until they became profitable (even if "until" never arrived for many of them). Regulatory changes made it easier for companies to compensate workers with stock options, and companies were allowed to account for mergers and acquisitions in ways that would encourage more speculative big deals.[24] These rules applied to every American company, but at the time the biggest beneficiaries—and often the most vocal section of the business world seeking these changes—were tech firms that were trying to draw large numbers of highly talented workers and large pools of investment capital into an industry where many companies had yet to prove they could earn even a single dollar in profit. The economic gains from computer technologies were undeniable, but the precise scale of the gains would prove debatable. Even today economists aren't sure exactly how much of the productivity boom of the 1990s actually existed, versus how much represented nutty, money-losing ideas that should have stayed in a garage somewhere. Meanwhile, alongside the superficial boost to investment in IT, personal consumption had continued to drift upward as a proportion of GDP throughout the 1990s, reaching a postwar high above 66 percent in 2000.[25]

The dot-com stock bubble that burst in 2000 should have prompted some questions about all this, but the policy approach that had helped create that bubble would prove astonishingly durable. The George W. Bush years again saw ultralow interest rates—the federal funds rate sat well below 2 percent for most of Bush's first term, ostensibly to help the economy recover from the dual shocks of the dot-com bust and the September 11 terror attacks—and again saw reductions in capital gains taxes relative to other forms of taxation, with the top capital gains rate falling to 15 percent, while the top corporate-income rate remained stuck at 35 percent. Financial engineering exploded again.* Fixed investment hit a blistering 5.4 percent growth rate during the five years of Bush's two terms when it grew, excluding the tail of the dot-com recession in his first year and the downturn in investment that presaged the financial crisis starting in 2007.[26] But the growth rate in output per hour worked was starting to drift downward again from its 1990s peak (which already had failed to match the mid-twentieth-century boom), hitting an average of 1.9 percent per year in Bush's

---

* For a polemic on this topic from a former budget director in the Reagan administration, see David A. Stockman, *The Great Deformation: The Corruption of Capitalism in America* (New York: PublicAffairs, 2013), particularly Chapter 21, "The Great Financial Engineering Binge," 443ff.

first seven years.[27] The big boom was not in productivity but in housing—one of the less productive sectors of the economy, since once a house is built, it contributes only weakly to output growth. Chapter 4 will examine in detail why this happened and what it meant to the economy, but the key point here is that investment once again was not flowing into the types of capital spending that create good jobs that last for the long-term.

So putting all these policy trends together, what went wrong? It's an important question partly because it speaks to how fair it really is to blame the Boomers for these mistakes, and also because nailing this down will help to understand why things got so much worse for Millennials after 2008.

Surveying the evolution of the US economy during the Boomers' lifetime, the overarching theme that emerges is that Americans forgot how to save and invest—meaning that we grew less willing or able to direct our own resources into investments in boosting productivity for the future, and instead became ever more reliant on borrowing to fund just enough investment to deliver quick hits of economic growth. Oren Cass, an economist at the right-leaning Manhattan Institute for Policy Research, makes a convincing argument in *The Once and Future Worker* that over this span the United States transformed from a production economy into a consumption economy. The supply-siders of the 1980s might disagree with that characterization, since so many of their policies were intended to boost productive investment—indeed, they often viewed themselves in opposition to the Keynesian focus on stimulating consumption. But in practice they only partly arrested the slide away from job-creating investment and toward debt-fueled, short-term growth. The reality is that whichever policies the Boomers tried, and whichever political party they elected, they became less and less effective at stimulating the productive investments America's economy and its workers needed the longer they were in charge of running the country.

Millennials would be left to pick up the pieces after 2008.

The "Same Old, Same Old" and the New Young

The thing about the global financial crisis that hit in 2007–2008 and the Great Recession that followed is that they were bad but not necessarily *uniquely* bad. Modern economic crises invariably arise when an economy has become too reliant on debt and suddenly can't borrow anymore. The United States had definitely become reliant on debt, with mortgage debt alone reaching 73 percent of annual output in 2007.[28] And suddenly it couldn't borrow anymore. Households started struggling to repay their mortgages, which sparked concerns about who else might not be able to repay. Banks started writing down the value of the loans they held as assets on their balance sheets, which raised even more concerns about who else might struggle to repay debts. The financial system froze. And when people could no longer borrow to the extent they had needed to borrow to keep the good times rolling in the years before 2008 (since they hadn't been relying on genuine investment to fuel the boom), the good times stopped. Economic output shrank by 4.3 percent from precrisis peak to recessionary trough.

In retrospect, at least some of the doom-and-gloom about the financial crisis turns out to have been overdone. The mortgage meltdown was confined to relatively few geographic areas—and even among homeowners who were stuck owing mortgages worth more than their homes, many were prepared to keep repaying their mortgages to ride out the soft market. The government claims it actually made money on its bailouts of banks, auto companies, and other firms: compared to a total of $439 billion disbursed from the controversial Troubled-Asset Relief Program (TARP) since the crisis, the US Treasury purports to have made a cumulative profit of $49 billion as of 2017.[29] To the bailout's critics, this suggests that perhaps the large precrisis debts in the economy weren't quite as unsustainable as they looked in the depth of the crisis.

This isn't to second-guess politicians and policymakers who had to make snap decisions *without* the benefit of hindsight. And they'd argue that many of their choices helped to stabilize the economy precisely so that the crisis wouldn't become worse than it did. But it does make the point that a lot of what has gone wrong for Millennials since 2008 isn't necessarily the fault of the crisis itself. Rather, it's the result of choices Boomers made before and during the crisis—and kept making for years afterward.

One of the most disastrous decisions for Millennials concerns monetary policy and the Federal Reserve. The special sauce America had been missing since the 1970s was productive investment. Yet instead of trying new policies to finally lift investment out of its generation-long funk—let alone its Great Recession stagnation—the Fed tripled down on the monetary policies that had distorted investment for decades already.

In the depth of the crisis, Federal Reserve chair Ben Bernanke responded in the orthodox monetary manner, slashing interest rates to make it as easy as possible for companies and households to borrow. The federal funds rate would stay at essentially zero for nearly seven years between December 2008 and November 2015, a low never witnessed before for a duration never experienced before. And when that didn't provide sufficient stimulus, Bernanke's Fed also started buying financial assets to pour more cash into the economy and reduce borrowing costs even further. Bernanke injected money into the economy by expanding the Fed's balance sheet with policies collectively known as "quantitative easing," and by the time the Fed stopped buying bonds and other assets, it had expanded its balance sheet to roughly $4.5 trillion, from around $900 billion before the crisis. The stated goal of these asset purchases was to dramatically reduce long-term interest rates on corporate bonds and mortgages in order to stimulate more investment to lift America out of its slump.

The Fed's record is decidedly mixed on this score. After the level of annual nonresidential fixed investment fell 15 percent between 2007 and 2009, a mini-investment boom in 2010 and 2011 left the annual level of investment where it had been before the crisis. That's arguably a victory for the Fed. But despite the Fed's extraordinary monetary-policy efforts, business investment only grew by around 3.4 percent per year after that—the same investment growth as in the economic expansion of the early 2000s, but with significantly more effort from the Federal Reserve.[30] And again, there are different types of investment. This policy wouldn't necessarily stir up the right kind of investment to help Millennials.

As a first-order problem, there's mounting evidence that the Federal Reserve's policies stoked more financial engineering than productive investment. A 2013 study by economists at the Organization for Economic Cooperation and Development noted that long-term capital investments by companies fell significantly after the 2007–2008 financial crisis, whereas financial maneuvers such as share buybacks spiked. Once the economists took into account interest rates and tax policies and compared data on investment and financial behavior from thousands of companies, an explanation emerged: cheap debt financing and low expected returns made long-term investments less economical than debt-funded share buybacks. The low long-term interest rates that were supposed to stoke investment in the wake of the crisis had the opposite effect.[31]

Making matters worse, when Federal Reserve policies did stimulate investment rather than financial engineering, it tended to be the wrong kind of investment for real, sustained job creation. A large proportion of the assets the Fed bought to increase the money supply and lending were mortgage-backed securities. We'll see in greater detail in Chapter 4 how this affected the housing market, but it also had a major, negative impact on the job market, too. Because banks knew the Fed was eager to buy mortgage-backed securities, many banks had an incentive to boost their mortgage lending. That was what the Fed had intended, since policymakers hoped that putting a floor under the housing market would contain the recession. But what the Fed hadn't counted on was that much of this mortgage lending would come at the expense of lending to small- and medium-sized companies to fund job-creating investments. Recent research has shown that banks tended to shift away from corporate lending and more toward mortgage lending in response to Fed policies.[32] This was pumping "investment" back into the less productive housing sector of the economy, while depriving the smaller firms—where, remember, Millennials would ordinarily have hoped to get their start.

Millennials also would suffer from more subtle consequences of postcrisis monetary policy. Economists in recent decades have noted two surprising trends. One is that changes in labor productivity since the 1980s haven't tracked changes in overall economic health as closely as they used to. For most of the postwar period, recessions coincided with (in fact, may have been partly caused by) temporary declines in labor productivity, and conversely, productivity increases fueled economic recoveries. But starting in the late 1980s and early '90s, this relationship broke down. Labor productivity has started to grow faster during recessions—and yet that productivity gain doesn't trigger an economic recovery. Millennials saw this firsthand after 2009, where an early growth spurt in output per hour worked (4.6 percent in 2008 and 3.3 percent in 2009) failed to spark anything more than an anemic recovery in overall GDP growth after the Great Recession.[33]

The other surprise, meanwhile, is that the labor share—the proportion of GDP paid out to workers in compensation—has generally fallen over the past fifty years, despite occasional improvements from time to time. It plunged to an average of 60 percent in the five years after the Great Recession and so far shows little sign of improving again.[34] Conventional economic theories had always assumed this labor share would be roughly stable—that it might change from time to time but would return to its average level over a period of a few years.

The quest for explanations to these two riddles has led some economists to new conclusions about how companies decide which investments to make—and especially whether companies in recessions invest in technologies that make their labor more productive, or whether they invest in technologies that make their capital assets more productive. And it's starting to look like *the* big economic story of the past thirty years is that companies have been investing ever more heavily in technologies that replace labor and then make those labor-replacing technologies progressively more productive, rather than investing primarily in technologies that augment labor.[35]

Some early theories trying to explain this phenomenon assumed that over time more capital-augmenting investments would lead to more labor-augmenting investments too, to restore the economy to its long-run balance between the roles of machines and people.[36] That was always cold comfort to those unlucky enough to be in (or entering) the job market during one of the more capital-intensive phases. And especially since the Great Recession, it's also beginning to look like these changes might be profound and long-lasting. In particular, companies may be responding to longer-term changes in the relative costs of capital and labor. The cost of capital (as measured by factors such as interest rates, taxes, future expected growth, and the like) relative to the cost of labor appears to have a strong influence on companies' decisions about what kind of technologies to invest in.[37]

Many of these are difficult phenomena for economists to measure, and it may still take years for enough data to emerge to say for sure what effects these capital-investment trends have had on the labor market. But for a start, these economic theories offer a plausible explanation for a striking trend since the Great Recession: the American economy grew significantly more capital-intensive during and immediately after the recession without experiencing a similarly dramatic uptick in hours worked. "Capital intensity" measures the ratio of capital inputs such as machines, computers, office space, or the like to hours worked—and America's capital intensity increased by 8.6 percent in 2008 alone.[38] Yet companies didn't avail of the productivity bounce new technologies should have provided to boost output by hiring more workers. Instead, the total number of hours worked by Americans in that year *fell* by 5.2 percent.[39] This suggests companies were trying to find technologies that would substitute for labor instead of augmenting it.

And that hangs a bright red shiny question mark over the wisdom of the Fed's post–Great Recession decision to go all in on doing everything it could to make capital investment as cheap as possible. Ben Bernanke, Janet Yellen, and their colleagues assumed this would boost employment. It may instead have had the opposite effect.

The Problem with Obama

But of course, Ben Bernanke wasn't the only leader in town in Washington while the Great Recession and its aftermath were unfolding. The crisis started on the watch of George W. Bush, but he was so near the end of his term that it's hard to argue his decisions had a significant impact on much beyond the response to the immediate crisis. That leaves a different Boomer—Barack Obama, elected in late 2008 and inaugurated in early 2009 while the economy was just trying to find its feet again after the crisis. And this section will make uncomfortable reading for a lot of Millennials, because we invested so much political hope in Obama, voting for him twice in large numbers. We flocked to Obama because he seemed to offer a generational change in Washington, to be more in tune with the needs of younger voters than the older, white candidates Republicans kept running against him. Yet Obama (born 1961) is a Boomer, and his plan for the economy would turn out to be Boomer through and through—at Millennials' expense.

The Boomers who swelled the ranks of the Obama administration were trying to re-create the working lives their generation thought they'd missed out on earlier in their careers. Candidate Barack Obama spoke directly to this nostalgia in his highest-profile speech of the 2008 election campaign—his acceptance speech at the Democratic National Convention—when he described his grandmother's journey "up from the secretarial pool to middle management" despite facing discrimination as a working woman in that era, and his mother's own progress from relative poverty to a college degree and a career. As he put it, one of the hallmarks of an economy that works for Americans is that American businesses "look out for American workers."[40]

What were the characteristics of that old, mid-twentieth-century economy the Boomers were trying to capture? The standout feature was a sense that the gains of economic growth were more fairly distributed between workers and companies. The transition to a high-skilled economy, which is actually a polarization toward both high- and low-skilled jobs, clearly was not pulling enough workers into the high-skilled category: one analysis found that a total decline in labor share of 4.4 percentage points in manufacturing industries was only partly offset by a 2.5 percentage point gain in labor share for more highly skilled business and professional services.[41]

Along with a yearning for the shared prosperity Boomers remembered from their youth, they also missed a greater sense of economic security. This would become most obvious in debates about health care. America's health insurance system, dependent primarily on employers to provide insurance for working-age people and their families, had developed in the era of stable employment. When the Boomers were growing up in the middle of the twentieth century, their parents were so productive that employers were willing (and profitable enough) to foot the bill for health insurance, and employees who expected to spend decades at a company had little reason to worry that a layoff might cut off their coverage. But this system was completely unsuitable for an economy where more and more people were working more and more different jobs over the course of a career, and where employment in general was becoming more precarious.

Where the Boomers went wrong was in viewing the relative equality and security of their youth as economic *inputs* rather than *outputs*. Strong unions, healthy wage growth, and a more labor-friendly distribution of economic gains were the result, rather than the cause, of investment and productivity growth. Yet especially under the Obama administration, Boomer politicians and policymakers tried to force the economy to again take on the outward trappings of that earlier, happier era. In the course of doing so, they would make labor ever more expensive, and investments requiring more labor ever less attractive, at precisely the moment capital investment was becoming cheaper and cheaper—at least for some investors in some industries.

To see why that approach was such a disaster, look no further than the Affordable Care Act, or Obamacare.

Obamacare was an attempt to solve a glaring problem: in a new economy of constant employment churn (and where there were fewer and fewer mid-paying jobs to support health benefits for large tranches of the working population) it just doesn't make a lot of sense to tie insurance to employment. It never made sense anyway. America's system of employment-based insurance developed the way it did only by accident. During World War II, wage controls made it hard for employers to compete for the ever shrinking portion of the population that wasn't engaged in fighting the war. But health insurance premiums weren't included in the wage controls, and the Internal Revenue Service in 1943 ruled that premiums would enjoy the same tax benefits for employers as wages.[42] A cockamamie health care market was born.

In some ways, Obamacare did try to break this nonsensical link between employment and health insurance. The marketplaces the law created for individuals to buy insurance, sometimes with subsidies, were billed as major boons especially to self-employed entrepreneurs, freelancers, and gig workers—categories that include a lot of Millennials. By allowing young adults up to age twenty-six to stay covered on their parents' health plans, the law at least severed the tie between Millennials' health coverage and their own employment, although it still left us beholden to our parents' fringe benefits at their jobs.

But that would prove only a partial victory, and one that still is plagued by questions about the affordability of some individual plans. Worse, in other important respects the Affordable Care Act doubled down on the old employment-insurance link in ways that were especially costly for Millennials who didn't work in the gig economy, or who didn't want to.

Any company with more than fifty employees would have to provide insurance or face a $2,000 per worker penalty. And the mandatory insurance premiums for employers who complied with the spirit of the law could be even higher for each employee. This provision and others created a dramatic new labor-cost cliff edge for businesses, especially smaller companies that would ordinarily play such an important role in opening up early-career opportunities for young workers. A firm that employed forty-nine full-time workers in middle-productivity jobs and was considering hiring one more employee would have every reason *not* to. The cost of the penalty under the employee mandate would be $40,000 without accounting for lost tax benefits, which the company would incur solely because of that one employee.* That $40,000 penalty would come on top of whatever salary the firm paid to that fiftieth employee, making her instantly one of the company's most expensive workers.† The bill would be significantly higher if the company decided to provide insurance for all fifty workers instead. The cold reality, especially for a manager trying to run a business during the anemic recovery, was that hiring that additional worker just wouldn't be worth it.‡ And if hiring new employees wasn't a viable option, companies had more reason to invest in technologies that would take the place of those unhired workers instead.

Other attempts to use legal diktats to provide economic security also backfired. One notable example was the Obama administration's attempt to implement a broad, updated overtime-pay rule. The 1938 Fair Labor Standards Act had created a forty-hour work week and mandated "time and a half" overtime pay for employees working beyond that limit. The main exemption was for executives and administration, which the law and subsequent regulations

---

* Since employers would be exempt from the penalty for their first thirty employees, they'd pay "only" for twenty.

† For a more detailed, and alarming, analysis of the "penalty arithmetic" that discouraged hiring under Obamacare, from which these numbers are taken, see Casey B. Mulligan, *Side Effects and Complications: The Economic Consequences of Health-Care Reform* (Chicago: University of Chicago Press, 2015), 40–57.

‡ The Affordable Care Act also introduced a complex web of penalties and subsidies for individuals and families that created its own burden on workers; those will appear in Chapter 5, when we look at how Millennials have been clobbered by Washington taxing and spending.

defined as anyone earning more than $30 per week whose duties satisfied certain criteria. That pay cutoff would increase periodically throughout the Boomers' childhoods, and for much of that era fully half of *salaried* American workers, let alone hourly wage workers, would be legally entitled to overtime pay, according to estimates from the Economic Policy Institute, which supports expanding overtime eligibility.[43] In 2004, the George W. Bush administration increased the pay threshold to $455 per week ($23,660 per year) but also made it easier to classify workers as "administrators" based on their job descriptions.

The rule President Obama introduced in 2015 increased the threshold to $913 per week, or $47,476 per year. This was a huge risk, since unlike the era of peak overtime coverage in the 1970s, productivity in the economy had generally been falling over the previous generation. We'll never know what would have happened if the Obama overtime rule had fully taken effect—it was blocked by a judge on procedural grounds in November 2016 and abandoned by the new administration of Donald Trump in 2017—but before the court froze the rule, many businesses already had started preparing to comply with it. The effects were decidedly mixed. Some workers did get raises, to push their pay above the new threshold and exempt them from overtime payments that would have been even costlier for their employers. But many other employers determined to find ways to do more with less work, by strictly limiting employees to forty-hour weeks. The law also created new incentives for employers to use contract or temporary work.

It didn't matter for Millennials, by the way, that many of these policies never or only belatedly came into effect. Proposed rules could still do a lot of damage to the labor market just by forcing employers to make decisions under a cloud of worry that the regulations *might* take effect. The overtime rule was nixed by the Trump administration in 2017. The Obama administration delayed enforcing the employer mandate for health insurance for years, and the IRS only started fining companies in late 2017 for failing to comply (although the fines could go back to 2015 if companies hadn't provided insurance already by then). But the damage had already been done and could last for a long time. Even if those rules didn't take effect, many employers had started to prepare for what seemed like the certainty that they would—limiting hiring, ramping up investments to make do with fewer human employees, and the like. Economists have come to view regulatory *uncertainty* as having just as many serious consequences as the regulation itself.

All of this starts to give Millennials some of the answers we crave about the bad job market we've faced. Of course Millennials stumbled into a jobless non-recovery as they tried to start their careers after 2008, because high labor costs and ultralow capital costs were encouraging businesses to invest in anything other than hiring and training workers. And of course young workers—who are generally less productive because they're less experienced—were most vulnerable to policies that threatened to jack up the cost of labor without increasing productivity.

It seems increasingly plausible that this transformation not only changed the mix between machines and labor within companies, but then changed the types of jobs companies created as they needed to hire employees with the skills to make use of the most up-to-date technologies.[44] This explains several of the labor market trends that have plagued Millennials: The most highly skilled cohort of young workers are prospering. But most younger workers are in greater risk of being crowded out of the labor market by older workers, who will have more skills and experience with which to make the best use of new technologies.

Gigs Bite

And of course we ended up with the biggest Millennial labor-market distortion of them all: the gig economy.

What exactly is the "gig economy"? One thing it *isn't* is new. Freelancers and part-timers have always been important parts of the economy. What also isn't as special about the gig economy as many people think is the thing that always catches everyone's attention about it—the technology. Smartphone apps like Uber or Lyft or Task-Rabbit make it a lot easier for workers to offer themselves as temporary employees without going through an agency, and the lower cost thresholds associated with hiring individuals to do jobs via an app mean that "temporary" can become as short as a single car ride.

But the technology is an important part of the story of the gig economy less because it has created revolutionary new gig work than because it proves the bigger point of this chapter: enormous quantities of investment capital have flowed into companies creating these apps because making an app that will take the middleman out of temporary hiring is currently a lot cheaper than investing in almost any business activity that would create a full-time job. Indeed, the entire appeal of companies such as Uber is that they do *not* have a large workforce that subjects them to expensive labor taxes, costs, and regulations.

Instead, the most important fact about the modern gig economy is its preoccupation with sweating capital as much as humanly possible—maximizing the profits from capital assets that a "sharing-economy" entrepreneur already owns—while investing as little as possible in labor. The central premise of Uber or Lyft or Airbnb or many other sharing platforms is that the app will allow a micro-entrepreneur (or the platform itself) to extract maximum profits from personal assets like a car or an apartment that otherwise would sit idle for large parts of the day. The companies are desperate to have as few employees as possible. Uber has waged a series of years-long legal battles to stick to its designation of taxi drivers using its service as independent contractors rather than employees eligible for benefits and overtime pay.*

---

* A related, and often underappreciated, aspect of new gig-economy apps is that they continue a long-term trend of shifting the burden of capital accumulation in the economy onto individual workers. This has been most controversial in the case of Uber: commentators have pointed out repeatedly that drivers are likely underestimating the cost of wear and tear on their cars—a cost that once upon a time would have been borne by traditional taxi companies that owned their own fleets. This theme of workers acquiring their own capital is something we'll revisit in the next chapter in the context of training, education, and "human capital."

The other thing that's new about this type of temporary work for Millennials is how pervasive it has become. This is controversial, because the government still struggles to measure this evolution in the labor market, and some data indicate that fewer workers might be engaged in gig employment than the media would have us believe. Official data suggest that around 95 percent of American workers are employed in the traditional, full-time way, a percentage that has held roughly stable in recent decades, and the percentage of people reporting that they're self-employed has actually fallen during the so-called ascent of the gig economy.[45]

But those indicators can be deceiving because they're based on survey data measuring what people say they do in the labor market. Or rather, surveys can be as confusing as the complex new gig economy itself, both for workers answering the questions and for the government data-collectors asking them. For example, will a full-time employee at a large company think of renting out her spare room on Airbnb for extra cash as a "job"?* Differences in how surveys phrase the question may account for differences in the number of gig workers various polls find. For instance, another survey found that 24 percent of Millennials had reported working a freelance or independent contractor gig in 2015, compared to only 9 percent of Baby Boomers.[46]

Meanwhile, measurements of what people actually do and how they actually work tend to point to a much bigger gig economy than surveys. The number of 1099 forms that record self-employment income for tax purposes has shot up by 22 percent since 2000, compared to a 3.5 percent decline in the W-2 tax filings that employers use to report pay for regular employment. There was a notable increase in 1099 issuance after 2008.[47] The gig economy could encompass a whopping 43 percent of American

---

* Writing this chapter taught me that I myself am now part of the "gig economy" by some definitions, since the money I earned from my publisher was in addition to my salary from the *Wall Street Journal*, and I wrote the book in my spare time around the obligations of my main employment.

workers by 2020, according to an estimate by Intuit CEO Brad Smith in 2017.*[48]

Certainly there are different kinds of gig work that allow different levels of skill development and provide different levels of job satisfaction. The problem is that the gig economy seems to be taking over large sections of the labor market, and Millennials will live with the consequences for the rest of their lives.

The most important benefit Millennials are missing out on as they get locked out of traditional employment is an employer's investment in their training and skills. Millennials as a cohort might have more education than any previous generation at this stage in our lives, but like any previous generation we still need to learn how to translate that education into real, on-the-job competence in the working world. Entry-level jobs in which an employer might start to invest in providing some of the coaching and mentoring that fully bakes a young worker are disappearing, to be replaced by gig jobs that exist precisely because employers don't think they can economically invest in providing on-the-job training to a promising but green full-time employee.

Internships have expanded into another way, besides long-term gig work, for Millennials to skirt around employers' reluctance to hire traditional full-time employees. Internships, unpaid *and* paid, primarily shift more of the financial risk of training an entry-level worker onto the worker herself. Even paid interns forego the commitments an employer would make toward an entry-level staffer— whether fringe benefits or longer-term training—in exchange for an "opportunity" to provide entry-level work. Unpaid interns essentially self-finance their own training in the workplace. This is a particularly pernicious trend from a social perspective because this method of entry-level training favors young adults whose families have the wherewithal to navigate the labyrinth of internship applications and the financial means to support a young adult who's

---

* Intuit owns TurboTax. Note that the company's definition of a gig worker in much of its research is broader than people working via smartphone apps and includes a lot more "traditional" freelancers and contractors.

working for free. Everyone else falls further and further behind in the labor market.

Boomer politicians and policymakers aren't unaware of the consequences of gig work and intern employment for younger workers, but those leaders are seriously blinkered when it comes to what has caused these phenomena and what to do about it. Too often, the response has been to extend to gig platforms such as Uber the same expensive employment regulations that apply to other companies—and that have helped push more and more investment into the gig economy in the first place. And in 2010, the Obama administration cracked down on unpaid internships by imposing a strict new legal standard that made it almost impossible for employers to avoid paying interns. That might have prevented some of the worst abuses in the internship job market, but none of these measures fundamentally improve the incentives for companies to invest in productivity enhancements and training for workers, instead of trying to replace as much labor as possible.

Talk about a major theft. Over the course of several decades, the Boomers transformed an economy that had worked for a relatively large number of workers into an economy that works for fewer and fewer. They were victims of this transformation themselves, but that's hardly an excuse. Especially after 2008, they should have thought more carefully about the lessons the economy was trying to deliver and reconsidered whether they'd been on the right track before. Instead, they doubled down on the same policies that already had contributed so much to their own problems. Millennials have paid the price for that bad decision for the past decade, and they are on track to keep paying for a long time coming.

CHAPTER 3

Human-Capital Punishment

SUZE ORMAN CHANGED MY LIFE.

I first got hooked on the charismatic personal finance guru's weekly CNBC show right around the time the 2008 financial crisis hit, and it was mesmerizing. Viewers would call or write in with their knottiest money problems—mortgages under water, retirement accounts nonexistent, bankruptcy looming—and Orman would offer what generally sounded like pretty good advice. Pare back spending on nonessentials. Build up an emergency fund—but not too big of one. Invest the rest. And whatever you do, don't buy whole life insurance, whatever that is.

One of my favorite segments was "Can I Afford It?" in which callers would dial in, divulge scads of financial information such as earnings, savings, debts, and living expenses, and then ask that all-important question: Could they really afford that new deck, kitchen remodel, or four-year college for the kids, or a sports car? If they could, hurray! If not, Suze would give them the real deal on what they'd need to change so that they could find the money. This quickly became a running theme in my household, so that whenever we were contemplating a major purchase, my now-husband and I would ask each other, "Would Suze Orman say we can afford this?"

What turned this from a fun TV guilty pleasure into a transformative experience was Orman's steely determination that everyone could manage money like a pro. When I first started watching, I was in my mid-twenties, and despite a moderately expensive education in economics, parents who seemed to be saving responsibly for retirement, and a job at a prestigious business newspaper, I knew embarrassingly—and frighteningly—little about how to organize my own finances. By that point I'd paid off the credit card debt I accumulated during college by scrimping in my first few years out of school. My parents were helping with my student loans, which were what seemed like a reasonable size because I'd gone to a state university (although as a higher-tuition out-of-state student). And I'd been saving religiously. But was I doing the right things with my money, and was I saving enough?

Along came Suze, with her bubbly personality, her can-do spirit, and a series of guidelines that seemed easy to follow. I've since found out that other personal finance gurus quibble with Orman's advice (and I'd now quibble with some of it, too). Of course they do. Personal finance, as with most things in economics, is more art than science. One big thing Orman understood, though—and this is an insight that's shared by all the most successful pop finance gurus—was that this wasn't really about money at all. She'd sign off each program with her rallying cry: "People first. Then money. Then things." She wasn't just fixing people's money problems. She was fixing their lives. Couples would sometimes come on together to talk about how one person's profligacy or another's excess of thrift was causing tension in their marriage. Suze intuited that the money woes were both cause *and* symptom of other problems. Working through their financial troubles could also help people sort through other difficulties.

I wasn't the only person my age to turn to Orman for advice. One of her biggest sellers was a book aimed squarely at young adults just entering the working world, which she published with what in retrospect looks like impeccable timing in 2005. *The Money Book for the Young, Fabulous, and Broke* quickly hit the *New York Times* bestseller list. In it she told Millennials (because who else was "young, fabulous, and broke" at that point?) to obsess over our credit scores; to start saving now, not tomorrow; and to go ahead and ask for a raise.

Her young target audience has followed her advice in the decade since—or we're all following *someone's* advice to save more. Some 85 percent of Millennials* had started to save as of 2016, according to a 2016 survey by Fidelity Brokerage Services, and those who do are saving more than their Baby Boomer parents.† The average Millennial in this survey had $9,100 stashed away in an emergency fund, most of that held either in hard cash or in a bank savings account, compared to $7,100 in emergency savings for the average Boomer.[1] A survey by Bank of America in 2017 claimed to find that 47 percent of Millennials had saved at least $15,000.‡[2]

So this is all good news for Millennials, right?

Only if your idea of a fun time is running on a treadmill for decades. Millennials are doing better than their parents by *some* measures today but face a much bleaker tomorrow. Some of us are more on the ball about the need to save for the future than our parents were at the same age. But that insight or intuition or whatever it is won't get us as far, because our financial futures are much cloudier than the prospects of any of the generations that came immediately before us. That's mainly the fault of our Boomer parents—Suze Orman's own generation, ironically enough. Boomers have created a generation that's embarking on adulthood already more heavily indebted than any previous generation, and with shrinking prospects of ever ending up back in the black. And as Suze Orman could tell you, this isn't only an economic crisis. It's an all-around life crisis for Millennials.

Understanding that crisis starts with a simple question: Just how much do Millennials have in their bank accounts anyway?

---

* Born 1981–1991.

† A major caveat for this survey is that the average salary of the Millennial respondents was $68,000 per year, well above the median salary for this age cohort. Of course it's easier to save when you're bringing in more cash to start with.

‡ Born 1980–1994.

Money-Mad Millennials

It stands to reason that a generation growing up in an awful economy where everyone struggles to get jobs is neurotic about money. Millennials have acquired a bad reputation for being spendthrifts (remember all that avocado toast), but it's not clear that we actually are. By some measures Millennials seem to be more financially responsible—and realistic—than our older cousins in Gen X, let alone our Boomer parents. For instance, 57 percent of Millennials in the Bank of America study quoted above reported they have a savings goal, compared to 42 percent of Baby Boomers, and 73 percent of Millennials have a monthly budget and generally manage to stick to it.[3] A Merrill Lynch survey in 2017 found that 85 percent of Millennials prefer to "play it safe" with their savings, which would explain why surveys consistently find Millennials stash money away in savings accounts rather than investing in stocks or other financial assets.*[4]

That said, these surveys don't speak to the financial lives of all Millennials—far from it. They focus on the most well-to-do Millennials, and broadening the sample to include everyone yields a very different picture. One 2018 analysis of Federal Reserve survey data found that even by 2016 and at the ripe old age of thirty-five, fewer than 40 percent of Millennials saved in any sort of retirement plan.†[5] A different survey, this time a broader sample of youngish adults from a range of income levels but all of whom had graduated from college, found that 28 percent had resorted to at least one emergency-lending facility such as an auto title loan, payday lender, or pawn shop within the five years leading up to the study.‡ That's a significant sign of financial stress, especially since college-educated

---

* Born 1983–1999. This Merrill Lynch survey focused on the wealthiest Millennials: those with investable assets above $250,000, or with an annual income of at least $50,000 and investable assets of $20,000–$50,000. This makes the result even more interesting, since it shows that even those Millennials who have "made it" since 2008 don't trust the financial system to protect and grow their savings.

† Born 1981–1991.

‡ Born 1977–1989.

Millennials already tend to be at the higher-income end of the scale among all Millennials. Maybe that result was skewed by the fact that the "previous five years" at the time that question was asked encompassed the Great Recession. But more recent behavior revealed by the same study raised similar questions about Millennials' financial health. Of the 87 percent of college-educated Millennials who said they had a credit card, 43 percent had used it in at least one expensive "emergency" fashion in the year leading up to the survey, such as taking out a cash advance, spending over the credit limit, or paying only the minimum due.[6]

These data complement rather than contradict those studies portraying Millennials as super-savers. The underlying message is that as we Millennials earn more money, we're borderline obsessive about saving. Yet many of us are still struggling to get to a point where we can save at all. This is a direct consequence of the depressing work-and-earnings picture in the previous chapters. That's not necessarily a fatal blow, since Millennials still have long careers ahead of them in which to try to catch up. And other studies call into question whether the earnings gap alone can explain why Millennials' household finances are so messy—by a different measure, Millennials* have barely deviated at all over the last decade from the average earnings benchmarks their Boomer parents and Gen X older cousins set.[7] But the bad job market matters because big job-related factors explain why Millennials are falling behind in the savings race.

Fringe benefits is one of them, and benefits affecting retirement are the best example of the problem. The changing nature of retirement plans in America over the last thirty years or so has had a profound effect on household savings and net worth. Companies have shifted out of offering defined-benefit pensions, under which the employer guarantees an annual retirement income based on length of service and working salary and then saves and invests its own pot of money to meet pension payouts. It's fair to say most Millennials who work for private-sector companies will *never* have

---

* Born 1980–1989.

a pension like that. Instead, a growing number of companies now offer defined-contribution plans, such as 401(k)s. Here, the company pays a percentage of the employee's salary each year directly into a retirement-savings account that enjoys various tax breaks. That money belongs to the employee, even if there are legal limits on her ability to access it immediately. Roughly 60 percent of American workers now have the option to participate in plans like this, and around 40 percent do,[8] and it means more and more household asset accumulation has shifted into this form of retirement savings. In 1989, around 37 percent of all households held money in a retirement account, and those were mostly households with higher incomes. By 2016, that had swelled to 52 percent of households, and the proportion of households in the lowest 40 percent of the income distribution with retirement accounts had more than doubled.[9]

In the best case, this is a decent deal for Millennials. Defined-benefit plans have proven to be not quite as stable as advertised: companies consistently fail to invest enough on behalf of the employees whose retirements the firms are supposed to support, and if the plan runs out of cash, the government generally won't pay the full benefit the worker was promised. Defined-contribution plans offer certainty about how much money a worker will have in retirement and also offer employees more flexibility to switch between jobs without being tied to one employer solely to rack up years in service toward a pension.

But there's one enormous catch when it comes to either method of retirement savings. A Millennial has to have a job with benefits in order to enjoy them. A dismal consequence of the labor-market dysfunctions Millennials have suffered is that they're dropping behind previous generations in terms of coverage by, or eligibility for, retirement plans. Looking at both men and women, a smaller proportion of Millennials* are covered by employer-sponsored retirement plans than was the case for either Baby Boomers or Gen Xers at the same age.[10] Another study based on a regularly conducted government survey found that a depressing 66 percent of working

---

* Born 1981–1991.

Millennials* had nothing saved for retirement, and not for lack of trying: although most of them worked for employers who offered retirement plans to some workers, 40 percent of Millennials weren't eligible to participate because they didn't work enough hours or didn't have enough tenure under their belts. Of those Millennials who were eligible, 94 percent did save for retirement, about the same proportion as the percentage of Gen Xers and Boomers who participate in retirement plans.[11] The Millennial spirit is willing. It's just the job market that's weak.†

Two things are happening here, which speak to both the economics and the psychology of Millennials' saving problems. First, we're objectively less well-off than previous generations. And second, we know it because the trend toward greater individual responsibility for saving makes it more obvious that we're falling behind. In the old era of defined-benefit pension plans, we probably wouldn't have realized until it was too late that our retirement income was going to be less than our parents' because our careers had been more disappointing. Now we see the freight train barreling down the tracks in our direction. At least we know we have a problem. But we are condemned to sleepless nights while we struggle to solve it.

And we're definitely losing sleep. The Fidelity survey quoted above found that 42 percent of Millennials worry about financial security "all the time" or "a few times a week or more," compared to 38 percent of Gen Xers and 35 percent of Boomers who fretted about money with the same frequency. Throw in the proportion of that survey's respondents who said they worry about money "a few times a month," and 65 percent of Millennials feel pretty frequent pangs about their financial prospects, compared to 55 percent of Gen Xers and 51 percent of Boomers.[12] And those surveyed were

---

* Born 1981–1991.

† The next section will discuss crippling Millennial college debt, but it's worth pointing out here that high debt doesn't necessarily directly affect the desire or ability to participate in a defined-contribution pension plan. Particularly if the employer makes an initial contribution each year without requiring an employee match, pension savings can amount to "free money" on top of salary that the employee wouldn't otherwise be able to access to pay down debt anyway.

the higher-earning Millennials! The study of college-educated Millennials mentioned earlier also found that 51 percent agreed with the statement "I have too much debt."[13]

As tempting as it is for Boomers to do so, don't go lecturing Millennials about how we could avoid this anguish if only we cut back on our consumption of avocado toast—because there isn't much evidence that Millennial overconsumption is what leaves us without any money to spare at the end of the month. On the contrary, Millennials are inducing a growing panic among a lot of retailers precisely because, while we do our fair share of spending, we're price-sensitive and value-conscious. In a working paper published by the National Bureau of Economic Research in June 2018, economists at the University of California, Berkeley, analyzed several large surveys of consumer behavior and compared the spending patterns of various age cohorts to what the economy had looked like when those cohorts were young. They found that if a cohort had early experiences of an economic boom (Baby Boomers), lifetime consumption tended to be higher than for cohorts whose early experiences were recessions (Millennials). This study looked at not only spending but other consumer behaviors, too, and the results jibe with some Millennial consumer trends. In particular, the more haunted by economic downturns a consumer was, the more likely he'd be to use coupons, increase purchases of sale items, or substitute lower-quality brands.[14]

While by some (although definitely not all) measures Millennials are better with money than their Boomer parents, we don't *feel* better about money. And that in turn may be because we've concluded our savings are particularly high-stakes for us because we won't have anything else with which to support ourselves as we age. We know our employers won't be there for us since we're not enrolled in old-fashioned defined-benefit pension plans. But we also don't believe the government will be there for us, either. A Gallup poll in 2017 found that only 25 percent of Millennials* expected

---

* Born 1988–1999.

Social Security to provide a major source of retirement income, compared to 44 percent of Boomers.[15]

No wonder Millennials appear to be the most financially cautious generation since the cohort who grew up in the middle of the Great Depression.* And there's a touch of rough justice to this. Millennials are now starting to hit what are supposed to be their prime earning and saving years, and doing it in an era when individuals are more directly responsible for their own retirements than any recent generation has been. Investment firms had assumed that these circumstances would make Millennials cash cows for them, as we started buying more investment advice, brokerage services, wealth-management products, and so on. So imagine these firms' dismay on discovering that we're just stockpiling our money in savings accounts instead. Anyone who thinks that Wall Street greed played a role in the financial crisis and ensuing Great Recession can appreciate the element of payback in this: the generation most directly traumatized by the financial crash will punish Wall Street for the next thirty years by denting banks' commissions and fees. It's not much consolation, but it's a nice thought.

Getting the Skinny on Sheepskin

What most definitely is *not* a nice thought is the next problem on any tour of Millennials' personal finances: student loans. Of all the words in this book, these two will strike the greatest fear into the hearts of Millennial readers. They should strike fear into the hearts

---

* A 2014 survey from UBS Wealth Management found that 13 percent of Millennials (born 1977–1992, and this is another survey of the wealthy set) described themselves as "conservative" when it comes to money management, compared to 10 percent of Baby Boomers—the highest percentage of "conservative" savers since the Depression generation, of whom 15 percent described their approach to money that way. The same survey found that wealthy Millennials hold around 52 percent of their savings in cash, versus only 28 percent in stocks. That contrasts with every non-Millennial cohort in that survey, who kept an average of 23 percent of their savings in cash and invested 46 percent in stocks (UBS Wealth Management Americas, "Think You Know the Next Gen Investor? Think Again," UBS Investor Watch series, 2014). A similar phenomenon shows up in survey after survey of Millennial saving habits.

of every other reader, too. Millennials' mountain of accumulated student debt is at the heart of most of what has gone wrong for us financially over the past decade, and what has gone wrong for us socially and emotionally too.

The numbers are shocking. Americans are sitting on $1.4 trillion in student debt as of early 2018. That's nearly 11 percent of all outstanding household debt, and second only to mortgages ($9 trillion) as a form of personal indebtedness. Americans owe more in student loans than on credit cards ($815 billion). And the struggle to repay is real. Since mid-2012, the percentage of student loans that are at least ninety days behind on payments has hovered officially between 10 percent and 12 percent. That's an understatement because at any given time a large proportion of student loans aren't yet due to start repayments or are otherwise excused for a spell. The delinquency rate for loans that the borrower is actually supposed to be repaying is likely around double the official tally.[16]

Now there are a few caveats. Not all of that debt is owed by Millennials. It's a cumulative total that includes student loans that Gen Xers (and even Boomers, in some cases) still are repaying. And although recent Millennial grads may have "benefited" from an outsized share of recent student-debt accumulation—the money paid for our educations, after all—we aren't necessarily on the hook for all of it, thanks to student loan programs that allowed parents to borrow for their children's education. This parental debt is why student debt for Boomer borrowers born in 1955 or earlier has skyrocketed in recent years. The number of borrowers in that age bracket grew to 2.8 million in 2015 from 700,000 in 2005, and by 2015 older borrowers accounted for 6.4 percent of student loans, up from 2.7 percent a decade earlier. They're borrowing more (an average debt of $23,500 in 2015 compared to $12,100 in 2005), which helps explain why this set of Boomers—not Millennials—has the highest default rates on student loans of any age cohort.[17] This is a crisis, no doubt, but unusually for this book, it's a crisis directly afflicting Boomers instead of their children. (Although the Millennial children will still pay in the end, as we'll see.)

Oh, and let's get real here: Most of the worst horror stories we've heard about student debt—the MFA grad who had to sell a kidney and his first-born child to repay a student loan equivalent to the national debt of Ghana—aren't all they're cracked up to be.* Six-figure student debt loads are rare. Borrowers who owe more than $100,000 in student debt accounted for only 5 percent of all borrowers as of 2016, even if their combined balances accounted for roughly 30 percent of all outstanding student debt.[18] Most people in this exclusive club have reached that echelon by attending graduate school.

And not all $100,000 debtors are created equal. Spending that kind of money on obtaining a master's degree in creative writing or a PhD in postmodern literary theory is probably a spectacularly awful financial decision. A Millennial who instead has spent that kind of money on an advanced degree in a hard science or on medical school will likely find repayments pretty manageable—and the degree very lucrative—over the course of her career. That's one reason why default rates for this tranche of borrowers tend to be lower than the default rate for all student borrowers together. (Any recent law school graduates out there should prepare to live on a knife edge, since sometimes law degrees pay off well and sometimes they don't.)

So the problem isn't precisely big-money debt. The majority of student loan debtors—some 65 percent of them—owed an outstanding balance of $25,000 or less as of 2016. Throw in people owing up to $50,000, and you've accounted for 84 percent of borrowers.[19] That roughly aligns with data on borrowing rates at an individual level. The average federal loan for a full-time-equivalent student in the 2016–2017 academic year was $4,620 (in 2016 dollars), down from a peak of $5,730 in the 2010–2011 year. The average total debt, federal and otherwise, to obtain a bachelor's degree for students who borrowed to finance their education was $28,400.[20] Even $50,000 in debt seems pretty manageable spread

---

* Ghana's debt is $31 billion, give or take.

out over the course of many years, especially when set against a potential seven-figure "college wage premium" that represents how much more income someone who earns a bachelor's degree can expect over a lifetime compared to someone with only a high school diploma. That wage premium is why college debt tends to be concentrated in households with higher incomes—72 percent of outstanding college debt in 2013 was owed by households earning more than $48,000 per year, the median income.[21] The debt itself theoretically helps to cause the income.

That's the foundation of the argument that there isn't really a student debt crisis. It's also a pretty shaky foundation. There isn't a crisis in the sense that legions of Millennials are buckling under six-figure debts they can't afford. But there is a very real crisis in terms of growing numbers of people laboring under *five*-figure debts, or less, that may never be affordable. And this has happened because Boomers consistently encouraged a lot of Millennials to borrow for college when we shouldn't have.

Reasonable-sounding data about average household debt levels shouldn't distract anyone from the fact that student debt has skyrocketed. One way to understand this is to compare how student debt relates to overall debt across generations. A 2014 analysis found that education debt accounted for a minuscule portion of total household debt for early Boomers when they were in their mid-twenties.* By the time later Boomers were that age, school debt accounted for 5 percent of household debt. But it was 22 percent for an early crop of Millennials by the time they hit their mid-twenties. Early Boomers took out mortgages instead, with housing debt accounting for an average of 43 percent of their household debt portfolios in their mid-twenties, compared to a housing share of only 20 percent for Millennials.[22] Boomers got a house when they borrowed. Millennials only got a piece of sheepskin with some Latin scribbled on it.

---

* "Early Boomers" in this study were born between the mid-1940s and the mid-1950s; later Boomers were born 1957–1965; Millennials were born 1981–1985.

This level of indebtedness has tended to track increases in the number of people going to college (many early Boomers just didn't, because the job market in their day didn't require it). It also tracks increases in college tuition. The average cost of tuition and fees at a private, nonprofit college in 2017–2018 was $34,740 (in 2017 dollars), which is what the tail end of the Millennial generation, born in 1999, is paying. Millennials born in 1989 paid $27,520 on average when they started college in the 2007–2008 year, whereas tuition and fees were $15,160 in the 1987–1988 year, as the first Gen-Xers were matriculating. And note that since these figures are expressed in inflation-adjusted terms, that increase is over and above the general upward drift in prices over the past thirty years.[23] Four-year state colleges are significantly more affordable, but saw similar rates of tuition increase—to $9,970 in 2017–2018 from $3,190 in 1987–1988. As college has become more expensive, Millennials have been willing to borrow larger and larger amounts of money to attend classes.

The amazing thing is that we take this phenomenon for granted. It seems so natural that more and more people would demand a college education and be prepared to pay almost any price for it. Yet viewed in a different light, these trends are astonishing. Millennials who have taken an Econ 101 course (at an average cost of $594 per credit hour, or $1,039 per hour at a private, four-year college) will know that for the vast majority of goods and services, demand declines as the price rises.[24] This is often true to at least a certain extent even for items like fuel or electricity that we tend to think of as necessities. And if a consumer doesn't demand less of something, he at least accepts lower quality—as prices on his favorite name-brand breakfast cereal rise, he starts buying the store-brand alternative instead. The biggest exceptions tend to be things like plywood in Florida two days before a hurricane is due to hit, when people are prepared to pay (and a lot of stores are prepared to charge) just about any price. An underappreciated aspect of the student loan crisis is that we Millennials became convinced that a four-year college education is just as important to our futures as bottled water is for survival during a tropical storm. The fact that Millennials have proven themselves desperate to buy a college education at any price should be prompting a different set of questions to start: Is college really that important? And why?

Millennials think it is, because Baby Boomers made it so. Boomers have created an economy where businesses have every incentive to invest heavily in capital goods like computers, and every incentive to avoid investing in workers as much as possible. That leaves would-be workers, desperate to make sure they land at the top end of the skills-and-income scale rather than the bottom, to invest in themselves.

Millennials have been taught pretty explicitly to think of college as an "investment"—that word pops up in almost every discussion of higher education and higher-education finance. It's *the* justification for taking on large quantities of debt to buy what otherwise would amount only to an intangible and dubiously intellectual four-year experience on a leafy college campus somewhere. One reason for this theory's popularity is that unlike many things that sound intuitive in economics, this thing has an aura of bona fide truth about it. There *is* substantial evidence that college graduates on average earn more than those who have not graduated from college.

That's why a distinguishing characteristic of the post-Boomer economy is an obsession, almost on the order of a fetish, with acquiring education. The proportion of the population attending college has risen steadily. When the oldest cohort of Baby Boomers started graduating from high school in the early to mid-1960s, typically around 50 percent of high school graduates in a given year would head off to college. The highest that rate ever got for the Boomers was 54 percent in 1981, for Boomers born in 1963. But for my classmates (born in 1982 and graduating high school in 2000, making us the most millennial of Millennials), 63 percent of those of us who got a high school diploma went straight to a two-year or four-year college, and the rate hit 70 percent of the high school class of 2009 for Millennials born in 1991.[25] As growing numbers of young adults have been going to the trouble of obtaining four-year undergraduate degrees, an ever-expanding number of slightly older adults have found themselves studying for even more advanced degrees. Looking only at the percentage of those ages twenty-five to twenty-nine who have obtained advanced degrees, the proportion of the population with a master's or above ballooned to 9.2 percent in 2017 from 5.4 percent in 2000.[26] And unlike the figures above for college enrollment among high school graduates, these grad school numbers only count people who actually finished the degree. Many people who started advanced education over the past decade ended up dropping out of it.

Millennials are the best-educated generation in human history, and this rate of college attendance is how it happened. Never in human history have so many known so much—and still been so underemployed.

Busting the Education-Investment Myth

That's the one small problem with the Boomers' obsession with education for themselves and their children: no one told Millennials what it really means, in economic terms, to view education as an investment. Millennials know that if we invest in the stock market, we might lose our money. Education, we've been told, is an investment in our "human capital"—in the knowledge and skills that will allow us to earn good livings for ourselves, in the same way our employers might invest in physical capital like computers or factory tools. But for our entire lives, we've been told that higher education is the one investment in human history that always pays off in the end.

That's preposterous, and a growing amount of data proves it. By now it's not even clear exactly what students are "investing" in when they go to college. In the generations since economists started describing education as a form of investment rather than consumption, the earnings disparity between college graduates and college dropouts has widened significantly. The implication is that employers value the degree itself more than the sum of the coursework that goes into it. This puzzled economists inclined to think of education solely in terms of a steady investment in increasing the student's human capital over the course of four years. Instead, it seems more likely that students are actually sending a signal not that they have the specific skills that come from acing Political Science 101 or earning a gentlemanly C in art history, but that they know how to run a rat race successfully. Economists call this the "sheepskin effect," and it's a signaling effect that happens because marching across a stage to "Pomp and Circumstance" tells employers not only that you have knowledge from your coursework but that you have soft skills like perseverance and organization, too.*

This accounts for what might at first look like one of the odder aspects of the student debt crisis: students are more at risk of suffering a personal financial crisis the *less* student debt they have. In 2014, for instance, 34 percent of people who owed less than $5,000 when they left school defaulted, compared to 18 percent of people who owed $100,000 or more.[27] That's because actually graduating, and not necessarily what a student has studied or for how long, makes all the difference to a student's likely earnings and ability to repay. For borrowers due to start repaying a student loan in 2011–2012, 24 percent of college dropouts had defaulted within two years, compared to only 9 percent of graduates.[28] Put another way, for each semester that a student is in school, the lifetime earnings value of whatever additional education she accumulates does *not* increase in proportion to the additional debt she takes on to attend school. She has to finish the full four years in order to enjoy any earnings benefit from the individual courses that have gone into that degree.

And even for Millennials with sheepskin in hand ready to hit the job market, how much of a return exactly could we expect to reap from our hefty investments in higher education? Better not to ask.

Estimates of a college wage premium are based on *average* levels of pay. It is *not* the case that all college graduates earn more than all

---

* For a coruscating book-length analysis of this phenomenon, see Bryan Caplan, *The Case Against Education: Why the Education System Is a Waste of Time and Money* (Princeton, NJ: Princeton University Press, 2018).

people who only have high school diplomas—and this is true even excluding obvious outliers like Bill Gates or Mark Zuckerberg or any number of Hollywood celebrities, worthless college dropouts that they all are. If you took all the people without college diplomas and all the people with bachelor's degrees and then ranked them in terms of earnings, the top 25 percent of high-school-only workers earn at least $50,000 per year, more than the lowest-earning 25 percent of BA holders.[29] There is considerable overlap on the earnings scale between nondegree and degree holders.

What a student studies, what job he gets, and simply how talented and hard-working he is turn out to have a big bearing on how much he earns. One study found that among entry-level workers between 2009 and 2013, the median wage for all college graduates (the wage at which half earned more than that and half earned less) was $33,000 per year, compared to a median of $22,000 for high-school-only graduates the same age. But that median for college grads obscured some huge variations. Those with degrees in the sciences, math, or technical fields, or those with health-related majors, enjoyed median wages of $43,000 and $41,000 respectively. Liberal arts and humanities majors? A median of $29,000.[30] That's still more than the median for high-school-only workers, but perhaps not quite as much more as someone who spent $20,000 per year on an undergrad degree—and will soon have to repay the loans—might have hoped for.[31]

Another important study in this field found data not just for average earnings differences between majors but also shed some light on the wide range of earnings within a lot of majors—and I mean *wide*. Just compare chemistry majors with students who study computers and IT.

Looking at the averages, chemistry is absolutely the way to go, with average pay of $45.37 per hour, versus $37.99 for the computer graduate. But those averages mask huge variations that can leave a lot of chemistry majors earning a lot less than a lot of IT majors. One way to look at this is to think about the wages for the middle 80 percent of workers with those majors, discounting the top and bottom

10 percent of earners. For chemistry, the cutoffs marking the bottom and top 10 percent are $13.73 and $87.13 per hour, meaning 80 percent of graduates with that major can expect pay within that range. But for IT majors the cutoffs are $17.16 and $58.82 per hour. There's less upside to an IT major, but also less downside. And the big caveat to these data is that they include chemistry majors who went on to earn graduate degrees, too. The lowest wage for the top 10 percent of chemistry majors *who didn't obtain a further degree* is $52.29, compared to $56.37 for the highest-earning 10 percent of IT majors who stopped after their bachelor's degrees. Similar patterns appear across a wide range of majors, where the average expected wages tell one story but the wide or narrow spreads around those middles send a very different signal.[32]*

That's a confusing amount of data, which is part of the point. Millennials have been encouraged to think about college degrees as a form of investment in ourselves that will always pay off. Yet, just like any other investment, with education a prospective student has to do quite a lot of homework before she knows how much and what kind of homework is worth doing. Some intuition would help here, if Millennials were encouraged to trust our own guts. Of course we'll enjoy a bigger "sheepskin effect" if the pieces of vellum in our back pockets say "Bachelor of Science in Robotics" rather than "Bachelor of Arts in Queer Literary Theory." And some students *are* trusting their guts—because they have to. There's some evidence that students' choices of college major are related to their families' economic backgrounds, with lower-income students filtering into more "practical" fields perceived to have better earnings potential. An analysis of National Center for Education Statistics data commissioned by the *Atlantic* magazine in 2015 found a discernible relationship between average household income and a

---

* This observation isn't necessarily at odds with the theory that a college degree is primarily a signal about soft skills rather than a measure of actual academic attainment, by the way. Features of a degree other than the specific facts the student learned—whether it's a quantitatively rigorous discipline, whether it's a field with a reputation for attracting more serious students—can send their own sort of signal to prospective employers.

student's choice of major, with students from lower-income house-holds more likely to major in law enforcement or education, and students from higher-income households more likely to major in history or art. The article's provocative title was: "Rich Kids Study English," since English majors seemed to come from families with the highest average household income of all.[33]

That trend represents a nascent attempt at Millennial self-help, but it doesn't solve the college-investment-not-paying-off problem. Not by a long shot. For one thing, it seems likely that students from lower-income backgrounds are making decisions based more on *perceptions* of potential earnings and job security than they are on genuine data. Consider the slight oddity that education is more popular as a major among lower-income households, according to the *Atlantic* report, despite evidence that it tends to be a lower paying major on average than some degrees favored by wealthier students, and also often requires a substantial additional "invest-ment" in postgraduate education in order to be employable in many school districts.* But students have no choice but to guess about a lot of this, because a lot of college administrators would rather not give students useful data to guide decisions about col-lege attendance and borrowing. The Obama administration in 2013 rolled out a website, called the College Scorecard, to give prospec-tive students very basic information about a college's cost relative to the national average, its graduation rate, the average earnings of re-cent graduates, and how many recent graduates managed to make payments on their student loans. Lobbying groups representing

---

* Consider some more data in the study I quoted earlier to compare chemistry and IT majors. Average pay for an education major in that study was $24.54 per hour, with 80 percent of *all* education majors earning between $12.75 and $38.64. For his-tory majors, in contrast, average pay was $36.12 per hour, with 80 percent of all his-tory majors earning between $12.65 per hour and $64.17. For very little difference on the downside, this implies students would enjoy more upside from a history degree. And the difference is even more striking for those without postgraduate degrees, where the top earnings for the 80 percent bracket was $32.68 for education majors but $49.02 for history majors. (Joseph G. Altonji, Lisa B. Kahn, and Jamin D. Speer, "Cashier or Consultant? Labor Market Entry Conditions, Field of Study, and Career Success," *Journal of Labor Economics* 43, no. 1, pt. 2 [2016]).

colleges and universities opposed the idea.[34] Higher-education lob-
byists succeeded in 2008 in persuading Congress to pass a law explicitly prohibiting the government from providing more detailed
information on earnings for various majors by matching government student-loan data with records of earnings from the Social
Security Administration.[35]

This lapse has had severe and long-lasting consequences for
Millennial college graduates and is at the heart of how levels of
per-person student debt that might almost look reasonable—if you
squint—can be so crippling. Those averages leave a lot of room for
a lot of vulnerable Millennials to get crushed by their loans.

The consequences are visible in data tracking the relationship
between student debt levels, credit ratings, homeownership, and
other life milestones. A lot of these figures are imprecise because
researchers struggle to account for the wide range of economic, social, and psychological factors that can influence individuals' financial decisions. That means what follows are more like "organized
anecdotes" rather than rigorous academic studies. But taken together a troubling picture starts to emerge. Having an outstanding
student loan balance does seem to weigh on credit ratings. A 2016
analysis by FICO, one of the companies that provides such scores,
found that some Millennials* who still owed on student loans had
an average credit score of 627 on a scale of 300–850, compared to
a score of 660 for those who had already finished paying off their
loans.[36] Another study, from credit-rating firm TransUnion and using different data, found 43 percent of Millennials† ranked as subprime borrowers.[37] Since total debt outstanding can reduce a credit
score, it's possible to surmise a connection between high student
debt and a relatively high number of Millennials with low scores.

Problems also show up when it comes to major life milestones,
especially homeownership. Chapter 4 will look at all the reasons
why Millennials have struggled to climb onto the property ladder,
but student debt is an important part of the story. A 2017 analysis

---

* Born 1982–1986.

† Born 1980–1998.

by economists at the Federal Reserve Bank of New York of consumer credit and education data found that yes, obtaining a college degree makes a young adult more likely to own a home than not having a degree. But among those who did graduate from college, student debt has a noticeable impact on the rate of homeownership: the rate of homeownership among those with no student debt was several percentage points higher than the ownership rate among those who had debt.[38]

That is why the discussion about student debt belongs in a chapter about savings more broadly. Rather than engaging in more traditional forms of saving and investment such as opening a savings account, buying a house, or investing in the stock market, Millennials have made enormous investments in themselves and their education. It's not at all clear that we've gotten our money's worth. Scholars who want to downplay the depth of this debt crisis for Millennials observe that a correlation between high levels of student debt and those bad financial outcomes doesn't mean the student debt has *caused* the bad outcome. This is also why universities generally argue against requiring disclosures on student outcomes to prospective students. The claim is that the factors that go into a graduate's success or failure are many and complex, and defy boiling down to a simple statistic or two that would rate colleges on actual outcomes. For example, as expanded student lending has allowed more lower-income students to attend college, maybe we shouldn't be surprised that those lower-income students then take longer to muster the resources to buy homes.

Maybe all that is true, but it's still not a great excuse for the way the United States does higher education—and the way that has clobbered Millennials. If it's the case that a wide array of personal factors influence whether college pays off for an individual student in the end, it raises a big question: What is the purpose of borrowing a large amount of money to go to college for people who would struggle to repay anyway, if going to college itself isn't lifting them into an income level that improves their overall financial health? The higher-education industrial complex consistently hypes the financial benefits of a four-year college degree for everyone *until* people start asking why some students don't benefit from those degrees. At that point, college administrators run for the hills.

Those questions also get at a particularly troubling aspect of Millennials' student debt morass: it's perpetuating and even deepening racial inequality. Research suggests African American students have been hit especially hard by the student loan mania. They're heavier borrowers than their white peers—one analysis of early Millennial borrowers* found that African American student borrowers held debt around 51 percent higher than that of white borrowers, even after controlling for factors such as the parents' income and educational attainment that also tend to influence the level of borrowing for all students.[39] African American students, especially after 2008, tended to take out loans that represented a larger share of their families' incomes and wealth.[40] Yet they also tended to complete degrees at lower rates than white students, putting them in the most vulnerable category of borrowers for a personal financial crisis—those who are heavily indebted but don't have a diploma to show for their financial strain.[41] These students are most at risk for all the negative consequences of the student debt binge.

The Boomer Give—and Take

It won't be a surprise to discover that things have gotten a whole lot worse for Millennials since 2008.

Even before the financial crisis, Boomers in Washington had become obsessed with sending more and more (and more) Millennials to college, and with encouraging borrowing to fund it. Governments have funded outright grants and subsidized lending for college costs since the 1950s, and the first major student loan program was created in the 1960s. Baby Boomers grew up with student borrowing themselves, and even had a student debt crisis

---

* Born 1981–1985.

of their own in the late 1970s, as the last Boomer birth cohorts to head to college found debt levels shooting upward after a brief policy experiment with letting students of all income levels, and not just the poorest, take out subsidized loans. That policy was reversed (for a spell), but by 1981, as Boomers born in 1963 were turning eighteen and graduating from high school, the value of subsidized loans for the first time overtook grants as the largest form of federal aid. Throughout the 1990s, Congress continued to expand loan programs by broadening eligibility for them and also by making it possible for parents to borrow to fund their children's college educations. By 2005, Washington had also expanded the ability to borrow for graduate school.[42]

This meant that heading into the 2008 recession, Millennials born in the 1980s had already taken on large quantities of student debt, and those born in the 1990s could expect to do the same— especially since President Obama set aggressive targets for overall college attendance and graduation. His first address to Congress, in February 2009, included a plea to all Americans to devote at least one year to post–high school education or training, and a promise that by 2020 America would boast the highest proportion of college graduates in its population in the world.[43]

President Obama's new administration at first looked like terrific news to the students who were being goaded into obtaining more education because in the depth of the Great Recession Obama's focus seemed to be on increasing *grant*-based aid for college costs. The stimulus bill passed and signed in February 2009 included an unprecedented $17 billion expansion in the Pell Grant program, the federal government's main vehicle for handing students money for tuition, and another $14 billion in expanded tax credits for (primarily middle-class) households that devoted their own money to paying for college. This was still debt-based aid in a sense. Since the $787 billion-and-counting stimulus bill was paid for with deficit spending by the federal government, Millennials as taxpayers will have to repay that bill at some point in the future. But it seemed like a handout to students at the time, and at least the interest rate on federal government debt is lower than the interest charged on a student loan.

The Obama administration also made some attempts to focus on both affordability and value for money. Obama frequently inveighed against colleges whose tuition fees were rising well ahead of the rate of inflation: "It's time for colleges and universities to get serious about cutting their own costs, because they, too, have a responsibility to help solve this problem [of spiraling tuition]," he warned in his State of the Union address in January 2010.[44] In 2013, he proposed a plan that would have linked a college's eligibility to receive federal student aid to various outcomes such as low student default rates.[45] That didn't go anywhere (the main result was the College Scorecard website for prospective students), and it probably wouldn't have worked anyway.* But the administration did try to cut off the subsidized-loan spigot to one set of institutions whose students consistently had significant trouble repaying the loans: for-profit colleges. From the perspective of protecting more vulnerable students from amassing crippling levels of debt (and protecting taxpayers from having to write off the value of defaulted loans), the administration was looking in one of the right places. For-profit colleges traditionally have lower graduation rates and higher default rates than similar nonprofit institutions such as community colleges.

But that was only *one* of the right places, since students at traditional community colleges also struggle to an unusual degree with failures to graduate and high default rates, even if those schools are much cheaper in absolute dollar terms than many four-year institutions. Rather than reforming the loan system itself, the Obama administration missed its mark by focusing primarily on the organizational structure of the school—for-profit or nonprofit—rather than on the outcomes for the students. And the Obama administration missed other important opportunities to fix the bloated and ineffective education system. The main lapse here was a failure to do

---

* Because the metrics the plan would have used to measure college "success" were so blunt, the government would have struggled to gauge the real quality of a school.

enough to encourage alternatives to a college education. President Obama often talked a good game about recognizing that a four-year degree isn't the only, or often the best, path to the right skills for the job market. His 2009 speech included vocational training in his target of boosting post–high school educational attainment. Yet in practice, the administration tended to become distracted by two- and four-year degrees. Major initiatives to promote innovative new models for vocational training such as new kinds of certificate courses arrived late in Obama's tenure (in 2015 and 2016) with considerably less funding than the administration poured into traditional higher education (tens of millions rather than billions) and when officials wouldn't be in office much longer to see them through.

And then there were all the other huge things Washington got wrong for Millennials after 2008, policies that were so wrong they arguably outweigh the benefits of Pell Grant expansion.

The fundamental problem all along has been that there is no market mechanism to warn colleges, lenders, parents, or students themselves that an individual student might be making a bad financial decision to go to college. For any other type of loan a person takes out—from a credit card to a payday loan to a mortgage—the lender assesses the potential borrower's creditworthiness and the riskiness of the loan (Does this person have a good credit rating? Is the loan backed by collateral?) and then proposes an interest rate that compensates for the risk. That interest rate in turn sends a strong signal to the borrower, forcing her to think about whether she'll really be able to repay. This market mechanism is missing in student loans, which are offered at one ultralow, subsidized interest rate to all borrowers regardless of the course of study, quality of the school, or likelihood that the student will ever be able to repay. And rather than fixing this market failure, the Obama administration broke the market even more.

In one major move, Washington chased private lenders out of the student loan market once and for all. Before 2008, private banks had accounted for at least 65 percent of the total student loan market, with the government itself issuing the rest. Calling these loans "private" in this sense is more than a little misleading. The government still guaranteed the loans, on the condition that the bank offer an ultralow interest rate at least several percentage points lower than unsubsidized loans—and substantially less than the interest rates banks charge on most loans that don't have any collateral. It was an absurd system under which private banks were able to make guaranteed profits with taxpayers taking all the risks of underwriting defaults. But instead of reforming that system to force private lenders to take on more of the default risks themselves (while giving them the freedom to set market interest rates), Washington moved in the other direction. In 2010, Washington effectively took over sole responsibility for student lending. This provision got wrapped up in legislation related to the Affordable Care Act, or Obamacare because the Obama administration hoped the "savings" achieved by "cutting out the middleman" in student lending could fund both more health care spending and more student-aid Pell grants. But thanks to this change, the United States moved from a system where the market might one day be able to warn some students off bad "investments" in education to a system where the government definitely never would.

The administration compounded that error with another loan-related provision that at first sounded like a great deal for Millennials: more generous income-based repayment plans, including a new public service loan forgiveness program. "Income-based repayment" is what it says on the package. Rather than calculating monthly payments the way normal loan payments are set—the amount the borrower needs to pay each month in order to pay off the full debt plus interest within a specified time—the income-based plan would allow recent grads to pay an amount equal to a certain percentage of their monthly income. From modest beginnings for students who started attending college in 2007 (whose loans would only be forgiven if their incomes were very low), the program was expanded with borrowers from 2014 onward, and with more generous terms. They'd only have to pay 10 percent of their monthly income (after basic expenses) toward student loans, compared to 15 percent under an earlier version of the program. Any loan balance that was still left after twenty years would be forgiven, at taxpayer expense. The public-service program contained a more generous add-on for students who took jobs with the government. Their loans would be forgiven after only a decade.

Great deals, right? Of course not. For one thing, they remove any last reasons that might have remained for prospective college students to worry about whether an education would be "worth it." In fact, an irony of the Obama years is that while the administration said it wanted to make colleges more accountable for results, it also introduced programs like these meant to insulate colleges and students alike from the consequences of low-earnings college outcomes.

Worse, note who would ultimately foot the bill for all this debt forgiveness. Not just taxpayers, but a certain kind of taxpayer: Millennial taxpayers. The time horizons for these programs mean that the taxpayer bills will only start coming due around 2027 at the earliest. Who will be working and paying taxes by then? Not the Baby Boom generation. The youngest Boomers, born in 1964, will all have reached age sixty-seven and retirement by 2031, and most of them will be long gone from the labor force before then. President Obama's big show of generosity toward Millennial students amounted to forcing us to make a gift to ourselves. Oh, and then Washington would take some of it away again by taxing any remaining loan amount that's forgiven as "income."*

Indeed, Boomer politicians of both political parties made extra certain to protect their generation's taxpayers from the one remaining student-loan risk they would have faced: bankruptcy on the part of the student-loan borrowers. Going back to the 1970s,

---

* This is also true, in a way, of all the Boomers we saw earlier in the chapter who took out education loans for their Millennial children. While those loans create a repayment burden for the parents and can have serious implications for their credit ratings, the reality is that all the default risk is ultimately borne by Millennials. As the Boomer borrowers retire, the taxpayer burden of subsidizing defaults will shift to the current taxpayers of the day, predominantly Millennial workers.

Washington had worried about students using bankruptcy court to avoid repaying debts that taxpayers were guaranteeing. Originally, lawmakers focused on preventing the worst potential abuses by making student debt slightly harder to clear. One provision, for instance, allowed an individual to discharge a student loan in bankruptcy only if she had already been making payments for five years—in order to prevent new graduates from making a quick trip to bankruptcy court so they could then start their careers debt-free. Over time Congress lengthened that window a bit. But then in 1998 and 2005, by which point Boomers were firmly in control in both Congress and the White House, changes to the bankruptcy law made it all but impossible to crawl out from under a student debt burden. Congress scrapped the time-limit system entirely, and instead imposed an almost-impossible-to-meet legal standard for the level of "hardship" a debtor would have to show in order to dispose of a student loan in bankruptcy. The 2005 law extended this form of student-loan tyranny even to private-sector loans not subsidized by the government and charging interest rates more closely resembling a market rate.

The main thing Millennials will note about these policies, taken together, is that they're immoral. In every other form of debt in an economy, society forces the borrower and the lender each to bear some responsibility for the outcome of a bad bet. That responsibility may be unevenly distributed—in normal times, an individual borrower will suffer more in terms of low credit ratings and mental anguish than a bank will suffer from writing off a debt that's wiped out in bankruptcy. But there's some pain on both sides, and that fact is supposed to impose at least some constraint on risky lending.

The consequences of the Boomers' self-opt-out of any responsibility for the student-lending binge, especially after 2008, run a lot deeper than a lot of people realize. The simplest—and deliberate—consequence is that this further dampened any warning signals to Millennials that maybe their student loans represented a risky, let alone bad, investment. The only plausible economic and political purpose of barring Millennials from clearing student debt in bankruptcy was to make more loans available, potentially at lower interest rates.

Dwell on that for a minute. Boomer politicians recognized that knowing what politicians, economists, educators, and bankers already knew about the returns or otherwise to a college degree, the market ordinarily would have demanded higher interest rates from borrowers to compensate for the risks that higher education would turn out to be a bad investment for any given student. Those higher interest rates would have discouraged some Millennials from borrowing to fund a higher-education bet at all and would have limited the amount that other Millennials could borrow. Boomers deliberately tried to thwart those market signals that might have discouraged at least some Millennials from making awful educational investments.

To President Obama's partial credit, he at one point proposed a limited reform of this system. But the emphasis here is on *limited*. In 2015, he suggested making it easier for student borrowers to discharge their loans in bankruptcy. But there was a catch: this would have applied only to private loans, the outstanding debt left over from the old subsidized private system he had already eliminated. The plan excluded government-issued loans, on the theory that those loans already enjoyed generous repayment options and forgiveness provisions.[46] The Obama answer on student-loan bankruptcy amounted to saying, "We Boomers won't bother fixing this problem now because you Millennials will have to pay for it later anyway."

Pennies from Heaven and Other Illusions

The worst thing about all this is that there simply doesn't seem to be any way Millennials can win this game. Just look at all the unconvincing things we're told to make us feel better about the financial holes we're in thanks to a poor job market and the student debt burden.

Consider what's probably the best bit of financial news of all for Millennials: the Baby Boomers will all die off eventually.

That's supposedly great news for us because it means we'll benefit from an unprecedented inheritance windfall. The numbers are astounding, in theory anyway. The most commonly quoted estimate is that Boomers will transfer some $30 trillion in wealth to their Gen X and Millennial heirs in coming decades. It's surprisingly difficult to pin down a source for that number—most consulting-firm studies or news reports that repeat it end up citing each other. But assume the best, since it's not entirely out of line with some other measures of this phenomenon. For example, Deloitte Consulting in a 2015 report estimated that Boomers will be sitting on some $29 trillion in financial wealth by 2029, which includes stocks, bonds, and mutual funds in retirement accounts and cash in the bank. Boomers' accumulated equity in their homes will be even higher than that.[47]

Call it the "pennies-from-heaven" strategy for Millennial financial security: your parents go to heaven, and you get their pennies. The phenomenon is nothing new in human history. But three things are unusual for Millennials as far as inheritances are concerned.

One is that as a form of wealth accumulation, inheritances have become pretty tenuous—because no generation up to now has lived as long in as poor health as the Baby Boomers are likely to do. As of 2014, the average 65-year-old (born in 1949) could expect to live another 19.4 years, to the ripe old age of 84.4. That life expectancy at age sixty-five has been climbing steadily upward for decades. Someone born in 1935 and turning 65 in the year 2000 would have expected to live on average another 17.7 years. Born in 1925? Remaining life expectancy at age 65 in 1990 would have been 17.4 years.[48] But these years aren't exactly likely to be "golden." Boomers are more likely to be obese, less likely to exercise, more likely to have high blood pressure, and less likely to feel generally positive about their level of health, relative to their parents' generation.[49]

This means one thing as far as the Millennial pennies-from-heaven financial strategy is concerned: there will be few pennies left. Boomers are likely to spend down their own pots of money and other assets before they ever have a chance to pass them along to the next generation. Since 2002 Fidelity has estimated how much a near-retirement couple is likely to spend on health care for the remainder of their lives, and the results are alarming. As of 2018, a sixty-five-year-old couple could expect to spend $280,000 on medical-related expenses over the remainder of their lives—excluding government benefits such as Medicare.[50] Do average Boomers have that kind of money? Does one even need to ask? As of 2018, only 33 percent of Boomers* reported having more than $300,000 in financial assets, whereas 58 percent have less than $200,000 in the bank or the retirement account.[51] That figure excludes home equity, so as long as Boomers are prepared to sell their houses to fund their retirement expenses and health care needs, Millennials might escape our parents' retirements financially unscathed. But we Millennials are notably skeptical about whether we'll really escape this burden. Another Fidelity survey in 2016 compared parents born before 1961 with their adult children born before 1991, focusing on families where the parents held at least $100,000 in wealth aside from their homes. While a generous 93 percent of the parents said they didn't think they'd need any financial support from their children in retirement, around one-quarter of the adult children said they figure they'll have to support their parents at some point.[52]

The second problem with the pennies-from-heaven strategy is the timing. One implication of stretching life expectancies is that younger generations will have to wait ever longer to receive whatever bequests manage to outlast their parents' health care needs. Go back to those life-expectancy numbers, and run some back-of-the-envelope calculations. A 65-year-old in 2014 could expect to live to the ripe old age of 84.4 years old. If he had a child when he was 30 years old, that daughter will be nearly 55 years old by the time she receives any inheritance. That is, by most measures, well beyond the point when an extra financial boost would be most useful, given what we know about Millennials' personal finances: past

---

* Born 1943–1960.

the age when her student loan burden is most acute, past the age when she'd ordinarily expect to buy a house, and past the age when she'd be raising a young family of her own with all the expenses that entails. That's not to minimize the enormous benefits of longer lives among the elderly, at least in most cases, in terms of advice given and received, grandchildren babysat, and holiday meals enjoyed together. No one can put a price on any of that. But it does mean that if the question is Millennial financial security, the reality that the Boomers are starting to pass from the scene now isn't going to be much of a solution to Millennials' most serious financial worries.

And all of this pales beside the biggest danger of relying on bequests to provide financial security for Millennials: it re-creates feudalism.

For centuries, the only sure-fire path to lifetime financial security was land, and the only sure-fire beneficiaries were a relatively small elite best positioned to profit from land ownership. Inheritances were the primary way to redistribute assets from one generation to the next, for those who had assets to pass to their children. Everyone else, for the most part, drudged on with work amid financial instability. Modern capitalism was supposed to change all this, by providing new assets that people could accumulate that weren't large tracts of land, and by allowing anyone a fair shot at building that kind of financial wealth even if your parents hadn't been rich enough to leave you a bequest. Inheritance was never not a fact of economic life, but it became a less important fact of life since with enough hard work one could aspire to build wealth even without wealthy parents or a rich long-lost uncle.

Returning to a reliance on Boomer-to-Millennial inheritances to bolster Millennials' future financial security means that a lot of Millennials will miss out. This is an inevitable function of the fact that very few Boomers seem to have enough money saved to cover the costs of their old age. It's particularly cruel to offer this as a solution for Millennials' debt problems, given that so much of that debt arises from attending college. Education was sold to us (figuratively and literally) as a great equalizer that would create new economic opportunities for all. What a terrible irony if it turns out that this isn't the case, and instead higher education is a great divider between those whose wealthy dead relatives can bail them out of student debt and everyone else.

All of this—the precarious job market, the student debt crisis, our Boomer parents' exploding health care budgets—leaves us Millennials with only one other financial option. We're going to have to work forever.

Millennials may never be able to accumulate enough assets to support a comfortable retirement, and we're starting to realize it. We already assume we won't be able to count on Social Security to support us if we retire. But we're not sure we'll have enough of our own money, either. Only around 50 percent of Millennials* in a PwC financial-health survey reported they are confident they'll be able to retire when they want to.[53] That percentage has increased from a low of 36 percent in 2013, but it's still a depressing result. Millennials can expect to have long working lives ahead of them during which to save and invest, yet large numbers of us worry about whether we'll have enough money for retirement. Boomers' own confidence in their ability to retire as reported in that survey was about as low as Millennials', but in their case it makes sense: as the financial crisis weighed on stock prices and the value of 401(k) plans, Boomers who had less time to make up any losses had more reason to worry. Why are Millennials already as concerned about their ability to retire, at least thirty years before the event, as Boomers, who were trying to retire in the middle of a Great Recession and slow recovery and newly concerned about whether stock-price gains since the Great Recession would last until they cash out their retirement funds? Perhaps this trend even explains some of the spending habits that drive Boomers up the wall, such as avocado-fueled brunches. If we expect that we'll never save enough to retire, we should at least aim for modest avocado-flavored consolation now.

---

* Born 1982–1997.

Besides, as financial plans go, working forever is a pretty bad one. We Millennials will probably live for a very long time compared to our forebears, even as life expectancy starts to plateau. And most of us simply won't be able to work for that long. As a journalist, I can probably keep going longer than many, at least to a certain extent. But will seventy-year-old Millennials want to continue working as construction workers or health care aides? The reality is that many jobs are physically and mentally demanding, making retirement as much a physical necessity as it is a financial luxury. Worse, the older we get, the harder it will be for people in those "age-limited" jobs to transition into something else.

This definitely isn't what we thought we were buying when we signed up for those expensive years in college.

CHAPTER 4

Millennius Domesticus

MILLENNIALS HAVE BEEN TAUGHT FROM AN EARLY AGE TO GO CRAZY FOR REAL estate. Home-improvement cable television came into its own in the 1990s, when the oldest tranche of Millennials were entering our prime TV-watching years. Housing was effectively a character on some of our favorite shows from our teens, whether it was the elaborate fun-houses of MTV's *The Real World* or those apartments on *Friends*. Another popular sitcom we grew up with was named, subtly enough, *Home Improvement*. That show made fun of an earlier, and far snootier, breed of home show, PBS's long-running *This Old House* with Bob Vila. The Tim Allen sitcom version worked because so many people were so familiar with the serious original.

These shows reflected ingrained ideas about housing and what it means to people, ideas Millennials fully absorbed: Your home should be a bedrock of stability in an otherwise crazy life. Your house should be an extension of your personality. Owning your home is the sign that you've fully "arrived" in adulthood. Your home, and your ownership of it, should be central to every other aspect of your life. Your home really is your castle.

And before we started learning those lessons from pop culture, Millennials already had received a master class from our parents. The epitome of self-satisfied homeowners were the Boomers, who owned their own homes in record numbers before the 2007–2008 financial crisis, accumulating record amounts of housing wealth in the process. Millennials grew up expecting to have the same love affair with housing that their parents had enjoyed—the economic and social stability, the status marking, the endless weekend trips to Home Depot.

Millennials have kept the faith even a decade after a financial crisis triggered by a housing meltdown wrecked the economy and stole our jobs. As of 2016, 80 percent of Millennials* who didn't own their homes planned to buy within the next five years.[1†] HGTV, one of the grandes dames of home-improvement soft porn, boasts that more than half of its audience is comprised of Millennials and their younger cousins in Generation Z.[2] We just can't get enough of shows like *Flip or Flop*, *House Hunters*, and *Property Brothers*.

But the housing market hasn't kept faith with us. After generations of expansion, homeownership in America is in decline, especially among Millennials. We're moving out of our parents' homes later than the previous few generations did. We're settling down in owner-occupied units later. As much as we still say we want to buy one day, an increasing number of Millennials may eventually need to abandon their dreams of homeownership entirely. Some worry that this amounts to a social crisis for Millennials, and maybe it does, but homeownership has become a trial for Millennials in a more quantifiable way too. Economically, we are losing out big because we're struggling to buy homes. Over the past century, housing has been the primary form of wealth accumulation for America's middle class. The Boomers wouldn't be where they are today if it weren't for homeownership, and that's true even after the financial crisis erased trillions of dollars of housing equity and pushed millions of mortgages into foreclosure. That's why it's a pretty big problem that Millennials can't buy houses.

And yes, there really is a Millennial housing crisis. This is the one area of any survey of Millennial misfortune where Boomers are likely to have the least sympathy. Millennials, who were too young to have bought houses in large numbers during the boom, didn't see

---

* Born 1981–1998.

† Note that the question is whether they *planned* to buy, not whether they would actually succeed at that goal in the end.

large amounts of home equity wiped out in the 2007 housing meltdown. Boomers and Gen Xers did. Millennials didn't directly suffer the emotional and financial traumas of foreclosures, and won't have those black marks on their credit reports for years to come (although Millennials suffered alongside the rest of their families if their parents were foreclosed on). Millennials also haven't suffered a lot of the other negative consequences of a housing boom-and-bust cycle. If "generation rent" Millennials can't find jobs in their neighborhoods, they can move at the drop of a trendy vintage hat. Boomers confronting a bad job market have often faced an agonizing choice between struggling to find work in the area where they've lived for years, or having to sell houses that might now be worth less than they paid for them just to have a chance at moving somewhere else where jobs are more readily available.

Unquestionably the Boomers were hammered by a housing crisis. But that doesn't change the fact that the Millennials have been, too. Or more precisely, Millennials have been hammered by all the steps the Boomers took to try to rescue themselves from their own housing crisis.

Meet Generation Rent

We all know the stereotypes about Millennial living arrangements—the basement-dwelling, couch-surfing, with-parents-living stuff of Boomer parents' nightmares. Well, it's all kind of true. Here are the facts about *Millennius domesticus*: As of 2014, living with parent(s) was the most common living arrangement for young adults ages eighteen to thirty-four—for the first time in a hundred thirty years. Around 32 percent of people in that age bracket have moved back home (or never left), compared to 31.6 percent who are living in their own household with a partner or spouse. The other third are living with roommates, with grandparents, or in a college dorm (or prison).*[3] It's not only that younger young adults

---

* Government statistics count living with grandparents separately from living with parents.

are struggling to launch—living at home is up among *all* age groups within the broad Millennial cohort. The proportion of people between twenty-five and twenty-nine living with their parents grew to 25 percent in 2014 from 18 percent in 2006.[4] While many of those "middle-age" Millennials eventually move out on their own, many others don't. Some 15 percent of older Millennials resided at Casa Mom-and-Dad as of 2016, compared to 10 percent of Gen Xers when they were the same age back in 2000, and 8 percent of Boomers in 1981. We're also living at home for longer: 91 percent of the oldest cohort of Millennials who lived at home had lived at their parents' address a year earlier, compared to 82 percent of the Boomers who had lived at home for at least a year in 1981.[*5]

There are some social or cultural reasons for the dramatic increase in living with parents, such as a long-term trend toward delaying marriage and having children (although a chicken-and-egg problem dogs any effort to understand the precise relationship between delayed family formation and delayed homebuying). Some of the new trend is a consequence of who American Millennials are—a generation of immigrants. Asians and Hispanics in America are almost twice as likely as whites to live in multigenerational households, meaning households that contain more than one adult generation, or where grandparents live with grandchildren. People who were born outside the United States are more likely to live in multigenerational households than those who were born here.[6] For some, living with parents for longer is a cultural expectation rather than an economic crisis. Other Millennials may be driven to live at home by more than their own economic concerns. Around one-quarter of Americans who care for an ill or disabled relative are Millennials.[†7]

But one of the biggest reasons for the return to the parental home for most Millennials is cold, hard economics. The rise in living at home has been driven first and foremost by higher unemployment and lower pay for young adults. Millennial men, who are

---

* Millennials born 1981–1991; Gen X born 1965–1975; Boomers born 1946–1956.
† Born 1981–1997.

more likely than women to live with their parents, have been especially hard hit. Median wages for men ages eighteen to thirty-four peaked in 1970, which not coincidentally is when the rate of men of that age living with their parents, started a long, gradual climb that turned into a spike after 2008.[8]

Not that Millennials need to be unemployed to have a reason to crash at their parents' place, literally and figuratively. Among twenty-five- to thirty-four-year-olds, three-quarters of those who lived at home as of 2016 had actual work or were studying.[9] An oft-repeated reason for living at home is that rents are unaffordably high, especially in vibrant urban areas where the job market tends to be strongest for creative, highly educated Millennials.* A paradox is that many of America's most expensive places to live have become so pricy because they're magnets for the kinds of creative, new-economy jobs that attract hyper-educated Millennials like moths to a flame (or like avocado to toast)—yet Millennials struggle to afford to live in these hubs partly as a result of rising rents and partly because our pay doesn't keep pace.

The moving-back-in-with-Mom-and-Dad trend represents an enormous backward step in the evolution of modern American adulthood. Sociologists and demographers have spent a hundred fifty years studying the question of why kids started moving out of their family homes—or more precisely, those researchers were studying why elderly parents stopped living with their children. Until the late nineteenth century, most American households were multigenerational. The most convincing theory for why that changed—why Americans started forming predominantly households that had only one adult generation—is that economic transformations after the Industrial Revolution gave the *younger* adults in families significant new freedom. Rather than toiling on family

---

* One study estimated that a 20 percent increase in average rent in a given metropolitan area would decrease the rate of household formation—an individual or couple moving out of a larger household arrangement to create their own independent family unit—by around 3.5 percent, for people of all ages. (Andrew D. Paciorek, "The Long and the Short of Household Formation," Finance and Economics Discussion Series No. 2013-26, Board of Governors of the Federal Reserve System, 2013.)

plots of land that they'd hang around to inherit, the growth of modern wage labor allowed young adults to strike off on their own and support themselves financially in independent households. What showed up most conspicuously in census data was a decline in the number of elderly people living with younger relatives in multigenerational households, but what those numbers meant was that the young-adult children had seized new opportunities to strike out on their own.*[10] Apparently today's young-adult children aren't finding the same opportunities beyond their parents' homes, or aren't able to grab at them.

Meanwhile, what of those lucky Millennials who actually have launched? They're mainly renting and paying dearly to do so. Median monthly rent in America increased more than 17 percent between 2007 and 2018, according to Census Department data— and that's *after* accounting for average inflation.† Young-adult wages simply haven't kept up with this, which is why according to one rental-listing service's estimate, Millennials‡ pay around 45 percent of their income in rent when they are between the ages of twenty-two and thirty—an average total of $92,600—compared to Boomers, who paid 36 percent of their income in rent when they were the same age.[11] It's not that Millennials don't want to move out

---

* This interpretation is at odds with a theory that was more popular in the middle of the twentieth century—that Americans abandoned multigenerational households because the *elderly* acquired the economic freedom to move out. But as economic historian Steven Ruggles has pointed out, the decline in multigenerational living arrangements predated factors such as the introduction of Social Security that gave the elderly more financial freedom. In fact, some of the creators of Social Security in the 1930s argued the program was necessary precisely because the elderly *already* were living independently but lacked the financial resources to do so comfortably. (Steven Ruggles, "The Decline of Generational Coresidence in the United States, 1850–2000," *American Sociological Review* 72, no. 6 [December 2007].)

† Data from US Census Bureau, Current Population Survey/Housing Vacancy Survey, July 26, 2018, and historical tables. Those numbers are in nominal dollars, not adjusted for inflation, but the US Bureau of Labor Statistics offers an online Consumer Price Inflation calculator through which one can convert historical prices into current dollars to separate out the normal effects of inflation on rent. And note that even if median rent had increased precisely at the rate of general consumer-price inflation over the decade, it still would have been rising faster than wages.

‡ Millennials born 1977–1995; Boomers born 1946–1964.

on their own. They simply think they can't, and they're probably right about that.

The one thing Millennials are not doing in the housing market is buying. The homeownership rate for those of us twenty-five to thirty-four in 2015 was 37 percent, compared to a 45 percent ownership rate for Boomers back when they were that age.[12]

What's alarming about this is that every single subset of Millennials seems to be losing out in some way. Ethnic groups that are increasingly represented among our ranks, such as blacks and Hispanics, historically have experienced lower homeownership rates, so maybe declining Millennial homeownership is a consequence of that longer-term phenomenon and not a recent crisis? Nope. Demographic change explains part of the decline in Millennial homeownership.* But white Millennials—whose racial group has always been most likely to own houses—also aren't buying as often as their parents did. And with the partial exception of Asians, homeownership rates *within* racial groups also are declining—black Millennials own homes at a lower rate than black Gen Xers did at the same age, and so on.[†13] Homeownership historically went hand in hand with getting married and starting a family. Millennials are doing less marrying and childbearing for our ages than Boomers did, but maybe homeownership at least is holding steady for Millennials who *do* pass those milestones? No dice: homeownership rates are declining across the board, whether Millennials are married or single. Not even *wealthy* white Millennials who are starting families are buying homes. The homeownership rate for white

---

* Which isn't actually very comforting considering historical problems with racism and lack of economic opportunities that account for part of the longer-term gap.

† Millennials born 1981–1997; Gen Xers born 1966–1982. There's some overlap because these data are actually measuring households headed by someone age eighteen to thirty-four in the reference years (I compared 2000 to 2015), but this doesn't sway the data too much because individuals born in 1981 or 1982 were less likely to own a home in the year 2000 anyway. Homeownership by young-adult households headed by an Asian increased faster between 2000 and 2005 when the Gen Xers were the main buyers than for any other ethnic group, so their postcrisis ownership rate for young adults hasn't fallen quite as low as the level in 2000, but the drop-off for Millennials still is steep.

adults ages twenty-five to thirty-four with household incomes of $100,000 or more and children is declining, to just below 84 percent as of 2015 (when that age range captures Millennials) from a peak above 90 percent before the crisis (when Gen Xers fell into that category).[14] In absolute terms, an 84 percent ownership rate is nothing to cry over. But the sudden downward trend even for this most privileged sliver of Millennials hints that something is going more broadly wrong in the market.

It's easy to lose track of how astounding and disappointing the ownership crisis is. For all the demographic and economic factors that might predict less homeownership, Millennials exhibit some traits that would ordinarily imply *higher* homeownership than previous generations. College graduates are significantly more likely to buy homes than nongraduates, and more Millennials have attended college than any previous generation. Yet our high levels of education aren't boosting our homeownership rates. On the contrary, the rate of homeownership for young adults now is lower than in previous generations even among those who have at least some college education.[15] This is a particular shock among people of color, for whom college was billed as an important boost into the middle class.

The first thing any good Boomer (or any crotchety Millennial) might do if confronted with these data, naturally enough, is to blame Millennials. There's a perception in some quarters that maybe Millennials are just being too picky. Tim Gurner—the Australian Millennial magnate of avocado-toast infamy whom we met in the Introduction—captured this point in his rant about Millennial homebuyers who need to be more "realistic" about what they should buy, including looking at cities where property is less expensive. It's tempting to think he was right, when news stories about a gradual uptick in homeownership among older Millennials (at long last) tend to note that we're leapfrogging past traditional starter homes into larger abodes in better neighborhoods—and with larger price tags to match.[16]

But the appearance of Millennial choosiness probably arises because, ironically enough, we have too little housing to choose from.

America's stock of starter homes is drying up.* Between 2012 and 2018, starter homes on the market declined both in absolute numbers (about half as many are available for purchase now as were available six years ago) and as a proportion of overall inventory (22 percent of homes for sale in the first quarter of 2018 were starter homes, compared to 30 percent in 2012). The average starter home available for sale now is older and in need of more fixing up than was the case even just a few years ago, yet the prices keep shooting upward.[17] These days, the best way for Millennials to get a starter home is . . . to rent one. By one estimate, more than a million starter homes that had been owner-occupied in 2005 became rental properties by 2013.[†18] Millennials have little choice but to hang on in our rented homes until we can afford the bigger, newer, more polished homes that actually *are* on the market.

Especially since Boomers have gone out of their way to make sure there won't be enough houses for us to buy in the parts of the country where we need to live. New-house construction as a percentage of the total number of households in America is the lowest it has been since data begin in 1957. This suggests that the supply of housing is falling further and further behind demand.[19] And there's a direct connection between where houses do and don't get built, and where Millennials need to live to be near jobs. It's possible to gauge in which cities it's easiest to build new housing and where it's hardest.[‡] And when researchers compare cities where the limitations are the tightest to the cities experiencing the greatest inflow of Millennials, they discover we're more likely to

---

* There is no universally accepted definition of "starter home." Both of the surveys I cite from here examine the entire housing stock in an area—not just those homes that are currently for sale—and divide those houses into three segments based on estimated value. Starter homes are the lowest-value segment.

† Defined as houses smaller than two thousand square feet.

‡ One method, used in the study cited in this paragraph, involves combining the results of a survey measuring how much land in a given city is available for development with a Wharton Business School index measuring the strictness of local zoning rules to develop an index for how easily housing supply can expand to meet demand.

live in cities that will produce the least new housing to accommo-
date us.*[20] Millennials aren't flooding into supply-constrained cities out of sheer bloody-mindedness or stupidity, but because those
are the areas where the jobs are, especially at the most highly educated, highly skilled end of the job market.† Boomers are capitaliz-
ing on that labor-market trend by limiting housing supply so that
they can profit from soaring Millennial rents and the high prices
Millennials pay to Boomer sellers in order to buy in these areas.
As one academic paper puts it, the rise of new zoning restrictions
starting in the 1970s changed cities "from urban growth machines
to homeowners' cooperatives."[21] Boomers paid a price for that tendency as first-time buyers in the 1980s, and Millennials are paying
even more now.

So Millennials' home woes boil down to one thing more than
anything else: affordability. No matter how far we reach, homeownership always seems to be just a little bit beyond our financial
grasp. Boomers are to blame, and it's time to dig into exactly how.

Weapons of Mass Construction

To understand what has gone wrong in the housing market, one
has to start with a fact that can seem surprising: homeownership
historically wasn't as significant in the United States as the Baby
Boomers grew up thinking it was. Between 1890 and 1930, the
homeownership rate—owner-occupied houses as a percentage of
all housing units—held steady at around 47 percent.[22] There are a
lot of reasons so many people didn't own in that era. The most important was that it was downright hard to afford a house. Banks
were extremely conservative when lending to homebuyers. In the

---

* In economics-speak, where the supply of new housing is "inelastic" because the
market won't or can't produce new supply even when rising prices would normally
prompt developers to build new properties for sale.

† There's a growing literature observing that job growth, and especially growth in the
highest-paying jobs, is geographically clustered in a relatively small number of urban
areas. See, for instance, Enrico Moretti's book *The New Geography of Jobs* (New
York: Houghton Mifflin Harcourt, 2012).

early 1920s, homeowners often needed to make a down payment of more than 40 percent of a house's value, and twelve years was considered a long mortgage.[23] Most mortgages were so-called balloon loans, where the borrower would make interest-only payments during the term of the loan and then pay off the principal in one enormous lump-sum at the end. Rates were variable, refinancing was common when the balloon payment came due, and banks were cautious about lending, owing to the risk that a buyer might default on the principal payment.[24]

So when homeownership really started to take off—just as the Baby Boomers were babies—it was nothing short of a revolution. The rate of homeownership began climbing rapidly, to 55 percent in 1950 and to nearly 63 percent by 1970.[25] Younger adults were buying homes in enormous numbers, with the ownership rate among heads-of-household ages twenty-five to thirty-five hitting 56 percent in 1960 from 19 percent in 1940, the biggest percentage-point increase of any age group during that time.[26] Rapid economic growth made homeownership affordable for unprecedented numbers of workers, and the Baby Boom itself encouraged parents to look for houses to buy as homes for their growing families.

But government policy also played a substantial role by totally overhauling the way Americans paid for homes. One cause of the financial crisis in the Great Depression had been that unemployed homeowners started defaulting on their balloon payments at exactly the moment a crash in property values wiped out the equity that mortgage lenders would ordinarily have recouped in a foreclosure. To solve this problem for both banks and foreclosed homeowners, Washington created a new agency (the Home Owner Loan Corporation, or HOLC) to buy defaulting mortgages from banks. Banks would get their money—and crucially, the government would convert the loans into a new kind of mortgage that would better protect homeowners. Instead of evicting foreclosed homeowners, HOLC transformed their mortgages into twenty-year, fixed-rate, amortizing mortgages, something that had never been common in the

United States before.* And then, Washington went one better. It created the Federal Housing Agency (FHA) to insure new mortgages, in the hope that banks would be more willing to lend to homebuyers if the government protected banks from the risks of default. The FHA would insure only amortizing mortgages—gone were the old balloon payments—and with durations of up to twenty years (extended to thirty years in the 1940s) with down payments as little as 20 percent (later cut to 5 percent for some buyers). For good measure, Washington also created the agency we now know as Fannie Mae to buy these mortgages from banks outright to free up even more cash for borrowing. After World War II, the GI Bill subsidized mortgages for millions of returning veterans with no down payment at all.[27] And as a cherry on top, this spike in mortgage borrowing meant that more and more households would enjoy the benefits of the mortgage-interest deduction in the income tax code. This loophole in the tax laws hadn't originally been intended as an incentive for homeownership—it arose from a broader exemption for all interest payments—but it became an important tax offset to housing costs that was available only if a family bought instead of rented.

These changes to the mortgage market had a profound effect on the American economy. Amortizing mortgages in effect became the American middle class's most popular form of saving.† That in turn reshaped the distribution of wealth between various households. If one thinks about all the household wealth in America as a pie, the middle class's piece of the pie steadily expanded from around 16

---

* In an amortizing mortgage, each payment includes both an element of interest and a bit of principal. Typically the earliest payments are primarily interest, but over the life of the loan the proportion of each payment devoted to principal increases.

† Economists have long debated whether this is a good thing. Maintenance costs can make ownership more expensive than renting, and house prices don't always rise as fast as the prices of other assets in which someone could invest, such as stocks. Maybe Americans would have been better off renting and then depositing the money they saved into a brokerage account to invest in the stock market. But the reality is that for a lot of people, that monthly mortgage payment to the bank was a form of discipline that no amount of academic studies about relative rates of return could replace. For anyone who lacked the self-discipline of a financial saint, the choice was often to buy a house or not save at all.

percent in the 1930s to 35 percent in the 1980s, even as the pie itself was also expanding.*[28] Homeownership and an explosion in pension wealth were the two biggest drivers of this increase. Before the homeownership boom, the main method for a middle-class family to accumulate wealth—if it ever accumulated any—was to take the risk of starting a small business. Now millions of people could enjoy the stability of a salaried job, while also having the means to accumulate wealth every month with their mortgage payments. The housing market had helped create a new middle class—and with it, a new American economy.

The problem is that in the 1990s, as they came into their own politically, the Boomers got greedy.

It all started with what at the time seemed like a housing crisis afflicting the Boomers. The homeownership rate started a gentle decline from above 65 percent in the late 1970s to less than 64 percent in the mid-1980s.[29] Far more worrying, homeownership among *younger* buyers ages twenty-five to forty-four fell during the 1980s from just above 60 percent in 1980 to just below 56 percent in 1990, a level lower than it had been in 1960. No one entirely understood why young-adult Boomers weren't buying. But the trend created a new fear among politicians: that too many people were being cut off from the benefits of ownership. In addition to concerns for new buyers, Washington had another major worry. The postwar housing boom hadn't boomed for everyone. Lower-income households and people of color had never managed to boost their ownership rates to anything approaching that enjoyed by the white middle class.

---

* The work of Emmanuel Saez and Gabriel Zucman, from whose influential 2016 paper on wealth inequality these numbers are taken, remains controversial. There's good reason to believe their method for estimating wealth underestimates the holdings of less wealthy families and dramatically overestimates the share of wealth held by the richest households. But to the extent that's true, it bolsters my claim that housing was a great equalizer for the middle class, since one weakness in the Saez and Zucman study is that it may significantly *undercount* the housing wealth accumulated by the lower 90 percent of households. (Jesse Bricker, Alice Henriques, Jacob Krimmel, and John Sabelhaus, "Measuring Income and Wealth at the Top Using Administrative and Survey Data," *Brookings Papers in Economic Activity*, Spring 2016.)

By the early 1990s, with Boomers fully in the electorate and growing more influential in politics and business by the day, this Boomer housing crisis seemed increasingly urgent. Politicians leapt into action. And they did so in a way that would fundamentally up-end the housing market and ultimately raise questions about why policymakers were encouraging homeownership at all: the Boom-ers doubled down on housing debt.*

In 1992, less than a month before Bill Clinton was elected Amer-ica's first Baby Boomer president, Congress passed a new law to sub-sidize mortgage lending for lower-income borrowers using Fannie Mae and her 1970s-vintage brother, Freddie Mac. Those agencies were created to buy mortgages from banks and then hold them or sell them to other investors, in order to encourage banks to lend by providing a ready market for mortgages. Fannie and Freddie had always been limited in the types of mortgages they could buy—with a focus on relatively modest-sized amortizing loans from borrowers with relatively good credit. But the 1992 law set quotas for Fannie and Freddie to buy mortgages that had been extended to low- and middle-income homebuyers even if those loans didn't otherwise satisfy Fannie's and Freddie's criteria. Now 30 percent of their mort-gage purchases would need to be loans that lenders had extended to low- or middle-income borrowers. That was roughly the propor-tion of these less secure mortgages that the agencies had bought

---

* The analysis that follows is based in part on the dissenting opinions included in the final report of the Financial Crisis Inquiry Commission (FCIC) in January 2011. Un-surprisingly, what caused the financial panic remains a controversial question, which unfortunately neither the majority report agreed on by the six Democratic members of the FCIC nor the two dissents filed by the panel's four Republican members fully answer. The majority report suffers from some particular shortcomings that should make Millennials wary of treating it as a definitive guide to the crisis. Its authors took a scattershot approach to listing many market and policy problems before the crisis, without articulating which factors might have been more or less important than others; and its members seem to have been politically devoted to the goal of boosting homeownership, leading them to downplay the negative consequences of government policies aimed at doing that. The dissents suffer from their own weak-nesses—they're perhaps a little too quick to downplay the role of old-fashioned greed in fueling the housing mania—but their approach to the economics of the crisis is more focused, and to my eye more plausible.

before anyway. But the law allowed the Department of Housing and Urban Development (HUD) to increase that target, and successive HUD secretaries under Clinton—Henry G. Cisneros and Andrew Cuomo, Boomers both—would raise the quotas aggressively, to 50 percent by 2001. The Clinton administration also steadily increased the proportion of those loans that had to go to the riskiest borrowers, those with the lowest incomes. And Fannie and Freddie generally exceeded their quotas.[30]

To meet those quotas, Fannie and Freddie—and the lenders writing the mortgages that would be sold to the pair—had to dramatically loosen lending standards. A simple fact had always helped ensure the stability of the US housing-finance market: so long as most homebuyers were required to make a down payment and meet requirements for the level of the monthly mortgage payment relative to monthly income, only a few buyers would end up defaulting. But those standards had been barriers for low-income households hoping to buy a home but struggling to raise a down payment. So in the 1990s the rules were eased significantly. The 1995 National Homeownership Strategy issued by HUD played up the importance of easing down-payment standards for the sake of enabling up to eight million more families to buy homes.[31] Mortgage lenders, working in tandem with Fannie and Freddie, were urged to find ways to reduce down-payment requirements and increase the number of mortgages made with very small down payments, and to "look beyond" traditional measures of creditworthiness (such as provable income or a manageable level of debt relative to income) when making loans.[32]

Boosting homeownership among risky mortgage borrowers became a bipartisan Boomer preoccupation. The Republican George W. Bush administration steadily increased the Fannie and Freddie low-income quotas, which reached 56 percent by 2008 after the financial crisis already was under way. Worse, in a 2004 regulation increasing these quotas, HUD Secretary Alphonso Jackson insisted that the increased quota be met by extending more loans to the riskiest borrowers—those with the lowest incomes.[33] It all worked, in a manner of speaking. In 1989, only 1 in 230 buyers made a down payment of 3 percent or less. By 2003, it was 1 in 7 and on the eve of the crisis in 2007, it was just less than 1 in 3.[34]

Those pro-debt policies lit a fire under the housing market, and the Federal Reserve poured on the accelerant. The 1990s was the era of Rubinomics and unusually low interest rates from the Alan Greenspan–run Federal Reserve—a policy that was supposed to stimulate more business investment to bolster the Boomer job market. But the short-term rate the Fed sets is intended to serve as a benchmark for *all* other interest rates, and sure enough the low federal funds rate in this era filtered through to the housing market one way or another. From just above 10 percent in the second half of the 1980s, the average interest rate on a thirty-year fixed-rate mortgage fell to around 8 percent for most of the 1990s. Mortgage rates fell again, to below 6 percent in the mid-2000s, after the dot-com bubble burst and the 9/11 terror attack prompted the Green-span Fed to cut interest rates even further.[35]

Low interest helped fuel the housing bubble in another way—by bolstering the market for those mortgage-backed securities (MBS) everyone started hearing about after the crisis hit.* Markets for securities of this sort had existed for a long time, but the market really took off in the early 2000s for a simple reason: There were trillions of dollars' worth of mortgage-backed securities available for investors to buy, they were supposed to be safe, and they offered a higher rate of return when returns for many other assets had been driven down by low Federal Reserve interest rates. Indeed, one way Fannie and Freddie's own lending quotas helped fuel the housing fire was by goading private-sector institutions to take more mortgage-lending risks of their own to achieve better returns even

---

* The concept behind an MBS is relatively simple. Banks that have made a lot of mortgage loans can lump those together and then sell groups of them to other investors. Those investors absorb the risks of the underlying mortgages—the danger that the buyer will default, or will repay the mortgage early before she's paid all the interest the MBS investor was expecting—but in exchange can enjoy the potential returns of mortgage loans when borrowers do repay on schedule.

while Fannie and Freddie were cornering the market for the "safer" mortgages extended to riskier borrowers.*

These housing policies had the desired effect. The overall ownership rate started climbing again, from 64 percent in 1993 to nearly 68 percent in 2001 and an all-time high of 69.2 percent in 2004.[36] But too few people stopped to ask whether this Baby Boomer housing boom really would—or could—transform America in the same positive ways that the first postwar ownership boom had.

Although more people "owned" homes, Americans owned smaller and smaller portions of the houses they lived in. In 1945, owners' equity had reached nearly 84 percent of the total value of housing.† That fell throughout the postwar boom period, to a low of 63 percent in 1966, as 20 percent-down, thirty-year amortizing mortgages came to dominate the market and slow-and-steady equity accumulation for existing borrowers didn't keep up with new lending. But it was clear that this generation of buyers took equity-building seriously. In 1966, as the first tranche of Depression-era twenty- and thirty-year mortgages ended and the Baby Boom itself

---

* There was another monetary factor in play here, for those who are more technically minded: one effect of inappropriately low interest rates was to depreciate the dollar relative to other currencies, and as a result to increase the dollar prices Americans paid for imported goods and commodities. This prompted one large economy—China—to accumulate enormous dollar reserves as Beijing tried to prevent its own currency from appreciating too much relative to the dollar. Meanwhile, commodity-exporting countries such as Saudi Arabia also amassed enormous dollar balances. They all needed somewhere to park their dollars, and America's housing market provided a ready outlet. Bonds issued by Fannie Mae and Freddie Mac ("agency debt" in financial parlance) were especially popular because foreign investors believed Washington would never allow the housing agencies to default, while the investments offered higher returns than normal Treasury bonds. As of July 2008, just months before Fannie and Freddie were placed into receivership for their bad debts, the Federal Reserve held nearly $890 billion worth of agency debts and mortgage-backed securities on behalf of foreign central banks and sovereign-wealth funds. America couldn't have produced quite so bubbly a housing bubble without this foreign investment in the mortgage market—which was really just recycling Fed-produced easy money back into the American economy.

† That high level was probably a result of the combination of high-down-payment, short-duration mortgages and the hangover from the Depression-era wave of foreclosures that had effectively transferred full equity in the homes of the most indebted owners to banks and other institutions.

wound down, total housing equity in America started climbing steadily, to around 68 percent throughout the 1970s.[37]

Starting in the 1980s, Americans' attitudes toward home equity and savings changed. Tax-law changes in the 1980s made mortgage interest the *only* interest a household could deduct from income taxes. The home equity line of credit was born. Suddenly it made an awful lot of sense for households to borrow against the value of their homes for many purposes—the interest rate would be lower than a credit card or personal credit line, and that interest would be more tax-efficient than any other loan. Older homeowners, whether from the Silent Generation or the first wave of Baby Boomers, used these loans somewhat responsibly at first: in 1991, 54 percent of households with a home equity loan outstanding used the money to finance renovations that increased the value of their homes. Within a decade, however, homeowners, now including large numbers of Boomers, were going to town with their home equity. Only 45 percent of home equity borrowers in 2001 used the money to pay for renovations, while the proportion using home equity to consolidate other debts (most often credit cards that had been used to finance consumption bigger than disposable income) rose to 26 percent from 21 percent a decade earlier. The rest used home equity for items such as car purchases or educational or medical expenses.[38] Cash-out refinancing would peak in 2006, when *prime* borrowers, ostensibly the most responsible credit risks, would cash out $320 billion from their home equity—nearly 30 percent of prime mortgage lending that year.[39] Housing was no longer a long-term investment in financial security. It was a piggy bank.*

---

* The fact that these equity-extracting homeowners were prime borrowers is a significant angle on the financial crisis that often gets overlooked. In calling the event the "subprime crisis," policymakers and the media have focused—as much of this chapter does—on the role of expanding lending to less creditworthy borrowers in the run-up to the crisis. But studies have found that large proportions of defaults in the crisis (nearly 40 percent in Los Angeles, according to one count) were by owners who had bought before 2004 and would have had positive home equity even after a steep fall in prices *if they had not borrowed against the additional equity in their homes created by rapidly rising prices*. One implication is that by pumping up the housing market via lending to riskier borrowers, Boomers in Washington inadvertently encouraged other homeowners to take bigger mortgage risks, too. (Steven Laufer, "Equity Extraction and Mortgage Default," Federal Reserve Board: Finance and Economics Discussion Series, July 2013.)

This explosion in mortgage lending was completely nonsensical from a public policy perspective. The economic and social benefits of homeownership arise from the ownership itself—the accumulation of equity, helped by an amortizing mortgage requiring a substantial down payment. A weakness of housing policies all along was that lending subsidies and the mortgage-interest deduction encouraged housing *debt* rather than housing equity. Traditional lending standards had kept some focus on equity by requiring down payments and an amortizing structure. Now, however, rather than helping low-income buyers accumulate equity through grants or other assistance, starting in the 1990s the government amped up the housing lending market. In the name of encouraging homeownership, many would-be buyers found themselves taking out loans for which they'd only repay the interest for the first few years, after they hadn't put any money down on equity in the house to start. *Unless house values continued to rise rapidly and permanently*, it would be years before this new cohort of homeowners truly owned anything at all. And that was one enormous "if."

Such doubts were too easy to ignore because in so many ways the housing boom seemed to be fueling phenomenal economic growth. New demand for more—and often bigger, more luxurious—homes fueled a construction boom. Equity release fueled a household consumption explosion. In fact, to an astonishing degree, housing *was* the American economy in the mid-2000s. Investment in housing rose to nearly 35 percent of total fixed investment by 2005, compared to around 25 percent throughout the 1990s. Housing loomed over consumer spending as new borrower-owners bought refrigerators, dishwashers, and other appliances to put in those houses.[40] But this was extraordinarily dangerous. Not only is housing itself a low-productivity investment because it doesn't directly generate as much future income as investment in a new factory machine, but Americans were borrowing in unprecedented quantities to "invest" in housing assets whose low economic productivity raised the question of where the new money to repay the loans would come from.

So a disaster was all but inevitable by the time the Federal Reserve started raising interest rates very slowly in June 2004 in response to fears the economy was overheating. Mortgage rates crept upward over the next couple years, gradually limiting the amount that prospective homebuyers could borrow and—by 2006—capping what previously had seemed like the unstoppable ascent of house prices. New and old homeowners alike who had counted on rising prices to create new equity out of thin air suddenly found the houses were worth less on the market than the mortgage the "owner" was repaying. Delinquency rates—the percentage of mortgages that were at least thirty days behind on their payments—started to inch up the same year.[41] The prices of mortgage-backed securities plummeted as investors woke up to this new risk, blowing holes in bank balance sheets around the world as the banks realized the assets they held— backed by risky mortgages—were worth less than they thought. The rest would be a particularly wretched bit of financial history.

The Boomer Property Protection Racket

When the crisis finally came, it started with a press release the significance of which most Millennials completely missed. On February 7, 2007, HSBC, the global bank based in London and Hong Kong, put out a two-page technical note warning investors that the losses on its portfolio of US mortgage-backed securities would be higher than it had previously anticipated. The bank blamed slowing house-price growth and rising defaults.[42]

In retrospect, those two pages marked the moment the global financial system stepped over the cliff edge and began its plunge into the unknown. More signs of distress would appear in quick succession. Hedge funds run by the investment bank Bear Stearns to invest in US mortgages reported heavy losses. French bank BNP Paribas prevented investors from withdrawing money from its own mortgage hedge funds because trading in those assets on global markets had frozen. Then, on October 1, 2007, it became clear that this wouldn't be any ordinary financial crunch. Swiss investment bank UBS, a global giant, wrote down the value of its mortgage-related assets by $3.4 billion. On October 24, Merrill Lynch announced a quarterly loss of $2.3 billion. This was more than a modest blip now. America's mortgage meltdown was going to inflict heavy losses on *all* major banks, and whether they'd survive the blows to their balance sheets was anyone's guess. Some of the biggest names in American finance—Bear Stearns, Merrill Lynch, Washington Mutual, Countrywide Financial—didn't. Mortgage giants Fannie Mae and Freddie Mac were put into receivership, a form of bankruptcy. And then there was Lehman Brothers, the venerable investment bank that just couldn't be rescued. Markets that had barely maintained their composure for a year and a half went into meltdown when Lehman tipped into bankruptcy in September 2008, with stock prices plunging around the globe.

The basic contours of the crisis weren't at all unusual in the annals of financial history. Investors buoyed by cheap borrowing had overextended themselves, and then the assets they'd bought had lost value. Because so many of those "investors" were banks holding mortgage-backed securities, the gaping holes on their balance sheets threatened to make it impossible for the stricken banks to lend to anyone else when the value of some of their assets evaporated. It was both a liquidity and a solvency crisis. In the heat of the financial panic, the supply of ready cash in the financial system—liquidity—dried up as wary banks were temporarily unable or unwilling to lend to each other even for twenty-four hours or less to grease the wheels of the financial system. Meanwhile, the resulting plunge in value of the mortgage-backed securities and related assets that banks held on their balance sheets meant that some of them were also insolvent. Even if they could get day-to-day liquidity, they'd still owe others far more than they could ever repay.

So Boomers in the White House (George W. Bush and then Barack Obama), the Treasury Department (Hank Paulson and then Tim Geithner), and the Federal Reserve (Ben Bernanke) quickly developed two distinct but related approaches to managing the crisis: shoring up Wall Street's *liquidity* by pouring extraordinary amounts of Federal Reserve and taxpayer money into the financial system and then fixing the *insolvency* crisis by reinflating the housing bubble on Main Street in the hope that this would help the economy grow its way out of the financial crunch and ensuing Great Recession.

They managed to get the first half of the crisis response at least partly right. The nineteenth-century English central banking the- orist Walter Bagehot taught that in the middle of a liquidity panic, the central bank should stand ready to lend to all comers against good collateral and at hefty interest. That's what Washington tried to do. Throughout 2007 and 2008, Ben Bernanke's Federal Reserve devised increasingly creative ways to make emergency loans to banks of all sorts, including often stretching the rules governing the kinds of institutions to which the Fed could lend. Congress also created the Troubled Asset Relief Program (TARP), a $700 billion financial lifeline intended to calm the liquidity panic while also starting to shore up the solvency of banks and other finan- cial institutions.* The government would give recipients cash for their balance sheets in exchange for preferred shares that would earn large dividends for taxpayers before the banks' private-sector owners—the holders of the common stock—would see any return. Bagehot would have recognized this type of bailout.

These bailouts became flashpoints both among political con- servatives in the nascent Tea Party movement and among politi- cal liberals, many of them Millennials, in the Occupy Wall Street movement that would eventually develop. But it's hard to argue Millennials were victims of the bailouts. Over time the government has profited from these taxpayer cash injections as the banks re- covered and bought back the government's preferred shares, so we won't be paying down this government debt into our old age. And these maneuvers almost certainly did help to contain the deepest fi- nancial crisis since the early 1930s, averting a deeper and longer re- cession. Since the crisis, the politicians and policymakers in charge at the time have tried to make themselves out to be heroes for these

---

* And, rather oddly, automakers such as General Motors and Chrysler, which both received rescue funding via TARP.

interventions, but it's fairer to say that at least they weren't entirely inept at putting out a financial fire they had helped to start and that still managed to catch them by surprise.

The problem, for Millennials more than anyone else, was everything else the government did during and after the crisis to fix the *solvency* crisis. Possible solutions to this problem could have run the gamut from partially nationalizing some banks, to giving them more time to work out the true values of their mortgage-related assets before reimposing capital rules, to encouraging a more leisurely pace of mergers and acquisitions, to simply allowing more banks to go bankrupt while continuing to provide emergency liquidity to soothe the markets. Some of those ideas would have been politically popular, others not. But instead of any of those options, the Boomers in Washington became convinced that the best path was to revive the housing market by keeping as many Boomers and Gen Xers as possible in homes they could barely afford, while propping up prices so that Millennials would *never* be able to afford a house.

Efforts to halt the flood of home foreclosures started early on.[43] In August 2007, President Bush and Treasury Secretary Paulson created a new voluntary program to try to encourage borrowers and lenders to convert unaffordable loans into new, fixed-rate mortgages insured by the FHA. That was followed a year later by a law encouraging lenders to write down the value of mortgages so that homeowners would gain at least a sliver of equity, in exchange for which the lender would benefit from FHA insurance on the new loan. That program was a flop owing to its complexity and strict conditions,* but the Boomers in Washington were just getting started. The Obama administration, coming to office in January 2009, kicked off a confusing flurry of mortgage-relief programs—HARP, HAMP, 2MP, HAFA, UP, HAMP Tier 2, PRA,

---

* All 760 borrowers out of an expected 400,000 modified their mortgages under the program (Katie Jones, "Preserving Homeownership: Foreclosure Prevention Initiatives," Congressional Research Service Report No. R40210, May 14, 2015).

and others. These all worked (or didn't) in different ways, some writing down principal, others providing incentives to lenders to reduce interest and monthly payments; some devoted to primary residences, others to rental properties; some loan guarantees and lender subsidies, other programs handing money directly to state housing agencies. The one thing they all shared was an absolute determination to spare as many precrisis homeowners as possible from suffering foreclosure. "It's in our interest that more people stay in their homes during this period of uncertainty," Bush had said in July 2008.[44] "All of us will pay an even steeper price if we allow this [foreclosure] crisis to continue to deepen—a crisis which is unraveling home ownership, the middle class, and the American Dream itself," a recently inaugurated Obama said in February 2009.*[45]

Another Boomer also seemed heavily committed to propping up the housing market: Federal Reserve chair Ben Bernanke. Aside from fulfilling its classical lender-of-last-resort function for Wall Street, the Fed set about trying to rescue Main Street, too. It started with short-term interest-rate cuts, from a federal funds rate of 5.25 percent as of September 2007 to effectively zero by December 2008. Fed statements announcing these interest-rate cuts generally focused on broader economic and financial market problems. But the

---

* In that speech, Obama articulated the most compelling economic argument for bailing out underwater existing owners: the concern that a tide of foreclosures could ruin a neighborhood—and neighboring house prices—especially if foreclosed homes were allowed to fall derelict. Economic research seemed to support this conclusion, although it wasn't always clear how big the negative effect of a foreclosure in the neighborhood (economists call it an "externality") might be in practice. But more recent work raises questions about these assumptions. One emerging theory is that it isn't the foreclosure itself that causes the problem, but the fact that a homeowner in danger of being foreclosed stops investing in upkeep of the property either because she lacks the resources—tight personal finances are a major driver of default—or because she knows the bank will own the house soon anyway. In this view, foreclosure is the *cure* instead of the cause of bad neighborhood effects because after a foreclosure, the new owner has more equity and more incentive to invest in upkeep. If further research supports this claim, it would mean the Boomers got the foreclosure crisis exactly wrong. By trying to delay foreclosures rather than speeding up the process, Washington might have exacerbated the neighborhood problems it thought it was solving. (See Anthony Yezer and Yishen Liu, "Can Differences Deceive? The Case of 'Foreclosure Externalities,'" George Washington University Institute for International Economic Policy Working Paper Series, November 2017.)

minutes of meetings of the Federal Open Markets Committee—
the body that formally sets monetary policy under the chair's leadership—show a growing preoccupation through this period with
how many new mortgages were being originated, and what effects
a drop-off in house prices would have on the broader economy.

Then came the asset purchases, or quantitative easing. Traditionally, the Fed's main "policy tool" was the federal funds rate, the
rate at which banks lend to each other overnight.* That rate, the
interest rate on the safest type of borrowing in the economy, then
becomes a benchmark for other interest rates.† When economic
growth slowed and inflation fell short of the Fed's target, the central
bank could cut its target interest rate to encourage more borrowing and investment. If growth seemed too strong and inflation was
starting to pick up, the Fed could increase its target rate to discour-
age borrowing and apply the brakes.

But the central bank would face a dilemma if the interest rate
was at or near zero and the economy still wasn't growing as desired. Bernanke had spent much of his academic career considering
what to do in that scenario. For a solution, he (and other monetary
economists) turned to an idea once proposed by Milton Friedman,
one of America's most influential economists and economic historians. If cutting interest rates didn't work on its own, pump as much
money as possible directly into the economy to trigger more inflation. Friedman had put it more colorfully by suggesting a central
banker could throw money out of a helicopter.[46]

On November 25, 2008, in the wake of the Lehman bankruptcy
and amid a global panic, the helicopter took flight. The Fed issued
a momentous announcement that it would buy bonds issued by
Fannie, Freddie, and their little sister Ginnie Mae, and mortgage-
backed securities they had created, to the tune of $600 billion. It
was the first time the Fed had ever bought any asset other than

---

* The Fed normally influences this rate only indirectly by buying and selling Treasury bonds or adjusting the interest rate it pays on the reserves banks hold at the Fed
in order to nudge the market toward the target rate.

† Lenders make a guess at how much riskier they think a given loan is relative to the
"risk-free" federal funds rate and add additional interest to compensate for that risk.

garden-variety Treasury bonds. And Bernanke was doing it for homeowners—most of them Boomers. "This action is being taken to reduce the cost and increase the availability of credit for the purchase of houses, which in turn should support housing markets and foster improved conditions in financial markets more generally," the Fed said in the press release announcing this, its first quantitative easing program.[47] Over time the program expanded to include hundreds of billions of dollars' worth of mortgage securities, and added new asset purchases (dubbed in the press "QE2" and "QE3"), for a total of nearly $3.5 trillion thrown out of the metaphorical helicopter. Along the way, the Fed also executed a maneuver that came to be called Operation Twist, in which it exchanged some of its holdings of short-term government bonds for longer-term bonds—another attempt to depress long-term rates on loans, including mortgages.

The plan worked, up to a point. Mortgage rates fell as the Fed hoped they would, to below 4 percent for a thirty-year, fixed-rate mortgage for much of the postrecession period from between 5.5 percent and 6.5 percent during the precrisis mania. The availability of this credit, which allowed many homeowners to refinance at lower rates for lower monthly payments, may have added around $76 billion in additional household spending power to the US economy.[48] But all of these policies to benefit the housing market helped certain kinds of homeowners and buyers more than others. Millennials became the biggest losers.

That's a bold argument, especially when both Boomers and Gen Xers are staking their own claims to the title of Housing Bust's Biggest Victims because those generations were the ones that owned houses when the crisis came in 2007. Gen Xers were especially exposed to the downturn as the most recent cohort of new buyers when the implosion came. Boomers, meanwhile, were between the ages of forty-three and sixty-one when house prices and homeowner equity took a dive—closer to retirement, when they'd be more likely to need to cash out the equity that had just evaporated.

But precisely because those two generations were in such dire personal financial straits, Boomers in Washington obsessed over saving the housing market *for those who already owned homes.* No one spared a thought for the rising generation of Millennial first-time buyers who would hit the market in the following decade. And sure enough, subsequent research has found that while low interest rates and quantitative easing did boost mortgage lending, most of that was for refinancing, not new purchases. In the depth of the crisis, lending for both new purchases and refinancing plunged, but after the crisis, only refinancing recovered significantly.[49]

That phenomenon created many unintended consequences for Millennials. Most immediately, the "correction" in astronomical house prices ended up not being much of a correction at all from the perspective of young buyers. While prices fell substantially from their 2006-era peak, they never came anywhere close to their level from 2000, before the housing mania had started—and have subsequently climbed even above their 2006 heights.[50] This was great for the Boomer and Gen X owners who managed to avoid foreclosure long enough to see some of their housing equity creep back. But this artificial boost to prices has pushed old-fashioned, 20-percent-down, thirty-year amortizing, equity-accumulation-machine mortgages out of reach for Millennials. We'll never be able to save that kind of down payment, so we don't. In 2017, the median down payment for a first-time buyer younger than thirty-seven was all of 7 percent,[51] and Fannie, Freddie, and the FHA still encourage first-time buying with down payments as low as 3 percent.[52] When it comes to the housing market, America hasn't learned anything from the crisis.

A related side effect for Millennials was to mute what should have been one of our great advantages in a recession—our mobility. A downside of homeownership is that the homeowner often gets stuck in an economic downturn. Plunging home equity makes it difficult to sell up and move from an economically depressed region to a healthier area, so struggling homeowners find themselves forced to take worse jobs in the region where they already live.[53] Millennials, who for the most part were too young to have bought homes before the crisis, enjoyed more flexibility to follow the job market than anyone else. The problem is that the benefits of quantitative easing for existing homeowners were following the job market, too. The biggest gains—measured by less drastic declines in house prices and more refinancing activity allowing existing homeowners to extract equity or benefit from lower rates—seem to have been concentrated in areas that saw the strongest employment during the Great Recession even before the Fed had stepped in with its extraordinary policies.[54] Put another way, instead of focusing its assistance on parts of the country where housing markets and the broader economy were under stress, the Fed was mainly driving up house prices in those already thriving parts of the country where mobile Millennials were most likely to be able to find jobs.

Given the negative consequences of ultralow interest rates and quantitative easing for Millennials, the obvious solution would seem to be to return monetary policy to something closer to normal—or at least to not focus so directly on pumping up house prices beyond what Millennials can afford. But not even that return to normal can help Millennials now. Mortgage rates for older homeowners were so low for so long that now that rates are slowly starting to rise again, older owners have less incentive to move out of their houses so Millennials can move in. It's an effect called "lock-in," and it's widespread. More than twenty million homeowners refinanced their mortgages between 2009 and 2012, when interest rates on the loans were at historic lows.[55] Even a modest increase in mortgage rates now can add hundreds of dollars per month to mortgage payments for owners who take out a new mortgage to move into another house. No wonder older owners don't move. Median housing tenure more than doubled between 2008 and 2016, eventually hitting eight and a half years. And the owners who do move aren't selling their old homes. Rents are so high and crisis-era mortgage payments so low that it can make more sense to rent out a spare property instead of selling it.[56]

Add all this together—the effort to keep Boomers and Gen Xers in houses they couldn't afford, the subsidies for mortgage refinancing at the expense of lending to new borrowers, the extra support for house prices in places with the best job markets, and a strong incentive for older owners to not sell their houses now that the economy is finally improving—and it starts to look like a pretty good explanation for what's going wrong for Millennial would-be homebuyers.

Locked Out

There's one other thing the Boomers did after 2008 to keep Millennials from buying houses. They changed a wide array of financial regulations to make sure that even if we manage to find a house we can just about afford in a place where we want to live and can find a job, we'll struggle to get a mortgage.

They didn't justify it that way, of course. Boomers did this in the name of financial responsibility. Early on in the crisis, a story took hold that the financial disaster and Great Recession were the fault of Wall Street's moral failings—the "arrogance and greed" of overpaid bankers, as Obama put it in the first weeks of his first term.[57] This theory had a whiff of truth about it. Bank executives and traders, egged on by their employers' salary-and-bonus policies that heavily rewarded short-term profits regardless of long-term risks, took more and more—and bigger and bigger—risks.

A lot of those bankers learned their lesson the hard way when their institutions collapsed and they got laid off. But soon enough, Washington had plenty of reasons to worry about whether out-of-control bankers might tank the economy again—3.5 trillion reasons, to be exact. That was the number of dollars the Federal Reserve poured into the economy via quantitative easing between 2008 and 2014, and if the Fed succeeded in making mortgage lending as easy as it had been before the crisis, it might be only a matter of time before the next disaster. Congress and other authorities would need to try to impose some semblance of discipline on markets.

The process started with a flurry of new rules intended to protect the economy from another solvency crisis in the most obvious way imaginable: make it harder for banks to become insolvent. Laws from Washington, based on new global standards,* would ensure banks held enough capital on their balance sheets—and enough safe capital—that not even a deep crisis that significantly dented short-term asset values could tip them into bankruptcy. No one will know until the next crisis—and there *will* be one—how well these rules have succeeded in preventing another near-total financial meltdown. For now, though, they've forced banks and other financial institutions to dramatically rethink their standards for mortgage lending. Banks must hold substantially more capital on their balance sheets in case mortgages default.† Mortgage-lending banks also were required to agree that if a borrower defaulted after the bank had sold the loan to Fannie or Freddie, the bank would take back the loan and bear a substantial portion of the loss—and then had to hold some reserve capital in the vault in case that happened.

Rules like this, and there are thousands of pages of them, have transformed the American mortgage market over the past decade. A lot of banks have gotten out of the mortgage-lending business entirely, leaving the field to nonbank mortgage companies. Those firms raise capital via financial markets rather than taking deposits, aren't subject to the same type of regulations banks are, and now

---

* These have come to be known as the Basel standards, after the Swiss city that serves as headquarters for the Bank for International Settlements, a financial and intellectual clearinghouse for the world's central banks. We're now on "Basel III," a set of rules proposed in 2010 in response to the 2007–2008 global panic, which had notably not been prevented by either Basel I or Basel II.

† They also must hold more safe assets to protect themselves in case so-called Mortgage Servicing Assets (MSAs) run into trouble. If a bank writes a new mortgage, the bank might then sell the loan to an investor or Fannie or Freddie, but will keep the right to "service" the mortgage, such as by collecting payments on behalf of the mortgage's new owner. Banks can collect a fee for providing this service (and can also use their mortgage servicing as a platform to sell the borrower other products, such as checking accounts or investments), and record their expected income from these contracts as an asset. But the more capital they have to hold in reserve against these assets—and therefore the less cash they have available to engage in other profitable lending—the more expensive servicing loans becomes.

account for around 60 percent of all mortgages issued in the United States.[58] And in general, every financial firm seems to be more cautious about lending to anyone. Some more caution is a good thing after the excesses before the crisis, but there are signs that wariness about lending is also higher than it was in previous, more normal eras. The Urban Institute, a think tank that tracks housing among other issues, compiles a Housing Credit Availability Index (HCAI) that estimates the percentage of new-purchase (not refinancing) mortgages that are likely to fall delinquent for at least ninety days at some point.* The higher that proportion, the more risks lenders appear prepared to stomach. Right now, they're tolerating a historically low level of risk. The current HCAI is around 6 percent, compared to around 9 percent in the late 1990s before the height of the housing mania.† And for private-sector loans, not counting those sold to Fannie, Freddie, or other government agencies, the HCAI has fallen from around 7.5 percent in the late 1990s to 2 percent today.[59]

After 2008 other rules made doubly certain it would be difficult for many Millennials to buy houses by making it far more difficult for banks to offer mortgages to people with the kinds of jobs Millennials can get. The problem here is the "qualified mortgage" (QM) standard written into the Dodd-Frank Wall Street Reform and Consumer Protection Act. Dodd-Frank placed new responsibility on mortgage lenders to confirm that borrowers could reasonably be

---

* Several important measures of credit availability are produced periodically, including a quarterly survey of loan officers at major banks conducted by the Federal Reserve and a Mortgage Credit Availability Index produced by the Mortgage Bankers Association. All of them can be useful in various ways, but I cite the Urban Institute survey here because it offers a more transparent estimate of the level of mortgage *risk* lenders seem to be prepared to take and how that has changed over time, and not just the number of loans they're writing.

† Another advantage of the Urban Institute HCAI is that it attempts to separate out how much of a mortgage's risk is related to attributes of the borrower (low income, low credit score, or the like) versus how much is related to the mortgage product (an exotic structure or extremely low equity making a default more likely for any borrower). The comparison I quote here is based solely on borrower risk—product risk has shrunk to nearly zero since the crisis, which is undoubtedly a positive development.

expected to repay mortgages, and those loans that met the strict-
est standards in terms of ability to repay would count as qualified
mortgages. In return for sticking to that standard, lenders originat-
ing qualified mortgages couldn't be sued later by defaulting homebuyers claiming they'd been misled about the terms of their loans
(a not infrequent occurrence during and after the 2007–2008 bust).
The new standards, formally implemented in 2014, were great in
theory. But they imposed particularly strict income-verification
rules in order to guarantee a prospective buyer wasn't borrowing
more than she could pay back—and self-employed or gig-economy
workers are most likely to struggle to satisfy lenders that they'd
qualify for a qualified mortgage. Meanwhile since nonqualified
loans expose lenders to greater legal risks and theoretically have a
higher default risk, lenders charge borrowers higher interest rates.
Given what we've already seen about the rise of precarious, gig-
style work among Millennials, it's easy to spot how Millennial-
unfriendly these mortgage rules are. Millennials with healthy but
irregular incomes and low credit scores but also good records of
reliability paying back their current debts are getting cut out of the
mortgage lending game entirely.

A fair question at this point would be, So what? It'll seem a little
rich to argue that Boomers are ripping off Millennials by making it
harder for us to take on the kinds of debts—in pursuit of the kind
of unreasonable homeownership goals—that caused the worst financial panic in generations. The homeownership rate before the
crisis was too high, and so were the debt levels Boomers and Gen
Xers accumulated to hit that artificial target. Surely it's a good thing
for Millennials, and for the economy, if we dial back a bit on the
homeownership binge.

It's certainly true that it'll be good for some Millennials not to
be able to buy. To the extent new rules have blocked some of us
from taking a bad gamble on housing, the policies are working. We
shouldn't aspire to the astronomical homeownership rate of the
mid-2000s. That was phony, built on too much unsustainable debt
and too little equity.

But Millennials should be worried, and angry, that the Boomer solution to the housing mess our parents created has been to double down on the types of bad decisions they already made once before. That's basically what has happened. Boomers in Washington have obsessed over sustaining artificially high house prices via Federal Reserve and other policies, and Boomers around the country have helped at the local level by choking off supply in the places Millennials need to live. For those of us who can manage to take out a mortgage, this market manipulation has forced us to take many of the same high-debt, low-equity borrowing risks the Boomers and Gen Xers did before the 2007 crash. And the Boomer "solution" to keep this from becoming another ruinous financial crisis is to make it hard for larger numbers of first-time buyers to jump on the ladder at all. It's fair for Millennials to ask: Will most of us *ever* be able to afford to buy a house with a traditional 20 percent down payment and a plain-vanilla thirty-year term? The answer, to all appearances, is no, and *that* is the biggest sign that something has gone terribly wrong for us in the housing market.

No one can say what the long-term consequences of this new housing inequality will be for Millennials. Prewar generations might not have owned many houses. But they also didn't live as long, or have as few children. The weight our society places on homeownership has become a form of positive peer pressure to save by accumulating equity in a home. If Millennials can't find a way to start buying in large numbers, we'll eventually confront a novel situation in history: a large class of people reaching retirement age who may or may not have sufficient savings to provide for their living expenses at the same time they still need to pay monthly rent—and shoulder the risks of rent increases despite the lower incomes households generally expect in retirement.*

The other unprecedented aspect of Millennials' housing problems is subtler. If you combine rising house prices and rents with

---

* Indeed, to the eyes of an economist, insurance against unexpected rent increases is one of the main benefits of homeownership—more so than wealth accumulation per se.

some facts about who currently owns homes and who would like to do so, you reach a startling conclusion: wealth flows in the US housing market have reversed. During long periods when house prices rose moderately, rents were reasonable, and older homeowners steadily paid down their mortgages, the housing market was mostly generation-neutral, or at worst only slightly skewed toward the old. Older owners who had steadily paid down their mortgages and accumulated equity could use that equity to meet their own needs in retirement or pass it to their heirs. Younger buyers might make an up-front transfer to the older generation when they bought a house from an older seller, but over time they, too, would accumulate more equity. And some might receive inheritances from their homeowning parents or grandparents.

What changed in the 1990s and 2000s is that older homeowners started borrowing more against the value of their homes than they would ever be able to repay. This cast doubt on whether homeownership would ever lead to a "downward" generational transfer. Instead, younger buyers are expected to transfer ever more wealth in the form of higher purchase prices or rents to the older generation in the hope that the older generation will manage to pay off its housing debt without triggering another financial crisis. Meanwhile, younger buyers themselves become saddled with enormous housing debts that will become unsustainable if house prices ever are allowed to fall to a more normal level relative to incomes. And while Millennials wait to take on those housing debts by buying their first home, they rent from older property owners at ever-increasing rents.

This trend could remove what has been a significant buffer for younger people. We already transfer significant resources from the working young to the retiring old in the form of government-run social benefits such as Social Security and Medicare. Housing used to countervail that trend by providing middle-class working households an opportunity to build their own nest eggs by accumulating home equity—and with tax advantages such as the mortgage-interest deduction that offset at least a small part of the tax payments that fund programs for the elderly. Yet even now that buffer is being removed for younger buyers, who own less of the homes they buy as house prices skyrocket and down payments can't keep up. For Millennials, both our tax payments and our mortgage payments are providing subsidies for older generations. What's left over for us?

CHAPTER 5

The Saturday-Morning Bank Heist

MY SIBLINGS AND I SOMETIMES JOKE THAT MY YOUNGER BROTHER IS OUR parents' retirement plan. I'm a journalist; it's not a field people go into to become fabulously wealthy so that they can support their aging relatives. My sister, Hannah, the baby of the family, works happily in communications with a side of novel writing and rock music. But David—well, David made better life choices than the rest of us. He graduated with a degree in electrical engineering while enrolled in ROTC. Now he's a pilot in the air force, and if he ever decides to retire from that he can look forward to a lucrative career at an airline or a defense contractor. He'll always have money to spare for Mom and Dad in their old age.

That's all a family in-joke because in fact our parents have saved for their own retirements and also, seemingly unlike so many Boomers, plan to have their home paid off before they retire. But pardon Millennials as a whole if we don't laugh—because to an astounding degree, we all really are our parents' retirement plans.

I've argued in this book that Boomers have stolen a decade (or more) from Millennials. When it comes to the job market, or the educational "investment" racket, or the homeownership crisis, Millennials have been mugged in broad daylight—we know immediately what has happened to us and can pick the offender out of a lineup. But now it's time to talk about a different kind of theft—the taxing, spending, and borrowing choices Boomers have made, for which their children will have to pay. Boomers' fiscal capers are more like a bank robbery in the early hours of a Saturday morning on Memorial Day weekend. The robbery is already over—the vault is empty—but no one will see what happened until the bank re-opens on Tuesday morning.

The Boomers' fingerprints are all over the crime scene, and the crowbar they used to clean out the vault is deficit spending. As astronomical as the US deficit and debt seem today, we Millennials ain't seen nothin' yet.

The real drain is the entitlements for the elderly, especially Social Security and Medicare. We've barely begun to pay these costs for the Boomers, and by the time they're done retiring, it's not clear we'll be able to afford to pay for anything else. Worse, Boomers have spent the last decade relentlessly expanding the entitlement bill we'll one day have to pay.

The Boomer Deficit-Attention Disorder

The numbers are stark: Washington typically spends around $4 trillion per year, give or take a few dozen billion. It collects around $3.3 trillion in revenues.[1] And although Boomer politicians have spent a generation claiming to be worried about that gap—which has sometimes waxed and sometimes waned but only very rarely been closed—the reality is that they've decided, upon most careful consideration, to punt this fiscal football to their Millennial children.

And we Millennials too often seem to take this kind of deficit spending for granted, since it's all we've ever known from Washington. So to understand what has gone wrong for us, we need to start with some history.

For most of America's history before the 1930s, the federal budget was balanced. Washington ran a cumulative surplus of $70 million (not adjusting for inflation) between 1789 and 1849.[2] The exceptions tended to be times of war. Then when peace returned, the government would tip back into a budget surplus and pay down the debt it had accumulated. Debt levels were modest by modern standards, with peaks of just shy of 40 percent of the size of the economy in the 1860s and 1920s, after the Civil War and World War I, and other long stretches when the debt was almost zero.[3]

This fiscal discipline was a deliberate political choice. When the Constitution was ratified, uncertainty over repayment of state debts accrued during the Revolutionary War hung over the new government like a cloud. Alexander Hamilton, the first Treasury secretary, argued the federal government should take on all that remaining state debt, even though that meant taxpayers in states such as Georgia or Maryland that had already largely paid off their debts would have to keep paying to fund the war debt of less fiscally responsible states such as New York and Massachusetts.[4] Hamilton believed the new government had to pay down all the debts of the states in order to make sure creditors would lend it money *in case of emergency* in the future. His "First Report on Public Credit," in which he made his case to Congress to assume state debts, refers repeatedly to borrowing during "exigencies," or "times of public danger," or "particular emergencies." The government, he argued, had to behave responsibly with its budget and its debt so that it could borrow "on good terms," as he put it.[5] The obvious subtext was that part of behaving responsibly was borrowing only when absolutely necessary. In the end, Hamilton succeeded in persuading Congress to take responsibility for the young country's debt—and then proceeded to pay it down. The debt had all but disappeared by around 1835, during the administration of the fanatically anti-debt Andrew Jackson.[6]*

---

* For some reason, Alexander Hamilton has become a hate figure for certain conservatives and libertarians in more recent generations. They appeal to a Jeffersonian complaint in Hamilton's own day that he favored the sort of "perpetual debt" that had become a fixture of British public finance during the eighteenth century. But the Jeffersonians either hadn't read Hamilton's writings carefully enough or, more likely, deliberately misrepresented his views for political gain. The reality is that Hamilton in his First Report insisted that new debt should only be incurred if the government had a credible plan for its eventual "extinguishment." And he devised a system for fully repaying federal debts within thirty-four years (later shortened to twenty-four by Congress) while leaving the new government with the flexibility to suspend principal repayment during emergencies—a flexibility Jeffersonians exploited to finance the Louisiana Purchase and again during the War of 1812 (Robert E. Wright, *One Nation Under Debt: Hamilton, Jefferson, and the History of What We Owe* [New York: McGraw-Hill, 2008]).

Clearly something has gone wrong if we now view a national debt of well above 50 percent of GDP as tolerable, and even normal. A lot of things have caused the change, both in the level of debt and in the public's attitudes toward it. One big change was the advent of Progressive philosophy in the late nineteenth and early twentieth centuries. Progressives believed in the virtues of a far more activist government than the United States had ever had before, and that meant a larger and more expensive government. Voters started taking it for granted that big government was desirable, at least to an extent. The transformation in public attitudes arguably was complete by the time state legislators across the country ratified the Sixteenth Amendment to the Constitution in 1913, giving Washington the power to impose a direct tax on individual and corporate incomes. That kind of direct taxation would have been anathema to Alexander Hamilton's generation and the generations after it and had been deeply controversial since it was first tried during the Civil War.

Then, starting in the 1930s, America faced around fifteen years of unprecedented emergencies. During the Great Depression, Progressives argued in favor of a dramatically more activist government response than Washington had deployed against any previous economic downturn. Spending skyrocketed to more than 10 percent of GDP for several years in the middle of the decade, which pushed the deficit toward 6 percent of GDP.[7] And before Washington could rebalance its books after that economic exigency, another global war broke out—a war of unprecedented scale that required an unprecedented mobilization of financial resources to fund. By 1946, debt had reached an unprecedented height of nearly 120 percent of GDP.[8]

But the expansion of spending—at all levels of government—wasn't only a function of a one-time Depression and a catastrophic war. If it had been, we wouldn't be fretting about a fiscal crisis now. Economists still debate whether various components of the New Deal during the 1930s helped or hurt the economic recovery, but at worst the spending blowout on public works would have constituted an expensive one-time experiment. Given the immense moral, political, and economic stakes, American victory in World War II—and the subsequent rebuilding of Europe and Japan as healthy democracies allied with America—was cheap at any cost. And anyway, Washington could have paid down the debt eventually, as it always had in the past.

The problem is that just as the Boomers were coming of age in the 1950s and '60s, the very nature of government spending started to shift. For most of America's history, the government had focused primarily on buying (or doing) physical things—building roads and bridges, or fighting wars. Earlier in the Progressive era the government started to augment those physical goods with the provision of services such as education. But by the 1960s, the government had started acting like a giant financial institution—a bank, or, more precisely, an insurance company. With the creation of Social Security and unemployment-assistance programs in the 1930s, the government offered a financial backstop for those who lost their jobs, or for the elderly who hadn't been able to save adequately for their retirements. That "insurance" role expanded dramatically barely a generation later as part of Lyndon Johnson's Great Society, just as the oldest Boomers were hitting their early twenties. Now the government would fund health care for the poor and the elderly, via Medicaid and Medicare. It would provide significantly expanded benefits for low-income families who fell on hard times, via expansive new welfare and social-housing programs.*

The government would also provide "insurance" for itself, or rather for all the individual people who worked for it. The rapid rise in government spending was accompanied, predictably, by

---

* Policy wonk Nate Silver draws an interesting connection between this phenomenon and changing public attitudes toward the government over the latter part of the twentieth century: "We may have gone from conceiving of government as an entity that builds roads, dams and airports, provides shared services like schooling, policing and national parks, and wages wars, into the world's largest insurance broker. Most of us don't much care for our insurance broker" (Nate Silver, "Health Care Drives Increase in Government Spending," *New York Times*, January 17, 2013).

a rapid rise in the number of people employed by the govern-ment.* The annual salaries all those government workers earned were one expense, and a significant one. But even more costly, over time those jobs accumulated some of the most generous in-surance benefits of any jobs in the economy, especially so far as old age is concerned: pension benefits and retiree health care pro-grams well in excess of anything available to most private-sector workers.

All this meant that government budgets—and deficits—would never be the same again. Before the twentieth century, govern-ment debt had amounted to one generation borrowing from its own future to tide itself over during an emergency. Borrowing was confined to narrow windows of time for narrow purposes, and the debts (measured relative to the size of the economy) were substantially repaid during the lifetimes of generations alive when the debt was first incurred. Borrowing to fund entitlements was fundamentally different—especially borrowing to fund entitle-ments for the elderly, because the beneficiaries were by definition retired from work and so would never have a chance to contribute toward repaying the debts incurred for their benefit.† The bur-den of the inevitable deficits the Boomers' parents started baking into the federal and state budgets would fall entirely on future generations.

The Boomers inherited these problems, which would have been difficult for them to solve no matter what they did. But instead of trying to find permanent fixes to what economists started calling

---

* Civilian employment by all levels of government had plunged in the immediate aftermath of World War II, by around 11 percent from the peak in 1943 to the trough in 1947, but then nearly tripled between 1947 and 1980, with some of the biggest single-year jumps occurring in the 1960s (US Bureau of Labor Statistics, All Employ-ees: Government, retrieved from Federal Reserve Bank of St. Louis, fred.stlouisfed .org/series/USGOVT, August 11, 2018).

† Even now that retirees have to pay taxes on Social Security benefits they receive, the revenue from that tax is only a very small portion of overall benefit payments.

"structural deficits," Boomers made things a lot worse by ignoring two major new realities.*

One reality was that to foster security and economic growth, the United States as a new superpower would have little choice but to play a much greater military role in the world. The Boomers' parents and grandparents made a serious fiscal mistake in the 1950s and '60s when they acted as if the higher level of US military spending during the Cold War was only temporary. That might have seemed true at the beginning, when some analysts expected the Soviet Union and Mao's People's Republic of China would collapse relatively quickly. But at a certain point, Washington should have realized that elevated military spending—which was almost 9 percent of GDP in the 1960s, and more than 5 percent of GDP on average through both the 1970s and the 1980s—was no longer what Alexander Hamilton would have considered an "emergency."[9] It was a new and ongoing fact of life, and other parts of the budget should have adjusted in response.

Boomers never solved the problem posed by permanently higher military spending, although for a spell in the 1990s they claimed they had. One reason the fiscal balance supposedly achieved by the Clinton administration in the late 1990s proved so short-lived was that it was premised on a belief among many foreign policy experts that the end of the Cold War meant America could at last permanently reduce its military budget. This so-called peace dividend involved Washington, now under Boomer management, reducing military spending to 3 percent of GDP by 2000.[10] Crucially, neither Clinton nor his Republican adversaries in Congress made any serious attempts to reform the biggest long-term drivers of domestic spending, the old-age entitlements. The welfare reform that they did pass in 1996 concerned benefits for low-income, working-age people, and overall government spending to help those households

---

* Economists use the term to denote the portion of the annual budget that arises from automatic spending such as entitlements—and politicians are happy to run with the term because it suggests the deficit is inevitable rather than a result of the politicians' own choices.

actually *increased* relative to GDP in subsequent years.[11] This set the United States up for fiscal failure after the September 11, 2001, terror attacks forcefully reminded Washington that it still needed to invest in a global military. Politicians to the Left of the ideological spectrum complain that if only America under George W. Bush hadn't become embroiled in two faraway wars at a cumulative cost of $5.6 trillion, there'd be more money in the federal budget for other priorities.*[12] But with military spending still only between 3 percent and 4.5 percent of GDP each year, those military expenditures aren't historically out of the norm, and arguably are too small to keep the military the United States needs fully staffed and equipped.[13]

The other reality Boomers never fully grappled with is subtler but will be the most crippling for Millennials as we get deeper into our own adulthood: Washington chronically flubs its estimates of future growth and other economic variables.[14]

Most people think about government budgeting in terms of adding up how much the government will spend, adding up how much money it will collect in taxes, and then shouting about how big the deficit is. But there's an important element lurking beneath that— lawmakers try to estimate how the budget will change over time. In order to do that, they rely on estimates about how the economy will or won't grow, and what effects that growth or otherwise will have on spending and revenues in the next few years. And starting in the 1990s, Boomers in Washington started significantly fudging estimates of future growth and revenues to suit political ends.[15] The Clinton administration habitually underestimated future revenues in an attempt to justify tax increases. Worse—and it pains me to say this as a conservative—the George W. Bush administration

---

* Totaling up the cumulative costs of the Afghanistan and Iraq wars is harder than many people realize. The estimate cited here is several times higher than official figures from the Pentagon, but includes the direct costs of military activities; related nonmilitary costs such as State Department activities in those areas; the expected value of medical treatment and other benefits for veterans of the wars; and miscellaneous items such as interest payments on additional debt Washington has borrowed to fund the wars.

generally overestimated future revenues to support its own pre-ferred tax-cutting policies.[16]

It's not precisely the case that the Boomers have been spending as if there's no tomorrow. In fact, a lot of Washington's budget rules theoretically require Congress to balance the budget over longer time horizons. The Boomers have just always assumed tomorrow would bring more growth—and more revenue—than turned out to be the case. This has been a particularly dangerous assumption when it comes to two of the biggest long-term drivers of government spending: the old-age entitlements of Social Security and Medicare.

"Dead Men Ruling"

Perhaps like many older Millennials, I first started hearing about the financial problems of Social Security and Medicare from *Saturday Night Live* in the autumn of 2000. I had just graduated from high school that spring, and a presidential election was under-way—the first in which those of us born in 1982 would vote. Little of that campaign sticks in my memory—with hindsight and more experience, I realize it's because it was an especially uninspiring campaign—but the thing I remember most clearly is a parody. *Saturday Night Live*, as ever, was ready after each debate with a spoof to send up the candidates, George W. Bush and Al Gore. And after the first debate, the aspect of Gore's campaign they fo-cused on was the "lockbox."

"Rather than squander the surplus on a risky tax cut for the wealthy," actor Darrell Hammond droned in his best impersonation of a leaden Gore, answering a question about tax policy, "I would put it in what I call a *lockbox*." That lockbox featured in every one of Hammond-cum-Gore's answers. He described in great detail the security arrangements for the lockbox. He warned hostile foreign powers that they'd never be able to find where he had hidden the lockbox. The one word Hammond drawled out when his Al Gore was asked to describe his campaign? "Lockbox."

It was funny because the Gore campaign had been focusing obsessively on the notion of putting Social Security and Medicare funds into a "lockbox," and no one knew what that meant.* We Millennials, political neophytes, didn't realize that we needed take that debate seriously and recognize that no Boomer politician was giving a good answer to the question of what to do about entitlement spending and the budget. That's because these two programs will shape Millennials' tax-paying futures more than just about anything else.

Some readers may think: "That's not true. Social Security and Medicare aren't like other government spending items. They're insurance. Boomers paid into these programs' trust funds via the 'insurance contributions' deducted from their paychecks. These programs aren't stealing from Millennials. They're giving Boomers what the Boomers already have paid for."

If only that were the case. Social Security and Medicare aren't "insurance" at all. When these programs were created, the government started acting like an insurance company. But it was only *acting*, in the sense that it was taking on a lot of the risks insurers assume when they sell annuity products or long-term care insurance. Those risks include that a person lives longer than the insurance company expects, meaning that it needs to pay out an income on the annuity product for longer than anticipated, or that an individual suffers a health problem that requires expensive health care for long periods of time.

But in other key ways the government is *not* like an insurance company at all. The benefits it pays out are only loosely related to what individuals pay into the system, as opposed to a real insurance company, which requires you to pay higher premiums to qualify for more generous payouts later. Worse, the government isn't actually saving and investing the taxes it collects. It's turning right around and paying out benefits to today's retirees with that revenue. Medicare doesn't even pretend to be trying to save for the future—most of its spending comes from general tax revenues, which "top up" a

---

* It will all become clear, or not, in a few pages.

"trust fund" whose meager payroll-tax revenues are wholly inadequate to the demands placed on the system.

Washington has gone out of its way to conceal these inconvenient facts from voters from the moment the programs were created. The law creating the payroll taxes that fund these behemoths is called the Federal Insurance Contribution Act, camouflaging a tax as an insurance premium. Every year, the Social Security Administration sends taxpayers a "statement" that's supposed to make it look like each individual has a certain amount of money stashed away in an "account," which he or she will be able to access once he or she retires. We talk about "trust funds" stockpiled with these "contributions," as if the money we've paid via payroll taxes sits there waiting for us to use it ourselves in our old age. But that's really not where the money comes from: each check the government writes to a retiree today is funded not by money that retiree herself paid into the system when she was working, but by a tax payment— not an "insurance contribution"—that a current worker has made. All those insurance contributions today's retirees made during *their* working years were actually taxes that funded payments to their own parents and grandparents.

This means there's no natural brake on the ability of people to take more out of the system than they put into it, so everyone ends up taking too much. One estimate considers couples earning average wages and finds that a couple born in 1950 who earned average wages during their careers could expect to receive Social Security and Medicare benefits worth $1,053,000 over the rest of their lives. But while they were working, they would only have paid $701,000 in taxes—a lifetime personal deficit of $352,000. A couple born in 1965 can expect to claim benefits worth $1,372,000 but will have paid lifetime taxes of $851,000—a deficit of $521,000.[17]* This imbalance has worsened, both before and after 2008, for two reasons: Americans are living far longer than they did when the programs were created, and they're doing so in worse health that requires ever

---

* The research quoted here uses constant 2017 dollars to control for inflation, and also calculates a discounted net present value of future benefits.

more expensive medical treatment. Not even economic growth can spare future generations the burden of this entitlement payout. Social Security benefits increase along with inflation, guaranteeing that the long-term fiscal burden will grow. Medical cost inflation, meanwhile, has driven up Medicare spending well beyond the rate of overall consumer-price inflation or economic growth.

Those dismal realities presage a fiscal crisis of world-historical proportions. Entitlements are eating the federal budget. Social Security, Medicare, and Medicaid already account for 54 percent of the federal government's noninterest spending, and that will climb to 67 percent in 2047.[18] So-called mandatory spending—primarily entitlements that run on autopilot with set benefit formulae, plus interest on federal debt—now accounts for more than 71 percent of total annual outlays, up from 38 percent in 1968, just as the Great Society entitlement expansion was coming online. That bite of the budget apple is projected to hit 75 percent by 2028.[19] Economist C. Eugene Steuerle has referred to this phenomenon as "Dead Men Ruling," capturing the way that programs designed by older generations of politicians increasingly limit the scope of budget choices younger generations can make.[20]

Part of the increase in such automatic spending is a consequence of demographic change. America is home to more old people than ever before—and will be home to even more as the Boomers age—so the number of people claiming benefits keeps climbing. The Social Security system's trustees estimate that by 2035, when the youngest Boomers are seventy-one years old, nearly 75 million Americans will be claiming Social Security's old-age pension benefit, compared to just under 51 million beneficiaries in 2017.[21]* The numbers are worse for Medicare, which had 58.4 million enrollees in 2017 but expects to have nearly 85 million enrolled in 2035.[†22]

---

* The Social Security Administration most often cites a figure of around 61.5 million total beneficiaries, which includes both recipients of the old-age benefit here and another 10.5 million working-age recipients of disability payments.

† This is the total number of individuals covered at least by Medicare Part A (hospital), Part B (regular medical), or Part D (prescription drugs), the three categories of benefit paid out of the two Medicare trust funds the government maintains.

How accurate those estimates will be is anyone's guess, since the Social Security Administration has a notoriously difficult time making accurate life-expectancy and payout projections.

Making a bad demographic situation worse, Boomers went out of their way as they approached retirement to make these entitlements as expensive as possible or, rather, to make the benefits for Boomers themselves as generous as they could manage. The best (or worst) example of this is Medicare Part D. This was a vast new entitlement passed by President George W. Bush and a Republican Congress in 2003 that dramatically expanded subsidies for prescription drugs for the elderly. In keeping with the long-standing rhetorical con of these entitlements, politicians talked about "coverage" for prescription drugs as if this Medicare expansion were another form of insurance. It's all a lie. The near-term beneficiaries—people who were retired when the provision passed in Washington, or even the older cohort of Boomers themselves—would never pay enough into the system to be able to pretend they had contributed to the cost of their own benefits. Prescription-drug "coverage" cost some $73 billion in general government revenue in 2017, compared to premium income—contributions paid by recipients toward the cost of their own prescription coverage—of $15.5 billion.[23]

It's true that since a reform in the 1980s, the government has collected more money via payroll taxes from current workers than it has paid out in benefits to current retirees for Social Security, although not Medicare.* But *on average* the amount that a worker contributes will fall far short of the amount that individual eventually will withdraw. Real insurers sometimes pay out more in claims than they've collected in premiums from some customers, but for others the insurer expects to collect more premiums than it will pay out. And an insurance company also aims to earn a reasonable investment return on its pot of premium money while it waits to find out whether a given customer is a "winner" or a "loser" for the firm. No insurer would stay in business for long if it always paid out more

---

* The reform centered on an increase in Social Security and Medicare payroll taxes.

than it collected, yet that's exactly the situation Social Security and Medicare find themselves in today.

One other entitlement also belongs in this discussion, even though it's almost never discussed as one: the overly generous pensions Boomers who work for state and local governments have promised themselves.

A long-term trend in American retirement planning has been the shift out of old-fashioned defined-benefit pension plans (where the employer saves and invests a large pot of money on behalf of its employees and then pays a guaranteed annual amount in retirement) and into defined-contribution plans such as a 401(k), where the employer pays a set percentage of salary into a tax-free investment account each year, which the worker can use in retirement. But one broad category of American worker has been largely exempt from this transformation: government employees, especially at the state and local level. Across the country, teachers, police officers, DMV employees, sanitation workers, and overall administrators have continued to be covered by defined-benefit plans, and often very generous ones at that, offering higher proportions of final salary as pension payments, and covering more health care with less out-of-pocket cost, than is available for most private-sector workers.

Governments are supposed to pay for these future benefits today, by stockpiling taxpayer cash in designated pension funds and then allowing trustees to invest that money to earn enough to meet future expected payouts. But of course, hardly any state capitol or town hall does this. Governments for decades have "underfunded" their pension plans. They pay in too little each year for the plans to have any hope of meeting obligations through a combination of those cash injections and investment returns. This allows politicians to divert money that otherwise would have shored up the pension fund into more politically popular current spending instead.

The funding gap is huge, although hard to estimate. State-government pension plan administrators themselves tend to claim they have a shortfall of "only" 34 percent, meaning that their current cash on hand and estimated future investment returns can cover 66 percent of what they expect they'll have to pay out over time. That amounts to an unfunded liability of around $1.4 trillion.[24] But there's ample evidence that those plan managers habitually overestimate the investment returns they'll earn over time, while underestimating how quickly their liabilities will grow. For instance, the median state retirement-plan administrator in 2016 assumed a future investment return of 7.5 percent, at a time when the interest rate on thirty-year Treasury bonds was barely above 2 percent.[25] Correcting for those implausible estimates can yield wildly varying guesses as to the true state pension shortfall. One of the more alarmist, but still plausible, estimates comes from the right-wing American Legislative Exchange Council, which pegs a funding shortfall of around $6 trillion using a discount rate of around 2.1 percent.* By their reckoning, states have only around 34 percent of the assets on hand that they'd need to meet their future obligations to current and future retirees.[26]

The one thing that unites all of these fiscal gaps, whether for Social Security, Medicare, or state and local pensions, is that someone will have to pay more for them in the future, or some beneficiaries will have to receive less. That means everyone—and especially Boomers—should be frightened that since 2008, the main entitlement trend has been that Millennials are losing the ability to pay for these benefits. The evaporation of a political willingness to pay won't be far behind.

The first factor affecting Millennials' ability to pay for their Boomer parents' Social Security, Medicare, and pension checks is a long-term problem: there just aren't enough Millennials. In 1950, America had 16.5 workers for every one person receiving Social Security old-age or disability benefits. That ratio held steady at around 3.3 workers per Social Security beneficiary for most of the Boomers' working lives, but the large size of their own cohort combined with their failure to produce enough younger workers (i.e., children) of their own, means that the ratio already had fallen to

* The interest rate that serves as a benchmark both for expected growth in plan assets via investment returns and also for plan liabilities.

2.8 workers per beneficiary as of 2017, and could fall as low as 2.1 by 2035.[27]

It gets worse. Both Social Security and Medicare are built on accounting frauds. Social Security in particular is supposed to be funded by a payroll tax on current workers and their employers, which is billed as a form of pension deposit or insurance contribution.* For much of Boomers' working lives in the 1980s and '90s Social Security was technically in surplus, with payroll tax receipts exceeding annual benefit payments. The extra money was stored in "trust funds."† That's no longer the case—in recent years, annual payouts have started to exceed annual payroll-tax revenues as the Boomers retire en masse—but in theory we'll still have another sixteen years until 2034, when the money in those trust funds runs out, to find a way to fix the program.[28]

But those trust funds don't really exist in the way that calling them "trust funds" leads most people to believe. During the years that Social Security was in surplus, as the extra cash came into the US Treasury from payroll-tax receipts, the government effectively borrowed the money. Instead of handing dollar bills to Social Security Trustees to stash in a vault (or invest the money in a wide range of private-sector assets, as state pension funds are supposed to), Treasury kept the cash and instead handed the Social Security Administration a stack of IOUs—a particular type of Treasury bond created especially for this purpose, which earns interest at a rate of 3 percent per year.[29] It's more accurate to say that the government has borrowed from itself to fund spending in years past that otherwise would have been funded with borrowing directly from the public. The Boomers took out a loan against their own retirement fund to finance their spending choices in the 1990s and 2000s.

So who pays the interest on the bonds, and eventually the full face value of the bonds to make good on Treasury's promises to

---

* Medicare's funding sources are far more complex, although in theory a smaller payroll tax is supposed to be part of that formula, too.

† There are two for Social Security—one for the pension portion of the program, which makes payments to the elderly and survivors of beneficiaries, and one for the portion of the program that provides benefits for the disabled.

the Social Security system? Today's taxpayers, which increasingly means Millennials. In fact, someone already is paying. In 2017, the interest that Treasury paid to Social Security on the bonds in the trust fund—interest paid out of general tax revenues—accounted for $83.2 billion in revenue just for the old-age portion of the program excluding disability insurance, helping to fill what otherwise would have been a $64.3 billion gap between tax receipts and benefits paid.[30] That interest payment is money from the government's general fund that isn't available for other purposes, such as roads, bridges, elementary schools, national defense, or even college tuition assistance. Moving forward, converting the bonds in the trust fund into cash that can be used to pay benefits will require redeeming more and more of them. That money will come out of the government's general fund—personal and corporate income taxes especially.* Boomers won't be paying most of that money by then, because they'll be retired.

The Bipartisan Bamboozle

The Boomers had planned to shovel entitlement debt onto the Millennials long *before* the Great Recession. Since the financial panic and economic downturn, the Boomer strategy has been to shift as much of the new fiscal burden of responding to the crisis as possible onto Millennials as well.

Depending on the listener, the numbers are either shockingly large, or else so hard to fathom that they sound numbing instead of shocking. In the wake of the financial crisis, government spending surged. The deficit ballooned to nearly 10 percent of GDP in 2009, and the publicly held debt grew by $1.4 trillion that year. And every

---

* This was the meaning of Al Gore's joke-worthy "lockbox." In the late 1990s, Boomers developed the idea that they should stop borrowing the "extra" money they were paying into Social Security and Medicare, so that the cash would be available when they needed it. It was a nice thought, but it also was pretty confused in Gore's telling. The main flaw was that Gore actually wasn't proposing to sequester the money at all—he wanted to use it to continue paying down the national debt. This still eventually would have left future taxpayers in the position of having to subsidize the programs out of general tax receipts, which is exactly what's happening now anyway.

year since the Great Recession, Washington has overspent its revenues by at least 2.5 percent of GDP.[31] By the time President Barack
Obama left office in January 2017, the national debt had risen to
nearly $20 trillion, from $10.7 trillion at the end of 2008 and $9.5
trillion just before the crisis. And lest anyone think this is a partisan
rant from a conservative author, the debt in 2017 and 2018 grew
even further, and the deficit expanded from its late-Obama level,
with Washington under Republican control. Total debt is now $21
trillion.[32] At 105 percent of GDP, debt is at levels not seen since the
years immediately after World War II.*[33]

The challenge for Millennials, surprisingly, is figuring out where
all that money went so we can bring it back under control (*if* we can
bring it back under control). It doesn't feel as if there should be any
mystery about this, given the explicit and controversial attempts
both the late Bush and the early Obama administrations made to
blow out government spending to boost the economy.[†] In 2008,
President Bush goaded Congress into passing a $152 billion stimu-
lus comprised mainly of one-off tax rebates of up to $600 per per-
son for low-income and middle-class taxpayers. President Obama

---

* There are different ways to measure the federal debt, and I'm not using the more
usual figures here. Fiscal analysts commonly cite the amount of federal debt held by
the public, which encompasses all Treasury bonds and other borrowings held by domestic and foreign investors, banks, and the Federal Reserve. That was $5.3 trillion in
2008, around $14.4 trillion in 2016, and has now climbed to almost $15.5 trillion. But
this measure *excludes* debt owed to government trust funds—most importantly, the
bonds held in the Social Security trust funds. Since what matters most to Millennials
in a discussion of fiscal policy is how repayment obligations will weigh on our future
taxing and spending decisions, it's important to include those trust-fund debts, as the
larger total debt numbers in the main text here do.

† This discussion will ignore measures implemented as a response to the immediate
financial crisis, such as the Troubled Asset Relief Program (TARP) discussed in the
previous chapter. This might be a controversial decision in the eyes of some readers
who remember the political uproar surrounding those spending moves at the time.
But with the benefit of hindsight, those programs look more like temporary monetary
maneuvers rather than fiscal policy as most people think about it. Taxpayers effectively
made loans available to troubled financial institutions and have profited on a net basis
as those loans have been repaid subsequently. (Technically the government bought preferred shares in financial companies that eventually were bought back, but conceptually
the effect is the same.) They didn't contribute to the long-term debt, or create any new
long-term spending obligations, in ways that are relevant to this chapter.

and Congressional Democrats followed that up with a $757 billion, ten-year stimulus bill (the estimated cost would eventually rise to $836 billion) in 2009, which focused on additional tax cuts but also on pumping up government spending.[34]

In the official telling, Boomers were responding to an economic crisis by deploying both of the fiscal tricks they thought had worked in the past—tax cuts to stimulate private spending and investment in a manner inspired by the 1980s, and a more old-school form of Keynesian stimulus akin to what FDR's Democrats had attempted in the 1930s.* But that was only part of it. In fact, some of the most hyped components of these stimulus bills were also the least signif-icant in terms of long-term spending and debt. The tax cuts totaling $440 billion across both plans, for instance, were one-off rebates or temporary cuts that automatically canceled after a short spell. As for the Keynesian-spending portion of the Obama stimulus, this drove conservatives nuts, but also was only a relatively modest part of the bill. Depending on how one counts, public-works spending accounted for only $115 billion over ten years, despite the adminis-tration's sales pitches about "shovel-ready projects" the government was ready to build immediately.† If economic growth had recovered quickly, these one-offs *might* almost have been manageable.

The problem for Millennials is that both administrations intro-duced many other, far costlier provisions that effectively shifted

---

* British economist John Maynard Keynes believed that recessions such as the Great Depression during his lifetime were caused by declines in overall demand in the economy—because people stopped buying things, companies stopped producing them, which meant companies stopped investing in new equipment and stopped giving workers raises, or even hiring them. A solution could be massive government spending, financed by debt, so that the government could replace the missing de-mand in the private sector.

† This very approximate tally, my own calculation, includes transportation spending, spending on government buildings, and some high-profile provisions such as a few billion to help make homes more energy efficient by weatherizing them. In practice, very few projects turned out to be ready to start construction within ninety days (the official definition of "shovel-ready"), and local agencies often were overwhelmed by a sudden influx of money they had no way to spend as quickly as Washington hoped (Michael Grabell, *Money Well Spent? The Truth Behind the Trillion-Dollar Stimulus, the Biggest Economic Recovery Plan in History* [New York: PublicAffairs, 2012]).

the financial burden of adjusting to the economic downturn from today's households to tomorrow's taxpayers—and that then slowed the economic recovery that would have made the taxpayer burden more affordable by expanding the economy and the tax base over time.

Laws signed by both Bush and Obama expanded eligibility for unemployment-insurance benefits, from a standard of twenty-six weeks before the recession—up to six months—to up to ninety-nine weeks, or nearly two years. New rules also made it easier to apply for unemployment benefits, including for people who quit their jobs. The Supplemental Nutrition Assistance Program (SNAP, or food stamps) expanded by judging the eligibility of more households based solely on their income rather than their assets and making it easier for able-bodied adults without dependents to claim benefits. More unemployed people were able to come onto the rolls of TANF, the main welfare program (created by the 1996 Clinton-era welfare reform), as Washington loosened requirements that most recipients seek work. And a host of other subsidies became available, such as a taxpayer-financed benefit for those who lost their jobs but wanted to keep their employer's health insurance coverage for an extended period. At the same time, Boomers in Washington also extended significant assistance to homeowners whose mortgages were underwater. We've seen some of the housing-market consequences of those programs, but there's a fiscal angle, too. Not only were they expensive, but they were designed to target lower-income owners with benefits that phased out as household income rose.

Debates about these programs over the past decade have focused on the immediate cost, but that's only part of the fiscal picture. Spending on social programs would have increased during a recession anyway, as falling incomes would mean more households became eligible for assistance even if the rules stayed the same. Instead, the place to focus is on how changes to the *design* of these programs allowed even more people to use them than otherwise would have been eligible—and how these benefit expansions shifted the economic burden of coping with the Great Recession, and how it changed the prospects for a quick recovery.

University of Chicago economist Casey B. Mulligan has done the heavy lifting of examining the consequences of expanding benefits and has reached some startling conclusions. Making higher levels of benefits available to more people for longer had the effect of replacing more of the income a household might lose when a worker lost his or her job—for more households. For someone on the cusp of either working or nonworking, more generous benefits added $311 per month to household income relative to what those programs would have paid before 2007.[35] And because many of these benefits—which also included some taxpayer-funded programs to modify mortgages—were means-tested, they constituted a hidden tax.* Economists have long understood that a consequence of this type of program is that for some workers, an additional dollar of personal income can restrict benefit eligibility in a way that effectively acts as a tax on that dollar of income. Mulligan calculates that for workers on the cusp, more generous means-tested benefits increased the effective marginal tax rate to as high as 48 percent, from 40 percent before the Great Recession.[36] That high marginal tax rate provided an incentive for some households to stay on benefits longer, at taxpayer expense, because employers would have had to offer significantly higher pay to replace the total value of lost benefits.

Mulligan argues that these labor-market distortions slowed the recovery, a phenomenon he calls the "redistribution recession." The implications for Millennials are serious. All this additional stimulus spending, especially on the transfer payments to help households, was funded by debt. As a result, the net effect was to shift some of the economic burden of the Great Recession from the current generation onto future generations of taxpayers. Households right on the edge between working and continuing to collect benefits would continue to collect benefits at future taxpayers' expense instead of swallowing a slight reduction in pay. A certain amount of that kind

---

* Meaning that eligibility for aid is based on income—the more one earns, the less assistance one receives.

of burden-shifting is the point of social safety-net programs, and Millennials benefited from that safety net, too, if our parents (or we ourselves) fell on hard times and needed a boost. It's fair to expect us to pay back some of the expense of those benefits in the future. But the Boomer innovation was to dramatically expand the safety net, in the process shifting even more of the costs of adjusting to the Great Recession into the future than would normally have been the case. Changing the designs of the programs revamped the previous generational balance embedded in their rules—often on the fly, without a full debate about the long-term consequences, and in ways that mainly benefited Boomers and Gen Xers.

And then came Obamacare.

This isn't a book about everything that was and remains wrong with America's system for providing and financing health care. It would be hard to find anyone on either side of the political aisle who thought the system worked properly before Obama signed the two laws collectively known as the Affordable Care Act (ACA) in March 2010. And I'm not going to wade into the long and bitter argument about whether the structure of the ACA was the only or the best way to achieve the goal of providing more affordable health care to more Americans.

But Millennials do need to have a frank conversation about the ACA's costs before we decide whether we're willing and able to shoulder those burdens—and how we could design something better if we want to try—because the Boomers who passed the law didn't. Whatever else the 2010 health care overhaul did or didn't achieve, it created substantial new fiscal obligations on future generations, and Boomers in Washington were characteristically truth-shy in how they presented those trade-offs.

Broadly speaking, the ACA was designed to increase insurance coverage for Americans in several ways, all of which implied some fiscal consequence. The law imposed a new mandate on many employers to offer health coverage or pay a penalty. This meant that either the private sector would provide insurance or would effectively pay a tax to help the government provide the benefit.* Washington also would offer subsidies to individuals who bought insurance on government-run exchanges—a fiscal cost, although one that was hard to predict since it would depend on how many employers complied with the employer mandate instead. And states were encouraged to expand eligibility for Medicaid to house-holds with higher incomes than traditionally were covered. Again, it was surprisingly difficult to predict the fiscal effects of this, which would depend in part on how many low-income households gained insurance from their employers versus how many bought subsidized insurance on exchanges versus how many registered for Medicaid instead.

The Boomers who passed the legislation weren't ignorant of the need to pay for these obligations, but they were embarrass-ingly overoptimistic (to put it charitably) in their plans to offset the costs of the new subsidies. For instance, ACA as passed envi-sioned a gradual reduction in the rate at which reimbursements under Medicare would increase, with cost savings to be enforced by a new expert panel if necessary. It imposed a "Cadillac tax" on employer-provided health insurance plans with premiums above $10,200 (for an individual) per year, in part to offset the tax deduc-tions employers claim for insurance premiums for their workers and indirectly to help control overall medical costs by discourag-ing employers from providing "too much" insurance. It rolled out two supplementary Medicare taxes on salary income and capital income, such as dividends for wealthier households with income above $250,000 (for a married couple filing jointly). And it created new taxes such as a medical-device tax of 2.3 percent on products ranging from surgical gloves to pacemakers.

After putting those two halves together and consulting a bunch of Magic 8 balls to overcome the enormous number of hard-to-predict variables involved, the Obama administration and other

* Although the typical subsidy for an individual to buy insurance via a state-level exchange is several thousand dollars more than the employer penalty.

government economists came up with multiyear budget projections. When the law was passed in early 2010, the expectation was that it might contribute to the federal budget deficit in its early years. But over the longer term, especially as the revenue measures fully kicked in and cost controls started reducing the growth in health care spending, the picture would improve. The Congressional Budget Office predicted that the ACA would help *reduce* the deficit by $124 billion over ten years.[37]

But the ACA is yet another manifestation of an age-old Washington trick: roll out a new spending commitment that front-loads the benefits and back-loads the costs . . . and then avoid ever actually imposing those costs because doing so is politically unpopular. If one sets aside any of the other policy arguments surrounding health care, one almost has to admire Boomer politicians' adeptness at wriggling out of paying for the health care law they themselves passed less than a decade ago.

Political opposition quickly delayed implementation of the employer mandate, which removed one major fiscal corrective.* The Cadillac tax on high-cost employer-provided insurance has been delayed several times, from 2018 to 2022, and hardly anyone expects it will ever actually be imposed. After being imposed for a few years early on, in 2016 the medical-device tax was put on hold at least until 2020. The Medicare cost-control panel has yet to be convened, since Medicare spending increases haven't yet crossed the threshold that would trigger that provision in the ACA, but Millennials shouldn't hold their breaths waiting for Boomers to accept a bureaucratic decree that they receive less Medicare spending. Members of Congress already have started trying to repeal this part of the law.

---

* In practice, this delayed implementation created the worst of all possible worlds. As we saw in Chapter 2, since the provision was never formally repealed and *is* now being implemented, it cast a pall over the labor market by discouraging some firms from hiring to upsize beyond the fifty-employee payroll threshold that would subject an employer to the mandate. Yet in the meantime, it wasn't actually requiring any employers to provide insurance or generating any penalty income to offset the other ACA costs that already were kicking in.

Boomers also almost immediately canned the single major aspect of the law that would have front-loaded revenue collection from Boomers in exchange for back-loaded benefits. This was the Community Living Assistance and Support program, or CLASS, which would have allowed individuals to contribute to a government fund that would then support long-term care costs in their older age. More the half of the alleged deficit reduction over ten years—around $70 billion—was supposed to arise from individuals paying more into this program at first than it would disburse. At least Washington quickly admitted that this budgetary benefit was a fiction (among other fiscal holes, no one had properly accounted for the fact that after the first decade, CLASS would face bankrupting claims on its resources), but this meant that the long-term finances of the ACA overall would be even more tenuous than originally estimated.

A special mention goes to the Medicare surcharge for higher-income taxpayers, because it turns out we have a pretty good idea what will happen to that over time. The income threshold at which the tax kicks in isn't indexed to inflation. That means that as the years pass and the general level of wages and prices increases, more and more people will cross the $250,000 income minimum at which they start owing the tax. But precisely because those earners won't *feel* richer—their $250,000 salaries will buy less at that point than $250,000 buys today—they'll lobby their members of Congress to lift the threshold. We already see this happen every few years with the Alternative Minimum Tax provision of the regular income tax—that tax, originally introduced to ensnare only the wealthiest taxpayers, came with an income cutoff that wasn't indexed to inflation. And politicians have spent decades periodically raising the threshold to exempt taxpayers as inflation boosts wages. Millennials will "benefit" from this to the extent that we can lobby our own way out of this tax obligation if and when our earnings climb to that level. But that only means we'll need to come up with some other way of financing the ACA's fiscal demands.

And that, really, is the great fiscal con of the ACA so far as Millennials are concerned. Boomers voted themselves enormous new benefits. But their "plan" to pay for them involved sliding out from under the taxes they claimed would fund it and instead leaving Millennials to find some other means of footing the bill. Either we'll have to subject ourselves to the full brunt of tax increases and cost controls written into the law but never imposed by Boomers on themselves—and even then there's a significant question about whether those taxes will be enough—or we'll have to scrap the ACA and forego its putative benefits while still paying down the debt the Boomers racked up in the ACA's early years for benefits they had no intention of paying for.

Paying the Piper

Even after all the terrible policy decisions we've discussed so far in this chapter, it's worth asking a basic question: Exactly how unfair have the Boomers been to Millennials as far as fiscal policy is concerned?

One irony of so many fiscal policy debates is that politicians and pundits usually don't look in the right places to spot the generational unfairness in the ways the government writes its budgets. Yes, budget deficits pose unique intergenerational problems because in the worst case they represent today's spenders borrowing against the future work of today's children. Yet some critics of this way of thinking about fiscal policy are right that taking too crude and judgmental an approach toward deficits will miss the fact that today's young or unborn can benefit from the spending they'll have to repay, too. Deficit spending for roads and bridges, or *perhaps* for education, can sometimes pay off in higher economic growth down the road. That creates more opportunities for younger generations, and also more resources from which to pay down the debts.

So not all of the deficit spending since 2008 has represented a theft from Millennials. Some portion of those allegedly shovel-ready projects genuinely benefited the economy, and created physical infrastructure Millennials now are able to use. Military spending also presents significant challenges if you're trying to sort out generational fairness. A strong military benefits all Americans, young and old, by providing a measure of the global security that allows the American economy to thrive.

But acknowledging this complexity doesn't mean it's impossible to draw *any* conclusions about generational fairness when it comes to taxes and government spending. Economists increasingly are trying—and their assessments about what has happened to Millennials and younger generations (including those who haven't yet been born) since 2008 are bleak.

One way to think about fiscal fairness between generations is the idea of generational accounting, first developed in the 1990s by economists Laurence J. Kotlikoff, Alan J. Auerbach, and Jagadeesh Gokhale. The basic concept is to add up how much everyone currently alive is likely to pay in taxes over their lifetimes, and then add up the benefits they're set to receive under current laws and current assumptions about lifespans and degrees of healthiness. If the expected benefit payouts are greater than the expected tax payments, the deficit is called a "fiscal gap." Don't bother asking what a surplus is called in this accounting system—no one has yet identified a developed country anywhere in the world where future expected tax payments are *greater* than expected benefit payouts.*

Generational accounting gives us a way of thinking about the rough scale of the future impact of various taxing and spending policies, by offering a broad idea of how fiscal policies will or won't balance in the future. For most developed economies those estimates are terrifying. In one of their first papers introducing the concept, Auerbach, Gokhale, and Kotlikoff estimated in 1991 that a boy born in 1990 would have to pay net lifetime taxes (after

---

* One point to note when interpreting technical economics papers on generational accounting is that the method often compares tax payments and benefits of all generations currently alive to expected payments and benefits of those not yet born. While the numbers quoted in this section give a sense of how the generational balance has deteriorated over time—with younger currently living generations such as Millennials bearing much of the burden—it can be difficult to extract firm numbers.

subtracting benefits received) around 21 percent higher than a boy born in 1989.[38] By 2001, Gokhale and Kotlikoff were estimating that the generation *about* to be born would pay a net lifetime tax rate roughly double the net lifetime tax rates expected for the generation *just* born.[39] Phrasing things a bit differently a decade later,* Kotlikoff and co-author Scott Burns estimated that restoring *federal* finances to long-term intertemporal balance (meaning matching total taxes for currently living generations to the benefits they'd receive) would require either boosting total government revenue by 64 percent and then sustaining that level permanently, or reducing all spending by 40 percent. Waiting twenty years, until the oldest Millennials are pushing fifty, would require revenues to then increase by 72 percent or spending to fall by 46 percent.[40] Correcting widespread state- and local-level generational imbalances would require even steeper tax hikes.

This method helps to better understand the fiscal trade-offs the old are foisting on the young, and how sensitive America's long-term fiscal prospects truly are to economic growth and entitlement promises. For instance, one way to define fiscal fairness would be to say that younger generations shouldn't have to pay a larger share of their income in taxes than older generations did, in order to fund spending promises the older generations made to themselves. By this standard, the Boomers have been miserable failures at budgeting and are imposing a miserable fiscal burden on their children.

That leads to a troubling conclusion: the greatest fiscal theft of all that the Boomers have perpetrated over the past decade is to rob their Millennial children of fiscal choice. Millennials increasingly find ourselves left with no good options for fixing all these problems.

One obvious option would be to just increase taxes. Unsurprisingly, this is often what Baby Boomers recommend since they're least likely to bear the full brunt of the tax hikes. For instance, a common argument about Social Security reform is that all we need are relatively modest tax increases—perhaps another 2 or 3

---

* And after Medicare Part D and the Affordable Care Act.

percentage points added onto the payroll-tax rate,* and an increase in the level of income subject to the tax, perhaps to include all wage income rather than just the first $128,000—and the system would return to balance.[41] The Congressional Budget Office figures an immediate payroll-tax increase of around 4.5 percent could make Social Security solvent for seventy-five years, if you believe it's possible to make accurate forecasts over such a long span.[42] More plausible plans tend to focus on balancing the books for shorter terms of only a few decades. Alternately, maybe to solve *all* our fiscal problems we only need to increase general income taxes on the rich or on corporations. In the 2016 Democratic presidential primary, Bernie Sanders proposed a top personal income-tax rate of 54.2 percent.[43]

Those plans don't come close to the answer Millennials need. None of these tax increases would generate enough revenue to begin to cover the sort of gap generational-accounting estimates have revealed. In practical terms, most Boomers would be exempt from most of the consequences of a payroll-tax hike. And because most of these proposals make Social Security solvent only for another thirty to fifty years, Millennials still would confront an empty Social Security trust fund by the time *we* are retiring.

The tax increase that would make a difference would be a national consumption tax, akin to the value-added taxes European governments have used for decades to help fund their own (still underfunded) social-welfare systems. The lack of a consumption tax helps explain why America's government revenues tend to hover at around 25 percent of the economy (for federal, state, and local combined) compared to between 35 percent and 50 percent in most European countries.[44] But politically, it's not clear Americans are ready to pay that level of tax, or we would have a consumption tax already. And in terms of fairness, this kind of tax hike is a moral mess. Consumption taxes disproportionately target poorer households, which spend a larger proportion of their incomes. The only benefit to this, so far as Millennials are concerned, is that the

---

* This would be an increase in the total payroll tax, split evenly between employers and employees as the current payroll tax is.

elderly also consume a larger proportion of their incomes—so a consumption tax might be the one revenue raiser we could actually force Boomers to pay. Still, any tax hike to fund existing benefit payouts will almost by definition fall hardest on younger taxpayers, who will pay more of their income in taxes over a longer stretch of their working lives in order to fund benefits for Boomers that the Boomers themselves weren't prepared to prefund by paying higher taxes during their careers.

Plus, there's one more problem with increasing taxes. I was tough on Republicans earlier for frequently cutting taxes without keeping spending under control. But one has to admit that tax cutting historically has been a political winner for Republicans because it's been an economic winner for the country. There's ample experience to show that tax cuts stimulate economic growth, and that's why tax cuts tend to produce higher revenues. Republicans' fiscal fault is that they habitually overpromise on revenue creation (and on tax cuts' capacity to "pay for themselves"), not that tax cuts don't create any new economic growth and revenue at all. This implies, however, that a strategy of raising taxes dramatically to fund entitlement spending will affect economic growth for the worse. Younger generations would end up "paying" for Boomers' entitlements not only with higher taxes but with long-term slower economic growth than their Boomer parents or grandparents enjoyed. That sounds abstract, but it will be very real. In Chapter 2, I argued that underinvestment in job-creating activities has hobbled Millennials over the past decade. It is essential we don't make that problem even worse with more bad tax policies. Slower economic growth means fewer good job opportunities and fewer and smaller pay raises. It also, incidentally, means less government revenue over the longer term.

If we're not willing or able to raise taxes, of course there's another option: Millennials can spend less on other things so that we can fund benefits for Boomers without having to increase taxes on ourselves and our own children. This might work for a while. But the enormous chunk of the government budget that entitlements already eat means that we're fast running out of other spending we could pare back in order to meet the entitlement bill for Boomers and still have any hope of balancing the budget.

That leaves benefit cuts. Boomers like to think this would never happen. They've expended considerable political energy trying to make it seem impossible to cut benefits. They always talk about Social Security and Medicare as a political "third rail," that electrified track on a subway that's deadly to touch. But it's starting to look like generous benefits aren't sacrosanct after all. State and local pensions are the canaries in the fiscal coal mine. Most states have implemented pension reforms since the Great Recession, and as part of that process most states have reduced benefits.[45] Usually those reductions only limit future payouts that will be available for new hires when they retire several decades down the road. But increasingly, current retirees aren't as safe from cuts as they used to be.

When Detroit's city government filed for bankruptcy in 2013, its retirees were forced to take a 4.5 percent pension cut and will lose future cost-of-living adjustments. Some also lost generous medical benefits.[46] And a public-employee pension fund's government overseer doesn't need to be in extremis to put benefit cuts on the table. For instance, the Ohio Public Employee Retirement System (OPERS) board of trustees voted in late 2017 to try to reduce future cost-of-living increases for current retirees.[47] The state legislature ultimately saved the benefits,[48] but it's only a matter of time before some legislature somewhere can't. If nothing else, these and other cases show that what was once viewed as an ironclad rule of public pensions—taxpayers and politicians can cut benefits promised to new hires but not for people who already have retired—isn't so ironclad after all. In which case, how ironclad is the "rule" that it's impossible to cut other old-age benefits such as Social Security and Medicare?

Millennials don't want to do this, and we won't enjoy it. For one thing, some of the benefits will be illusory. We'll still be shifting onto ourselves personally some of the burden of supporting elderly parents who previously relied on Social Security. But if we can't pay, we won't pay. That's why Boomers should be deeply worried about the uncomfortable fiscal choices they've foisted onto their Millennial children. And why Boomers may yet find they have to pay some dues of their own for the unsustainable promises they made to themselves.

CHAPTER 6

Their Present, Our Future

THIS IS THE PART IN BOOKS LIKE THESE WHERE THE AUTHOR USUALLY STARTS TO offer some solutions. There might be a bulleted list or two, or a plan for a law or three that might fix things.

Not here, though, and not because I'm trying to cop out on my authorial duty. The reality is that to state many of Millennials' problems as this book has done already is to hint at possible solutions. In fact some of the problems we've looked at have been fairly well-known at least to some Boomer politicians and policymakers for a while. They've just chosen not to address them.

Instead it's worth taking a different tack. Call it the "scared straight" option. Millennials can look to other countries that have grappled with these problems to better understand what happens if we let intergenerational problems fester or, just as bad, try to solve them the wrong way.

If misery loves company, American Millennials certainly have a lot of company in the world—including a lot of Millennials who in their own ways are more miserable than we are. It's a much more surprising fact than a lot of people seem to realize. The world's economies, even the developed ones, tend to be pretty diverse. They're home to a wide array of industries; they trade with different partners; they impose different taxes and offer different social benefits; they regulate themselves in different ways. The one thing they all share in common, it would appear, is that *no one* has figured out how to make sure today's Millennial young adults get a fair shake.

A shocking statistic from the United Kingdom makes clear the spread of the crisis: The average working-age household in Britain enjoys around £20 less in weekly disposable income than the average retired household, the Resolution Foundation think tank reported in early 2017.[1] Apparently it's now more lucrative to have worked in the past than to be working in the present. As far as the study's authors could tell, this was the first time this had ever been the case.

What should be worrying for American Millennials is that this failure by other countries to do better for their younger generations isn't for want of trying. Other countries have been studying and debating problems of intergenerational fairness for longer than Americans have—that British income report was part of one of several major investigations of these issues that various UK think tanks have conducted in recent years, for example. Other countries have already tried some of the solutions we're often told will work for our own economy and yet still are inflicting a raw deal on their rising generations. It's an important message as debate blossoms in the United States over how to fix our own economy for future generations. We need to look at countries that have adopted some of the fixes American politicians (Boomer and Millennial alike) often propose for our own ills, and then to understand why those solutions have not actually fixed anything in the other places they've been tried. The value of looking abroad is that it should keep us from investing all our hopes in ideas that already aren't working somewhere else.

The examples that follow highlight either solutions that haven't worked or bigger problems that the United States urgently needs to try to avoid. These examples all come from developed economies. That's not because the challenges Millennials face in developing countries aren't serious, but because those challenges are so different from what American Millennials have to grapple with. India and many African economies, for example, urgently need to foster rapid economic growth to create more opportunities for their own large Millennial generations. But because their populations are still relatively young and fast-growing, they don't face the demographic transformation that complicates developed countries' efforts to maintain a fairer generational balance. China does face a demographic transformation already—Beijing's notorious one-child policy, in effect for the entire time that the country's Millennials were being born, has wrecked that country's generational balance. But Chinese Millennials will have to confront the demographic crisis their elders manufactured without the benefit of a fully developed economy, to the point where many observers now expect that China will grow old before it grows rich.

What follows isn't an exhaustive list of countries with Millennial problems. The tour will skip places such as Canada, Australia, Italy, Greece, Spain, and many others where Millennials are suffering particularly bad deals. Instead, I've picked out a few examples that speak to particular American concerns—the property market, fiscal balance, jobs—in ways that are especially relevant for American Millennials trying to understand our own problems. Each country or region I cover here has followed a script that at least some Americans think might help our own crop of Millennials. None of them have quite worked out as intended.

Nonworkers of the World, Unite

The 2007–2008 global crisis was miserable in most places, but it was especially miserable for Continental Europe because the crisis just went on and on.* By early 2009, Washington had managed to stabilize—more or less—America's financial system. The United States was in for a spell of recession and a long period of anemic recovery, but at least the panic was over.

In Europe the crisis started early and lasted seemingly forever. Some of the first tremors of the global crisis emerged in Europe. European banks had invested in bad American mortgages. As I mentioned in a previous chapter, one of the first harbingers of the

---

* The discussion of Europe in this section will exclude the United Kingdom, which was affected differently by the 2007–2008 crisis and recovered differently afterward.

global panic came when a French bank, BNP Paribas, limited withdrawals from hedge funds exposed to the US housing market. In the first phase of the global panic, German banks suffered losses on their own investments in bad American mortgage assets. Iceland's economy collapsed. Much of Europe tipped into a recession, thanks to the weaknesses in European banks and the drag a slowing American economy placed on European exports.

Then came the homegrown debt-and-currency crises in the eurozone. The creation of the euro currency in 1999 had encouraged investors to downplay the risk that some governments might one day struggle to repay their debts. Interest rates had plunged, encouraging some governments to borrow wildly irresponsibly, most often to fund social spending. When investors did finally catch on to the risks in the most heavily indebted euro member countries, other countries that use the euro—especially Germany and France—had to step in with bailouts of debtors including Ireland, Portugal, Spain, and Greece.* Those bailouts were conditioned on stringent economic reforms intended to boost long-term economic growth to make debt repayment more manageable—conditions voters in Greece and Spain especially tried to rebel against. Businesses, bankers, investors, and ordinary Europeans watched on anxiously year after year as the continent's politicians tried to invent, often out of thin air, the bailout funds and policy rules they needed to hold the euro together. Europe's economies limped along waiting for something to happen—either major stimulus, or major economic reforms, or a revival of the US economy that would allow Europe to export its way out of the hole.

And by now it won't come as much of a surprise that some of the biggest losers from all this were European Millennials.

The economic story of the past couple decades, almost everywhere in Europe except the United Kingdom, has been youth unemployment. The numbers are stupendously awful. As of mid-2018

---

* The first big moment of revelation came in late 2009 and early 2010, when the government in Athens admitted Greece's budget deficit and national debt were much higher than previous budget statements had suggested.

the unemployment rate for those under age twenty-five was around 15 percent. That's down from a peak of around 25 percent in the immediate aftermath of the eurozone economic crises of 2010–2012, and it's still worse than it looks. The denominator when calculating an unemployment rate is the total number of people either in work or looking for work, so that statistic misses people who have given up on finding work entirely. And "given up" is a huge cohort among European young adults. Another way European economists look at this is by examining the continent's NEETs—youths "not in employment, education, or training." In other words, this is the proportion of youths relative to the overall youth population who aren't doing any of the things young adults are supposed to do. Around 17 percent of European twenty- to thirty-four-year-olds fell in that category in 2017.[2] European countries have suffered higher unemployment than the United States for most of the past thirty or so years, but even so the problem of unemployed young people is something else.

The great mystery would seem to be why. Europe doesn't produce dumb kids. Like their American peers, European Millennials are the best-educated generation in history. The percentage of Europeans ages thirty to thirty-four who have completed university-level education or advanced technical training has swelled in recent decades, to nearly 40 percent in 2017 from 24 percent in 2002.[3] Europe also generally does a better job of preparing young people for a range of different careers across the skills spectrum. Germany's complex apprenticeship system is the classic example. Many young Germans skip university entirely, attending instead apprenticeship programs that combine on-the-job training with classroom learning.

This also isn't precisely a problem of slower economic growth overall. European economies by and large underperform compared to America, with the growth rate for the European Union overall struggling to hit 2 percent for most of the postcrisis period. But not *that* much, given that the US recovery also was slow during that span. What's notable here is that although youth unemployment waxes and wanes with broader economic changes, the young-adult unemployment rate always seems to get even worse than one might expect during recessions and always struggles to bounce back during recoveries. One plausible study estimates that Europe's generally weaker level of economic growth can explain only about half of the youth unemployment Europe has suffered since 2008.[4]

That means, of course, that half of Europe's youth unemployment since 2008 is explained by something *other* than general economic health. This observation offers the critical clue to what's going on here. Europe has managed to transform its young adults into economic shock-absorbers. Over the past decade especially, this means European Millennials have taken the inevitable knocks of the recession so that their parents didn't have to.

That on its own won't sound too out of the ordinary compared to the United States. I've noted that American Millennials bore a disproportionate share of the pain of the Great Recession. In this sense yes, we Americans have more in common with Europe than we might like to think. But several factors have made the problem a lot worse in some parts of Europe than the youth unemployment situation has ever been in America.

Economists trying to figure out why young Europeans struggle to get jobs have settled on several interrelated explanations. Some of those reasons have to do with the nature of the economy itself and might resonate in the United States. Continental Europe, like our country, is dependent on small- and medium-sized companies to create both economic growth and jobs. As I argued back in Chapter 2, a flaw in American Boomers' responses to the Great Recession was that Washington made it too hard for smaller companies to hire—monetary policies made it too difficult for those companies to get the financial capital they needed to invest, and tax and regulatory policies made each new hire too expensive. Europe had these problems in spades, especially when it comes to access to credit. The same study from the International Monetary Fund that found the economic downturn accounted for only about half of Europe's youth unemployment also found that younger workers are twice as vulnerable as older workers to suffering rising unemployment when small firms struggle to access capital.[5] Smaller European companies are much more dependent on bank loans for financing than American companies are, so those companies were even more vulnerable to a banking crisis.

But other parts of Europe's youth unemployment crisis are more distinctly European. One is that it's enormously expensive to hire someone—of any age—in many European countries. Relatively high income tax rates (that kick in at relatively low levels of income) and steep social-service taxes for pensions and health care take a big bite out of employers' wage spending. The most common way to measure this is the concept of a tax wedge. Economists calculate employers' gross spending on labor for a given worker, and then calculate how much of that money ultimately goes to direct income or payroll taxes or social "contributions." The bigger the tax wedge—the larger a percentage of an employee's gross salary that goes toward various taxes—the more expensive it is to hire that person.

Research increasingly finds that the higher the taxes on labor income, measured by the size of the tax wedge, the worse unemployment is for younger workers. IMF economists estimate this effect at an increase in youth unemployment of between 0.3 and 1.3 percentage points for each 1 percentage-point increase in the tax wedge. The basic economic problem is easy to understand. Younger workers tend to be less experienced and less productive when they start their careers. Big tax wedges can quickly make a young worker more expensive to hire than that worker's productivity justifies.

That's a recurring theme in a lot of analyses of Europe's youth unemployment crisis: European governments too often make young people too expensive to employ. Another example is European minimum wages. Perhaps surprisingly, not every European country has one,* but when they do, they tend to be relatively higher than the American version. The federal minimum wage in the United States is equal to about one-third of the median hourly

---

* Italy and Sweden are two countries that don't.

wage for a full-time worker—the hourly wage where half of full-time Americans earn more and half earn less. But in France, the minimum wage is equal to two-thirds of the median wage, and in Germany, the Netherlands, and the United Kingdom the ratio hovers between 40 percent and 50 percent.[6] As with high taxes, these minimum wages have the effect of raising the costs associated with employing lower-productivity workers. And here again, growing evidence suggests that younger workers, especially Millennials since 2008, have been the biggest losers.[7]

The final terrible trick a lot of European countries play on younger workers is to make *older* workers too difficult to fire. The stereotypes are somewhat true: it used to be well-nigh impossible to lay off a European—doing so would require hefty, legally mandated severance pay and expose a company to drawn-out litigation. By the 1990s, it was clear this web of legal protections for workers was strangling Europe's economies. If companies worried they'd never be able to fire a bad employee—or one whose labor they just didn't need anymore—they would resist taking the risk of hiring new employees. And the costs of maintaining legal lifetime employment guarantees would stifle investment. Governments across the continent eventually launched a string of reforms. Crucially, though, these plans rarely included a removal of the lifetime guarantees for older workers who already enjoyed those stringent legal protections for their jobs. Instead, governments created a second, less regulated category of worker, usually on a short-term contract of only a year or two, with significantly less job security and often lower pay and benefits, too.

Younger workers disproportionately find themselves in this less protected category. Around 18 percent of European workers ages twenty-five to thirty-four were in temporary positions as of 2017, up from 16 percent in 2008. In some countries the trend is even more pronounced: in Italy the prevalence of temporary work for this age group has grown to 27 percent from 18 percent in the same span.[8] That fact by itself isn't actually a bad thing, although critics often claim it is. Europe's experience before these reforms shows that for younger workers, the choice typically would be a less protected contract job or no job at all. But what does create a problem for European Millennials is that the coexistence of two different kinds of employee—older permanent workers and younger flexible hires—means that younger workers are the ones who *always* lose out. Whenever an economic downturn forces a company through a round of layoffs or a restructuring, the protections afforded for older workers grandfathered into the older system inevitably made it easier for companies to keep those employees and lay off younger workers.

What ties together all these European tales of Millennial-worker woe is a sad irony: policies that are intended to help all workers too often end up helping older employees at the expense of the young. And once the problem is phrased that way, the alarming fact is that some politicians—and even some Millennial politicians—in the United States want to repeat the same mistakes.

This is most obvious in the case of minimum wages. American economists have debated for years whether minimum-wage increases hurt or help all workers, and specifically the subset of younger, less skilled workers. To date, the evidence in the United States has generally been mixed, with some studies finding that younger, unskilled workers lose out and other studies finding that all workers benefit from relatively modest minimum-wage hikes. Europe's experience, however, offers some important food for thought on why America hasn't yet experienced big and bruising negative consequences from minimum-wage increases—but why we could in the future if we're not careful. As we saw, the crucial factor here is the gap between the minimum wage and the median wage. In recent decades, increases to the American minimum wage have tended to lag overall wage growth, which has allowed politicians to increase the minimum wage without narrowing the gap much at all. But a sudden and substantial increase in the minimum wage, such as the $15-per-hour level some American politicians support, would narrow the gap closer to the European level. And Europe's experience shows this isn't good for younger workers.

This pattern of inadvertently (or deliberately) copying the least Millennial-friendly aspects of European economies has repeated time and again in the United States since the financial crisis. The Affordable Care Act ratcheted up the cost of hiring new employees, especially among smaller and medium-sized firms. This starts to resemble the form of tax wedge that has driven down Millennial employment in many parts of Europe. And other popular ideas in the United States, such as bolstering the legal power of unions, have served mainly to create barriers to Millennial hiring when those ideas are deployed abroad. A study of developed countries between 1960 and 1996 found that the greater the role unions played in the economy—as measured by membership and other indicators of bargaining power—the lower the employment rate for younger workers. Part of the explanation is that unionized workers are able to price younger, less experienced workers out of the market.[9]

The punch line to all this, if there is one, is that while some American politicians keep trying to copy some of Europe's worst labor-market ideas, European Millennials keep trying to flee those same policies. The lifeline for European young adults trapped in bad economies has been a feature of the European Union itself: a citizen of any EU member state has the right to live and work in any other member state without needing to apply for a visa or suffer through any other red tape. And although precise data on this are surprisingly hard to come by, anecdotally hundreds of thousands of European Millennials—maybe millions—have availed of the opportunity to do exactly this, especially since 2008. Young adults from Italy, France, Greece, Spain, and other lagging economies have flocked to Germany, Britain, the Netherlands, and other relative success stories. If it weren't for this opportunity to vote with their feet, the youth unemployment rates in some European countries would likely be even higher than they are now.

This raises a question the next time an American politician suggests importing features of European labor markets, such as higher minimum wages, policy favoritism for unions, or heftier taxes on incomes: Why would we want to adopt the same rules European Millennials are busy trying to flee?

Cruel Britannia

American Millennials might occasionally complain about how difficult it is to buy a house. Our British cousins seem to be able to talk of little else. "Millennial Housing Crisis Engulfs Britain," blared one headline in the left-wing *Guardian* newspaper.[10] "Millennial Couples Making 'Heart-Breaking' Family Decisions Because of Housing Market," Huffington Post's British site has reported.[11] And proving that this is a bipartisan concern, sort of, the right-leaning *Daily Telegraph* has weighed in with its own spin: "Tories Fear Middle-Class Millennials Priced Out of Housing Market Could Sink Party at Next Election."[12]*

This amounts to a lot more than just a faraway sob story. Earlier in this book I argued that part of the housing problem young adults face in America is that we aren't building enough housing in the places where Millennials need to live in order to get good jobs. In the United States, these localized housing shortages are severe but not yet catastrophic. Our economy still is geographically dispersed enough that although the job market pulls many Millennials into regions where the housing supply can't keep up with the demand, many other Millennials escape. But in Britain, this crisis of housing scarcity already *is* reaching catastrophic proportions. Their fate will be ours, too, if our economy continues pulling us toward a relatively limited number of regions, and Millennials in hot spots such as New York City and Silicon Valley should pay particular attention to what's going wrong in Britain.

First, some facts on how bad a housing market can get for Millennials: The British market is objectively worse than the American market—a lot worse. A decline of around 7 percentage points

---

* Members of Britain's center-right Conservative Party are also known by the nickname Tories.

in the homeownership rate for American Millennials compared to Baby Boomers at the same age is a crisis in the United States. But in Britain, the gap is nearer to 27 percentage points—roughly 70 percent of British Baby Boomers already owned their home by age thirty-four, compared to barely more than 40 percent of Millennials who can say the same.[13]* The crisis is particularly acute for the middle class, where the homeownership rate for twenty-five- to thirty-four-year-olds right in the middle of the income distribution has collapsed to 27 percent, from 65 percent two decades ago.[14]† A plausible guess is that one-third of British Millennials will *never* own a home, compared to 23 percent of current retirees (Boomers and older) who don't own.[15]

America's homeownership shortfall is causing a social crisis for Millennials in the United States. But "crisis" might be too mild to describe the problem in the United Kingdom. Delaying home-ownership means delaying most milestones of adulthood: around one in six younger Brits in romantic relationships said in one poll that the struggle to find affordable housing (to rent or own) would cause them to delay marriage, and 22 percent of those in relationships said they'd delay having children.[16]‡ Those families who do take the plunge and start having children before they buy a house face years of uncertainty surrounding whether they'll end up continuing to live in the same school district or be able to afford a large enough home at all. Another study found the rise in moving back in with parents—mirroring the trend in the United States—weighs on self-esteem.[17] High housing costs, whether to rent or to repay an astronomical mortgage, account for a chunk of that £20 weekly difference in disposable income between retirees and workers I

---

* Baby Boomers born 1946–1965; Millennials born 1981–2000.

† Put another way, in 1995, 65 percent of middle-earning households headed by someone born 1961–1970 owned the home they occupied, but by 2015 only 27 percent of middle-earning households with a head born 1981–1990 owned.

‡ This poll included people born 1972–1998, so a mix of both Gen X and Millennials.

mentioned earlier.*[18] Speaking of retirees, as more British Millennials approach their own retirements without owning their homes, they'll exacerbate the fiscal challenges of an aging society. Since renting generally implies higher housing costs in retirement than owning, and since the lower a household's income, the less likely they are to buy, government spending on housing assistance for the elderly could skyrocket to £16 billion per year by 2060 from £6.3 billion now, according to a Resolution Foundation estimate.[19]

Underlying economic differences account for part of why British Millennials struggle to afford homes, but not all of the phenomenon. The British economy shrank more during the Great Recession (around 6 percent from peak to trough) than the US economy did (around 4 percent).[20] The British economy recovered more quickly, however, with growth frequently exceeding 2 percent over the past decade, a record the United States struggled to match. And although British economists often note that one problem facing young homebuyers is that wage growth has slowed dramatically for younger workers, those numbers require careful interpretation. Britain didn't suffer as severe a wave of youth unemployment as the one that afflicted the United States after the Great Recession.[21] Although wages are growing slowly, that's still better than the zero that a Millennial earns if she doesn't have a job at all.

This housing disaster is such a surprise now because for much of the twentieth century, Britain seemed to be *the* great homeownership society—even more so than the United States by some measures. As of 1971, 50 percent of households owned their own home. Reforms in the 1980s, and especially Margaret Thatcher's program to allow middle-class families in public housing to buy their homes and apartments, finally pushed homeownership into overdrive. By 2001, the ownership rate was 69 percent—a peak the United States itself wouldn't hit until 2004.[22]

---

* As in the United States, rapidly rising rents, especially in the economically thriving London and Southeastern regions of Britain, also weigh heavily on Millennial personal finances.

That dream of a homeownership society is slipping away from British Millennials now, and for a reason so obvious it could almost be comical. Britain has neglected to build enough homes. Estimates vary widely on how many new homes Britain needs each year, but almost everyone agrees it's not building anywhere close to that number. Researchers try to estimate how many new families are being formed each year—children reaching adulthood, couples getting married or having children, and so on—and compare that rate of household formation to the rate at which new housing stock comes on the market. Depending on who's guessing, England alone will need anywhere between 210,000 and 250,000 new housing units per year for the next couple decades.* It's building, at most, 190,000, including both new construction and conversions of buildings such as schools and churches into housing.[23] Every year that Britain falls behind its housing construction needs, the backlog of housing demand grows even larger.[†]

This overall supply shortfall for both sale and rental units has created a financial vortex for British Millennials that will be all too familiar to growing numbers of their American cousins. Rents have tended to rise faster than either overall inflation or wages, especially in job-rich urban areas—which in Britain primarily means London, London, and London. Those regions also are the areas where the supply of new housing for sale is most limited. We've seen that American Millennials tend to be drawn for economic reasons to urban areas, where it's relatively harder to build houses for them, and that phenomenon is equally apparent in Britain, or more so. The proportion of Millennials living in an area where average house prices are four times or more higher than average earnings

---

* Along with Wales, Scotland, and Northern Ireland, England is one of the constituent countries of the United Kingdom, and for administrative reasons data of this sort often look at England in isolation.

† There is a contrarian viewpoint that Britain doesn't suffer a supply shortfall at all, because by some counts new housing exceeds household formation, even in London. But these analyses, so far as I can tell, generally don't account for new households that *would* form if more housing were available—such as Millennials living with their parents who would have moved out on their own if they could afford an apartment.

has grown to 87 percent, from just under half for late Boomers and early Gen Xers. Nearly 40 percent of British Millennials now live in an area where the average house price is ten times greater than average earnings, compared to 9 percent of people who were our age two decades ago.[24][*]

And the thing about this is that everyone already knows why supply is so constrained. The prime culprit is Britain's Byzantine zoning process. As in the United States, local governments are responsible for approving construction applications, and in Britain they're exceptionally bad at it. Developers must spend months—and often years—negotiating the smallest details of major projects before construction can begin, ranging from specific building materials to the precise location of litter bins on the building site.[25] Objections from neighbors—some possibly legitimate, but just as often existing owners trying to save their views or maintain their own property values—can gum up the planning process. And large tracts of land are completely off limits for development, notably the "green belts" that by law surround major urban areas. Some 1.25 million acres of land in a large band around London are unavailable for new housing. When green belts were first designated between the 1930s and '50s, the goal was to preserve a clear demarcation between built-up urban areas and the countryside. But as the demand for housing has swelled, desperate homebuyers—especially first-timers like Millennials—find themselves pushed to new construction *beyond* the green belt, with the long, time- and carbon-guzzling commutes that entails.

This makes Britain an instructive, and frightening, proving ground for grappling with the politics of a problem that is steadily growing more urgent in the United States. The striking feature of this from an American Millennial's perspective is that the debate about zoning reform is so much more advanced in Britain compared to what it's like here. The young-adult flight into economically vibrant cities is more acute, especially because while the United States boasts many potential new-economy centers, London

---

[*] Late Boomers/early Gen Xers born 1961–1970; Millennials born 1981–1990.

is the focus of most of Britain's economic energy. And yet no one in Britain has managed to do anything about the new housing needs of Millennial families. Successive governments have promised to reform the zoning process, and over time it has become a little better, if one measures the time it takes for local councils to approve zoning applications and the number of applications that are approved. But not better enough to meet Britain's rapidly increasing demand for homes.

Meanwhile, Britain also offers some warnings about what not to do to "help" Millennials buy in areas where supply is strictly limited. Because while Britain has struggled to build more houses, it also has tried aggressively to subsidize first-time buyers to help them climb onto the property ladder. The results of pouring more taxpayer money into a limited market have been predictable—or at least easy to predict for anyone who's not a politician.

Most attempts to boost Millennial homeownership (or any first-time homeownership) have focused on making buying more "affordable." The signature program is known as Help-to-Buy, and it started its life in 2013 as a government-subsidized loan guarantee covering 15 percent of the purchase price of a house—an effort to encourage banks to extend more mortgage credit. In its current form, Help-to-Buy offers outright government loans equal to 20 percent of a home purchase price (40 percent in pricey London) with only a 5 percent down payment from the first-time buyer. Britain also offers subsidies for savings toward a down payment in special accounts and even "shared ownership," in which some buyers can buy part of the equity in a house and rent the rest from a housing association, gradually buying more equity over time.*

And this hasn't been solely a preoccupation of elected politicians. The Bank of England has gotten in on the act. Its own response to the global financial crisis of 2007–2008 and Britain's subsequent recession almost exactly tracks the Federal Reserve's interventions—unprecedentedly low interest rates and large-scale asset

---

* Housing associations are nonprofit organizations that manage subsidized housing on behalf of local governments.

purchases. The central bank slashed interest rates during the crisis, from a 2007 high of 5.75 percent to a historic low of 0.5 percent by 2009, where it stayed until another cut, to 0.25 percent, in August 2016 amid the uncertainty after Britain's vote to leave the European Union. And Britain has had its share of quantitative easing, centered around the purchase of some £435 billion of government bonds. Unlike the Federal Reserve, the Bank of England wasn't preoccupied with the housing market specifically, at least not at the start. But it's now clear that the housing market is where a lot of this new money ended up. Mortgage rates plummeted, along with other long-term interest rates, to around 4 percent as of 2018, from 7.5 percent before the crisis for a standard variable-rate mortgage.* Mortgage lending accelerated to the point that the central bank in 2014 needed to impose a regulatory cap on the size of mortgages relative to income that Brits could borrow in order to tamp down worries about another housing-induced financial crisis.

No prizes for guessing how this effort to support demand without increasing supply has worked. Estimates vary on the extent to which Help-to-Buy programs have pushed house prices further skyward. Left-leaning housing advocacy group Shelter in 2015 calculated the program had added £8,250 to the price of the average home. Since Help-to-Buy subsidies were available only for new-build homes, economists were able to study its effects in part by comparing price differences between new and existing houses. Sure enough, while new homes had always commanded a modest price premium, that premium expanded rapidly under Help-to-Buy to almost exactly the level of the government subsidized loan a home-buyer could receive. In other words, prices for houses eligible for the program increased quickly to absorb as much new money as the government was making available. That implies that on net terms, housing wasn't any more affordable for new buyers than it had been

---

* American-style fixed-rate mortgages are unheard of in Britain—a typical mortgage features a fixed rate for the first two, five, or ten years and a variable rate after that.

before (indeed, it might have been less so), and at best there was mixed evidence that the program stimulated more house building.

The main conclusion is that without any serious—and success-ful—effort to boost the supply of housing, attempts to make hous-ing more affordable for new buyers tend to backfire. But one group of buyers *does* benefit: those who already own homes. A significant trend in Britain in recent years is that more people are buying sec-ond (or third, or more) homes. One in six Boomers owns a second home, one study found in 2018, while another survey released a year earlier concluded that Boomers accounted for about half of the household wealth held in the form of second properties.[26] A large proportion of British Boomers are expected to hoard their prop-erty, too—only about 40 percent of them are projected to move out of their current houses before they die.[27]

That points to another serious problem emerging in Britain's housing market that should trouble British and American Millen-nials alike. What started as a crisis of affordability has rapidly be-come a crisis of economic opportunity.

Britain's property economy is reverting to a form of landed feu-dalism that had seemed to be receding. The great promise of the Thatcher-era housing reform, which allowed millions of low- and middle-income renters to become homeowners, was that Britain would become an ownership society. Economic security would no longer be restricted to a landed or professional class. Any individ-ual who worked hard enough could get ahead on his or her own merits. It's hard to square that vision with the growing evidence that Britain's housing market is becoming more and more reliant on family wealth, especially to help first-time buyers on the ladder. More than one-third of first-time homebuyers now accept finan-cial help from their families to climb onto the property ladder, a historic high. And Millennial buyers who can tap their families for financial help are able to buy properties at younger ages—in Lon-don, more than four years younger than buyers who don't enjoy that kind of boost.[28]

This exploration of the British housing market adds some important color to American debates about Millennial homeownership. The problem isn't only the prices or "affordability." The problem is availability—having the right kinds of houses in the right places. As both America and Britain have lost the capacity we used to have to build new homes when and where they're needed, younger generations have suffered worse and worse squeezes on their economic opportunities. Anyone who thought US zoning and construction woes are only a small part of our housing difficulties should look at what has happened in Britain as those problems have been allowed to fester.

German Zeroes

If only we could raise taxes a bit more, Americans are often told, we'd be able to balance our budget and continue providing social benefits to the poor and the elderly. Many of the Millennials who flock to politicians like Bernie Sanders and Alexandria Ocasio-Cortez believe it's true. Not so fast. It turns out a European country is helpfully offering an experiment in how to manage taxing, spending, and borrowing for maximum fairness and responsibility. That country is Germany, and how is that experiment working? Not well.

Germans will bristle at that characterization, because their budget balance has become legendary in recent years. Germany provides an advanced, Western European–style welfare state that by most measures is far more generous than America's. Yet its budget is in surplus and it's paying down its debt, which is set to fall soon to below 60 percent of GDP from a high well above 80 percent of GDP during the eurozone crisis after 2010. That budget balance— they call it the *schwarze Null*, or "black zero"—is a point of pride for German politicians of both major political parties. American politicians have paid lip service to deficit-cutting and budget-balancing for decades. The Germans actually do it.

They do it in a way that some Americans are inclined to view as a model. The key fact is that although social spending is high, taxes also are high. Germany collects revenue equal to nearly 38 percent of its economic output in a typical year (at all levels of government), compared to 26 percent for the United States.[29] The top corporate profits tax rate averages around 30 percent, compared to nearly 40 percent in the United States before the late-2017 tax reform and around 27 percent now.* Another major revenue raiser is the consumption tax, or VAT, which adds 19 percent to most purchases.

Americans to the Left of the political spectrum might note approvingly that Germany's top personal income tax rate is 45 percent, compared to 39.6 percent in the United States before the 2017 tax reform and 37 percent now. Those American politicians might be less inclined to warn Americans that a larger number of middle-class Germans pay Germany's highest rates—but this is an important part of Germany's fiscal story. Germany's method of calculating income tax is characteristically complicated, but the point is that taxpayers hit the second-highest rate, which is 42 percent, at much lower levels of income than an American needs to earn before she starts paying higher rates. Taxpayers earning as little as €55,000 per year pay 42 percent of each additional euro of income in tax; at that level of income an American would pay only 22 percent. That's because the Germans have figured out that the middle class is where the real money is when it comes to generating revenues.

And social taxes—sorry, "contributions"—also are higher in ways that some Americans might approve of. The total burden of taxes to fund old-age pensions, health care, unemployment benefits, and the disability insurance system is a whopping 40 percent of an employee's gross wages, with employers picking up around half that tab. The portion for pensions alone is around 19 percent, which is not so far off from the level of payroll tax some people advocate for the United States to "fix" Social Security. These social taxes are integral to the way Germany funds its government

---

* Both the German and US tax rates here include both the federal tax and an average of state and local taxes.

and balances its budget. Around 38 percent of government revenue comes from these "contributions," compared to an average share of 26 percent among all developed countries.[30] Even after accounting for benefits middle-class households receive in return for their tax payments, Germany pays high net rates. The average net tax rate for a two-parent household with one working parent and two children is nearly 22 percent, compared to an average rate of 14 percent across all developed economies.[31]

Most miraculous of all—at least from the perspective of left-wing American politicians such as Bernie Sanders, Elizabeth Warren, and Alexandria Ocasio-Cortez—is that the Germans by and large seem to be pretty happy paying all those taxes.

Promises to cut taxes are a bipartisan fixture of just about every political campaign in the United States. The only thing our two major parties argue about is which taxes to cut, and by how much. But not so in Germany. Germans had a national election in September 2017, and the remarkable thing about that campaign was that tax-cut pledges hardly resonated at all. The center-left Social Democratic Party (SPD) tried to promise tax cuts for the middle class, to be offset by a tax increase on those with higher incomes. That wasn't enough to spare the SPD from its worst election result since West German democracy restarted in 1949. As for the center-right Christian Democratic Union (CDU) of Chancellor Angela Merkel, anyone who thought the functional equivalent of the US Republican Party would make a big push for tax reform was sorely mistaken. Merkel started the campaign not wanting to promise any tax cuts at all and had to be dragged into promising a very small package of tax cuts by some right-wing malcontents in her party's leadership.

The simplest explanation for this is that Germans seem to think the tax system—and the entitlement spending all those taxes support—is working for them. A poll ahead of the 2017 election found that only around 20 percent of Germans supported tax *cuts*. Most of the rest either wanted even more government spending or to pay down the debt faster.[32] That matches other surveys that have found widespread public support for balancing the budget and paying down debt, but not for tax reductions.*[33] The one party in the September 2017 election that did support cutting taxes, the pro-business Free Democrats, ended up faring a little worse than expected in the final results. It's hard to tell exactly what accounts for this German insistence on fiscal rectitude, but most observers—including Germans—attribute this phenomenon to Germans' fondness for responsibility and a tendency to want to hoard resources, including hoarding cash in government treasuries. Germany is a fiscal conservative's dream. There's enormous support for balanced budgets. It's all a stark contrast to the United States, where voters seem to expect politicians to promise to balance the budget but never hold them accountable when they don't.

But there's a catch, as there always is whenever it comes to fiscal policy. Germany's budget isn't actually balanced at all—not in a generational sense, anyway.

To see why, it helps to understand how Germany got to *schwarze Null*, since as recently as fifteen years ago Berlin was still running high annual deficits and debt was climbing rapidly. The main strategy was a major round of reforms for working-age entitlements in the early 2000s. Those measures significantly dialed back unemployment payments and welfare benefits, and created new incentives for companies to hire at least on a part-time basis.† One crucial reform was to scale back programs that had allowed older workers to "retire" early by claiming generous unemployment benefits until they qualified for regular pensions. This wasn't directly a fiscal policy or even billed as a money saver. But the economic

---

* Another popular fiscal view in Germany that will warm some American politicians' hearts is an endemic belief that Berlin spends too much on the military—despite the fact that German military spending relative to the size of the economy already is on the low side compared to the rest of Europe—and that further cuts to the military budget should fund other spending priorities such as education and social-welfare benefits.

† They were implemented by SPD chancellor Gerhard Schroeder but are known as the Hartz reforms after Peter Hartz, the former Volkswagen executive who led the panel that proposed the overhauls.

growth the reforms helped to stimulate by encouraging more work has been one of the main ingredients in Germany's return to a balanced budget over the past decade.

Those welfare reforms left something out, though—old-age entitlements. Berlin has spent the past twenty years tinkering around the edges of its pension system, including increasing the retirement age to sixty-seven from sixty-five. And thanks to the welfare reforms, more workers in their fifties are working and paying taxes. But for the most part, Berlin focused on balancing the budget *for now* and letting the future worry about itself.

Which means that over the longer term, Germany's budget is terrifyingly unbalanced. Germany faces the second-worst demographic future in the developed world, after Japan, thanks to decades of falling birthrates. Depending on how one measures (and how one accounts for the wave of Middle Eastern migration that reached Germany from 2015 onward), Germany is only a year or two away from a situation where people older than sixty outnumber people younger than thirty.[34] By 2035, only one worker will be supporting each retiree, compared to an expected ratio of three workers per retiree in 2020, according to an analysis prepared for the Bertelsmann Foundation think tank.[35] In theory, the recent wave of immigration could help improve the age balance of the population, but in practice it's hard to predict what the economic effects of that inflow will be. Migrants currently are placing large burdens on German taxpayers to provide housing, welfare assistance, and education and training. No one knows how economically productive the recent arrivals will end up being—how much they'll actually contribute to economic growth.

As a result, the *schwarze Null* is more like a *schwarze* lull before aging Germans create a new era of unstoppable deficits and debt. Spending on government-funded pensions and health care for German retirees is expected to grow to between 29 percent and 33 percent of GDP by 2060, compared to 26 percent as of 2014.[36] From a surplus in the late 2010s, Berlin will start seeing annual deficits as large as 9 percent of GDP by the late 2040s. Debt could blow past 80 percent of GDP in 2040 and could reach 208 percent of GDP in 2060, the Bertelsmann report warns.[37]

German politicians who claim to care about budget balance are predictably uninterested in fixing *this* imbalance. Instead, German Boomers have spent the past few years competing to make their future retirement benefits even more generous—which just goes to show that this sort of entitlement blowout is universal. Conservative chancellor Angela Merkel in 2014 cooperated with her left-wing coalition partners in the SPD to lower the retirement age to sixty-three from sixty-five for some workers, at a time when the law already had been changed to increase the age to sixty-seven.* And in the 2017 election campaign, she categorically ruled out any proposal to increase the retirement age to sixty-nine or seventy, as some economists—including at the German central bank, the Bundesbank—have proposed to reduce the long-term fiscal burden of the old. Not to be outdone, the SPD also is busy making pension spending for today's old and soon-to-be-old more generous. The party has insisted on guaranteeing no cuts to pension benefits until 2040, and in August 2018 the Social Democrats got Merkel to agree to lock in benefits at least until 2025. There are limits to Berlin's devotion to fiscal rectitude.

These trends should worry American Millennials, since what Germany shows is that one of the most commonly proposed solutions to our country's fiscal woes simply won't work. As much as we increase taxes today, and even if we managed to balance Washington's annual budget tomorrow, we'll never be able to raise taxes enough to pay our parents' entitlement bills the day *after* tomorrow—and we'll definitely never persuade Boomers to sacrifice any of their benefits willingly. Precisely because Germany's budget already is balanced, the problem is cast into stark relief. We could pay 50

---

* After elections in both 2013 and 2017, Germany emerged with an unwieldy "Grand Coalition" government made up of the main center-right and center-left parties, and the finance minister in her government after 2017 was from the opposing party. This explains why a conservative such as Merkel can end up implementing policy ideas advocated by the Social Democrats.

percent or more of our income in various taxes in the United States and yet not solve the entitlement crisis our parents have created.

No Country for Young Men

In some countries Millennials struggle to get work; in others they struggle to buy homes; in others they face a lifetime struggle to pay their taxes. When you combine all of those problems, you get Japan.

There's probably no place on earth where it's worse to be a Millennial than Japan, and Japanese Millennials know it. Japanese Millennials are less confident about their future career prospects than their counterparts in Germany, India, or the United States—fair enough—but also are less confident than young adults in recession-addled Italy and Greece. Some 37 percent of Japanese Millennials believe they'll have to work until they die because they'll never be able to afford to retire, compared to only 12 percent of American Millennials who feel the same way.[38] Some in the media have dubbed Japan's adults the "world's gloomiest Millennials" as a result, and the shoe certainly seems to fit.[39]

This is more surprising than many younger Americans probably realize. When American Baby Boomers were entering their prime in the 1980s, everyone assumed the future would be Japanese. Japanese cars were cracking into the US market in a big way; Japanese companies were investing in America. The Japanese even bought some of America's most famous real estate, including Rockefeller Center in Midtown Manhattan. Now, thirty years later, the Millennial generation that should be inheriting a booming, world-beating economy is stuck in the doldrums and may never escape. What on earth went wrong?

Much of Japan's seemingly unstoppable economic growth in the 1960s and '70s happened because a country whose industries were heavily damaged during World War II was rebuilding itself quickly. In retrospect it's clear that there was less to the Japanese "miracle" than met the eye—a lot less. While America's own high priests of industrial declinism warned darkly about Japan's superior efficiency and management techniques, a real estate and financial crisis in the early 1990s would reveal that Japan actually faced many of the economic problems that dogged the rest of the world, or worse.* Growth had been buoyed by credit instead of across-the-board productivity gains, and in many ways the economy was—and remains—overregulated, underproductive, and in too many cases corrupt.[†]

But if one had to pick two things that are now going especially wrong for Japanese Millennials in an economy that never fully recovered from its first crisis of nearly three decades ago, those things would have to be jobs and taxes.

Nothing weighs on the minds of Japanese Millennials as heavily as the job market, which in most ways is the epitome of everything that has gone wrong for Millennials around the world. In Europe, onerous protections for older workers coupled with partial reforms of labor laws created a two-track labor market that leaves younger workers behind. This duality is more pronounced in Japan than anywhere else. Around one-third of all Japanese workers are now in "nonregular" work.[‡] Many of those are women, especially

---

* Lester Thurow, the dean of MIT's Sloan School of Business in the late 1980s and early 1990s, built a career around warning that Americans were failing to keep up with Japanese competitors who in his telling were better at just about every aspect of economic leadership and corporate management; the timing of his most famous book, 1992's *Head to Head: The Coming Economic Battle Among Japan, Europe, and America*, now seems unfortunate in light of the fact that when it came out, Japan was entering into what has now become two decades of near-stagnation. None other than Donald Trump also was a prominent critic of Japan, and America's relationship with Japan, in the 1980s, when he frequently complained the Japanese were free-riding on America's military and outnegotiating American businesses at every turn.

† Japan, Inc., has suffered a growing list of corporate scandals in recent years, ranging from Olympus to Mitsubishi to Nissan and many others in between, sometimes relating to efforts to fudge quality-control test results, and other times exposing long-running corporate efforts to conceal losses dating back to the 1980s and '90s.

‡ "Regular" employment in Japan is generally considered to satisfy all three of the following conditions: the worker is hired directly by the employer instead of via a temping firm; the employment is full-time; and the worker is on an open-ended contract. Anyone whose job doesn't satisfy at least one of those conditions is considered "nonregular." (Chie Aoyagi and Giovanni Ganelli, "The Path to Higher Growth: Does Revamping Japan's Dual Labor Market Matter?" International Monetary Fund Working Paper WP/13/202, October 2013.)

middle-aged, who reenter the labor force on a part-time basis after having children. But growing numbers appear to be young people, including young men. Between the late 1980s, when late-vintage Japanese Baby Boomers were entering the labor force, and the mid-2000s, when Japanese Millennials were starting to work, the proportion of men taking a nonregular position as their first job after graduation nearly quadrupled, to 29 percent from 8 percent.* And while many of those men eventually find their way into "regular" jobs, a growing proportion don't. Around 80 percent of late-Boomer Japanese men were in regular work by their thirties, compared to 70 percent of thirty-something Millennials now.[40] Anecdotally, growing numbers of young men report being shunted into the nonregular segment of the labor market, especially since the global financial crisis and recession of 2007–2009.[41]

That's because Japan's economy still struggles with the legacy of a lifetime employment system that is further and further out of touch with the demands of a modern economy. For the first several decades of the postwar period, Japanese jobs were for life. Workers would accept lower salaries than their foreign peers, but in exchange their companies would implicitly promise never to lay anyone off and to provide generous pensions. Workers themselves would avoid job hopping in search of higher pay elsewhere. Some of this was enforced by law—especially Japanese laws making it harder than in many other developed countries to fire workers, and courts that are especially likely to force companies to rehire workers deemed to have been unfairly dismissed. But a lot of it was cultural. Workers and companies alike faced significant social stigma for breaking the deal.

The economic crisis of the early 1990s changed things. Companies realized they could no longer afford not to have the flexibility their foreign competitors did—to hire and fire as needed to

---

* Note, however, that Japan didn't experience a demographic boom in the way America and some Western European countries did—the true Japanese "baby boom" lasted only for three years between 1947 and 1949, after which childbearing plummeted again. For convenience, I'll use the term here to refer to the entire cohort of Japanese born during the span of the American Baby Boom.

reconfigure the business in light of changing market conditions. And the government realized it needed to loosen the laws that had helped to cement the old lifetime employment system. So Tokyo created new types of employment, making is possible for more employers in more industries to hire nonregular workers. But the lifetime model has never gone away. In fact, the number of regular workers has held more or less steady over the past several decades. Instead *new* jobs have overwhelmingly been created as nonregular positions.[42] It's not entirely clear that Japan has the largest second-tier labor market of any developed country, but it does seem to be harder in Japan than in some European countries to climb out of precarious contract work into a "proper" job.*[43] And not everyone seems to have an equal shot at making the transition: those who are better educated stand a better chance of finding their way into secure employment eventually.[44]

That makes Japan a fascinating case study in what happens when Millennials face being trapped in a perpetually awful job market, and the conclusions aren't pretty. A growing problem is that companies and workers alike underinvest in jobs when those jobs are nonregular. Workers who feel helpless or hopeless about their long-term prospects at a company have less incentive to stick around, while companies worry they have less reason to invest in training for precarious workers. A 2006 survey of around one thousand Japanese companies found that while more than 90 percent provided training for regular employees, fewer than half provided any training for nonregular workers.[45] This increasingly is becoming a drag on the economy as a whole, as flagging productivity growth suppresses wages and lower wages dampen consumption.

---

* This is surprisingly difficult to compare across countries because every government measures precarious forms of employment in different ways—although it's notable that surveys finding Japan does *not* lead the world in the size of its second-class labor force often include a warning that their methods may undercount precarious employment in Japan. (Chie Aoyagi and Giovanni Ganelli, "The Path to Higher Growth: Does Revamping Japan's Dual Labor Market Matter?" International Monetary Fund Working Paper WP/13/202, October 2013.)

The job market is bad enough, but older Japanese politicians have gone out of their way in recent decades to create another problem for Millennials, too. A linchpin of Tokyo's attempts to rescue the economy from the 1991 crisis and ensuing lost decades has been massive government spending. The effect of this has been to shift onto future generations of taxpayers bigger and bigger burdens, while the economic growth those generations will need to make the debts affordable remains elusive.

The numbers are astounding, even for Americans accustomed to trillion-dollar deficits and tens-of-trillions-of-dollars national debts. Since the 2008 global crisis, Japan's government habitually has run annual deficits between 4.5 percent and 9.5 percent of GDP. Debt has soared, to 1,088,985,100,000,000 yen as of mid-2018[46]— that's a quadrillion*—an explosion to more than 235 percent of GDP from a "modest" 64 percent of GDP in 1991 just as Japan's protracted economic stagnation was beginning.[47]

A lot of that has gone to ill-fated attempts to stimulate the economy by building public works. We saw in the previous chapter that for all the talk in Washington about "shovel-ready projects," America's own fiscal-stimulus plans relied heavily on expanding transfer payments. Japan went the other way: it really did build infrastructure. A lot of it—some $6.3 trillion worth of roads and bridges between 1991 and 2008, and billions more in the decade since.[48] Yet these immaculate roads and new airports still have never managed to boost economic growth in a sustained way. Older Japanese politicians have merely left the younger generations heaps of economically unproductive infrastructure and mountains of debt. And as one would expect for a rapidly aging population, Japan's oldsters are also leaving behind an enormous and growing old-age entitlement burden, with spending on pensions and health care for the aged already eating up fully one-third of the government's budget each year and growing. At least in this area, Tokyo is exercising a little

---

* It's just short of $10 trillion, give or take a few billion dollars here or there.

restraint. Successive reforms since 2004 have pared back on automatic cost-of-living increases in benefits and have created stronger financial incentives for Japanese to work longer before they retire. Although the system is still unsustainable over the longer-term, Tokyo ekes out better marks for effort than most developed-country governments in this regard.

To be fair to older Japanese, they do understand that someone needs to pay the bills. A recurring debate in Japanese politics for decades now has concerned using a consumption tax—like a European value-added tax or the sales taxes American states levy—to help close the fiscal gap. The tax was first introduced in 1989 at the low introductory rate of 3 percent. But efforts to boost revenue from the tax always run into a small problem: increasing the consumption-tax rate in a weak economy is a great way to slow economic growth even further. In April 1997, the tax was increased to 5 percent, a move that was blamed, alongside the onset of the Asian Financial Crisis later that year, with tipping Japan into a recession. After he was elected in 2012, Prime Minister Shinzo Abe promised to double the consumption tax, to 10 percent, in two steps. But after the first of those increases, to 8 percent in 2014, Japan suffered yet another recession. The next stage of increase has been delayed, until October 2019 as of this writing. It's hard to say whether it will ever happen, though—or whether it should.

If Japan's older voters aren't willing to tax their way out of debt, they could always try to grow their way out of the hole. Abe has attempted to do exactly this with his famous "Abenomics" plan to revive the economy, centered on "three arrows" of monetary expansion, even more short-term deficit spending on stimulus projects, and economic reforms to boost productivity and growth. But only the first arrow fully took flight within his first years in office, with a (dis)honorable mention for attempts to boost deficit spending on infrastructure projects. The economic reforms definitely have not materialized, but they're crucial to achieving the economic growth that would matter for the future of the debt. Because Japan's total population already is shrinking, achieving economic growth now would require much faster and sustained increases in productivity per worker than any developed economy has managed in recent decades, to make up for the decrease in workers. Most "plans" for Japan to grow its way out of debt generally figure that an average annual GDP growth rate of around 3 percent will do the trick, which is fanciful for an economy like Japan's and especially so when governments in Tokyo have spent decades failing to deregulate domestic markets to stimulate more productivity-enhancing investment.

That leaves one last tax Japan can try to impose on its Millennials to pay its bills: inflation. Normal people think of inflation merely as price increases, but economists see inflation under some circumstances as a tax, particularly if a government is heavily in debt. Inflation is a great benefit for debtors because each yen they owe becomes less costly to repay in terms of true purchasing power. And if inflation increases nominal salaries and corporate profits, it can also create more actual tax revenue. So it stands to reason that a heavily indebted government like Japan's has become obsessed with creating more inflation. When he laid out his three economic-transformation arrows, Abe framed the monetary promise in terms of achieving 2 percent consumer-price inflation.

But here too Japan's debt poses enormous risks, since no one knows—or can predict—how well inflation might or might not work to reduce the burden of a debt like Japan's. The one advantage Tokyo has had going for it in recent decades has been extraordinarily low interest rates—sometimes less than 1 percent on government bonds that come due in thirty years. Since inflation tends to produce higher interest rates, one consequence of imposing an inflation tax on Japan would be that its debt would become more expensive to repay, and no one can predict how quickly the cost of interest payments might increase relative to inflation in this scenario.* If Millennials want this all to work out well, they'll have to trust the same government that created this fiscal mess to achieve precisely the right balance of inflation and modest interest-rate rises to extract the government from its fiscal hole. No wonder Millennials seem glum about the future.

But perhaps this discussion misses the point somewhat. It's almost too easy to talk about these problems in economic terms. The biggest lesson Americans can and should learn from Japan instead concerns the *social* costs of failing to give young adults a fair shake in the economy. The most alarming aspect of Japan's situation is the growing sense of hopelessness many young adults report feeling, which weighs on their own lives and on their society.

Hopelessness about the job market is stunting many aspects of Japanese Millennials' personal and social development. It appears to be a central factor in delayed marriage and is a major reason why a growing number of Millennials seem unlikely ever to have children of their own. Astoundingly large numbers of young adults— 42 percent of men and 44 percent of women—report never having had sex, a proportion that is both disconcerting (it encompasses people who are in their prime marriage-and-childbearing years) and increasing.[49] Men and women alike report that young Japanese women are reluctant to marry men who have not yet established themselves in the regular labor force, which hamstrings the marital chances of the growing proportion of men who will never be able to make that leap. That's one explanation for why the proportion of young Japanese saying they want to get married at some point is falling, to below 40 percent among men and below 60 percent for women.[50]

---

* The older generation will end up twisting this fiscal knife a bit, too: One reason interest rates have stayed so low in Japan for such a long time despite a rising pile of debt is that most of the bonds Tokyo issues are currently held domestically—typically by banks and pension funds that use the cash deposited by heavy-saving Japanese households to invest in Japanese government bonds. However, as the population ages and older households start withdrawing their savings during their retirement, Japan will have to turn to foreign investors to finance its debt. Many observers expect those foreigners to be less forgiving of Tokyo's fiscal excesses than domestic savers were, and therefore to demand higher interest rates.

Some of these trends are related to economic and social phenomena that long predate Millennials and Japan's current crisis. For instance, one barrier to marriage and childbearing for Millennial women is Japan's long-standing cultural hostility toward working mothers. But it also increasingly looks like bad economic decisions made over the past two or three decades are exacerbating those trends, creating too few opportunities for durable economic advancement for younger adults. Which itself raises a provocative question for American Millennials as we turn to our own challenges in coming years (and in the next chapter): Will the solutions we develop bring out the best in our society—and ourselves—or the worst?

CHAPTER 7

Millennials in Charge

IT'S NO COINCIDENCE THAT IN FALL 2018, AS AMERICA REACHED THE TENTH anniversary of the Lehman Brothers bankruptcy, Alexandria Ocasio-Cortez was elected to Congress.

Ocasio-Cortez's campaign in a House district in New York City made national news for a lot of reasons. In the Democratic party primary in July, she unseated Joseph Crowley, a long-serving representative who had reached the upper echelons of his party's leadership in the House. Her policy positions—she describes herself as a Democratic Socialist and favors expanding Medicare to cover all Americans, abolishing the Immigration and Customs Enforcement (ICE) Agency, and a government-guaranteed job for everyone[1]— fall well outside what has been the mainstream of American policy debates, at least until recently. And she's a Millennial, born in 1989. Her unconventional views bolstered a stereotype held by many that Millennials are trending inexorably toward the political Left, and the sense of a dramatic and unexpected generational changing of the guard inspired a lot of breathless reporting about Millennials' political ascendance.

Ocasio-Cortez isn't the first Millennial elected to Congress. The Constitution requires that members of the House be at least twenty-five years old. Taking 1982 as the first birth year for a true Millennial, that means our first shot at Capitol Hill arrived in the 2008 election. The youngest member of the 111th Congress, which took its seats in January 2009, was Republican Aaron Schock of Illinois.[2]

His 1981 birthday was enough for some to award him the title of "The First Gen Y Congressman."[3] The misuse-of-public-funds scandal that eventually engulfed him might lead some Millennials to say that Gen X can have him instead, thank you very much. In which case the first properly Millennial member of Congress was Democratic representative Patrick Murphy of Florida, born in 1983 and elected in 2012.[4] In the Congress elected in 2016, Millennials could count four representatives, using 1982 as the birth-year cut-off.[5] We have yet to crack the Senate, although we came extremely close (by some definitions) in the November 2018 midterm election. The youngest senator elected in that vote is Republican Josh Hawley of Missouri, born in 1979—on December 31. Those of us born in 1982 first became eligible to run in 2012, when we turned thirty, so a Millennial is sure to win his or her way into the world's greatest deliberative body any election now. (Murphy, the Florida Millennial, and Jason Kander, a borderline Millennial born in 1981 and running in Missouri, both tried and failed in 2016.) And hold onto your hats—the oldest Millennials are now constitutionally eligible to run for president.

American politics isn't quite suffering a youthquake yet—in fact, the average age of members of the House has trended upward in recent elections, and now is among the oldest on record, with members averaging 57.8 years old as of 2016. Senators average a sprightly 61.8 years old, down slightly from 62.2 years in the Congress elected in 2010.[6] While Millennials are starting to roam the halls of state capitols as local legislators across the country, it's still not in numbers representative of our proportion in the broader population.* But it's also true that those numbers don't tell the full story of political influence in a system as complex as America's—as was the case for the Boomers themselves, starting in the late 1970s and early 1980s.

---

* Data on this are predictably hard to come by, given the sheer number of state legislators in America, but a 2015 analysis from the National Conference of State Legislatures found that Millennials (born 1981–1997) held 5 percent of state legislative seats nationwide, while accounting for around 30 percent of the population.

That's because you don't have to get elected to wield at least a little influence. I first arrived in Washington as a bright-eyed Millennial journalism intern in the summer of 2001, before I was old enough to drink. Many of my peers were interning for members of Congress, and although those internships are unglamorous (to put it generously), many of the full-time staffers who research for committees or individual members, help manage schedules, devise media strategies, and field queries and complaints from constituents are under age thirty at any given time. As one commentator memorably and with only modest exaggeration put it in 2012, "The most powerful nation on Earth is run largely by 24-year-olds."[7] Ditto many of the political staffers who swell the ranks of a presidential administration—the young "political appointees" drudging away in the scores of policy-planning offices in executive agencies that help set the direction for tens of thousands of career civil servants.

Oh, and we vote, or at least we can if we want to. The first election for the oldest of us was in 2000, and if the birth range for a Millennial is 1982–1997, then all of the members of America's largest generation are in the electorate now. To date, Millennials are the electoral dog that's choosing not to bark—younger turnout has always been low, and there are signs that Millennials vote in lower numbers than Boomers did when they were our age.[8] But that may be starting to change. The 2018 midterm election witnessed historically high turnout among voters ages eighteen to twenty-nine (encompassing younger Millennials and older Gen Zers), surging to 31 percent of eligible voters from 21 percent in the last midterm in 2014. They may have shaped the outcome of several close contests for the House of Representatives and some governorships.[9] Youth turnout still is on the low side relative to our share of the population, but both major parties seem to be terrified of what will happen if and when Millennials do become more engaged in electoral politics.

All of which means one big thing so far as the subject of this book is concerned: the Boomers broke it, but it's rapidly becoming our mess to clean up. So it makes sense to cap off an exploration of

Millennials' economic ills with what ultimately is a political question. Will we manage to do any better for ourselves and our children than the Boomers did for us?

The Life of the Parties

The stereotype, of course, is that Millennials are all socialists. We created the Occupy Wall Street movement. We flocked to Bernie Sanders when he made his improbable run for the presidency in 2016, and we love dyed-in-the-wool liberals like California senator Kamala Harris and 2018 Texas Senate candidate Beto O'Rourke. We protest against Donald Trump. Millennials shout down conservative speakers on college campuses.

These caricatures of Millennials' politics are all sort of true, to an extent. Depending on the poll, Millennials trend heavily in favor of the Democrats, sometimes by margins of 30 percentage points or more.[10] One high-profile survey found more Millennials* would prefer to live in a socialist society (46 percent) than prefer capitalism (40 percent), and 6 percent would prefer outright communism. Little wonder, since 46 percent of Millennials think America's free market works against them, the highest proportion of any age group.[11] Other polls still peg Millennial† support for capitalism ahead of a preference for socialism, but the margin is closer than for other generations—52 percent to 42 percent.[12] Intriguingly, it's also not clear that Millennials actually know what "socialism" means when we're asked about it in these polls—which is one possible explanation for a puzzling finding that support for "socialism" is higher than support for a "government-managed economy" even though they are conceptually similar.[13]

But plenty of other evidence suggests we're still finding our political voice. That's the most plausible theory for why our political views are bafflingly self-contradictory—including how our

---

* Born 1981–1996.

† Born 1984–1996.

stated support for far-left policies and ideologies can coexist with our apparent (although modest) embrace of conservatism. A 2016 study, examining several major surveys, concluded that Millennials* are more conservative at this stage in our life cycle than either Boomers or Gen Xers were: around 27 percent of Millennial twelfth graders identified themselves as conservative, compared to 25 percent of Gen Xers when they were in high school and only 20 percent of Boomers.[14] Although the young-adult vote mostly went to Hillary Clinton in the 2016 presidential election, not all of it did. Some 37 percent of Millennials† voted for Trump, compared to 55 percent for Clinton—Trump won the same proportion of the youth vote that Mitt Romney had in 2012.[15] And notably, the group of Millennials who voted for Trump seems to have been more enthusiastic about their candidate than the group of Millennials who voted for Clinton was for theirs. Roughly one-third of Trump-supporting young voters said before the election that they were "excited" about the possibility of Trump becoming president, versus only 18 percent of Clinton supporters who felt the same way about their candidate.[16] Some of the political Right's highest-profile commentators these days are Millennials: Meghan McCain (born 1984), Guy Benson (born 1985), Ben Shapiro (born 1984), and Kristen Soltis Anderson (born 1984), among many others. Some of these and other commentators are periodically at the center of controversies on college campuses, where student protestors might try to obstruct talks or debates featuring conservative viewpoints. But it's important to remember that these speakers are on those campuses in the first place because they've been invited by other, conservative students.

So it's a mistake to think Millennials are uniformly on the political Left or the Right. It's probably more accurate to argue we're all contrarians. The biggest clue is that whatever else we say about our political views, we consistently tell pollsters that we're less likely to

---

* Born 1980–1994.

† Age eighteen to twenty-nine at the time of the election, so birth years 1986–1998.

affiliate with a particular party than previous generations were—or even than our younger selves. The proportion of young voters (ages eighteen to twenty-nine) self-identifying as Democrats plunged between 2008 and 2016, to 37 percent from 45 percent. But identification as a Republican increased only one percentage point, to 27 percent. The biggest gain was in the number of young voters describing themselves as independent.[17]

Other commentators have argued that one reason Millennials as a cohort tend to vote more for Democrats is that Millennials are so racially and ethnically diverse—which means that we include in our ranks more members of minority groups, such as African Americans and Hispanics, that have traditionally voted Democratic by larger margins than whites.[18] But it's not obvious that either party can take this trend for granted indefinitely. In polling around the 2016 election, Millennial African Americans were more likely than whites or Hispanics to say they "somewhat" or "completely" trusted the Democratic party—but only 47 percent of them did.[19] It's fair to argue that, having witnessed the economic and social failures of the Boomers, and having grown skeptical of institutions that we think embody many of those failures, all Millennials still are casting around for answers. Millennial politics is less about picking one side of the party spectrum the Boomers settled into and more about recentering politics around issues that matter more to us than they did to our Boomer parents.

This is especially noticeable on many social questions, where the fault lines that divided the Boomers so acrimoniously seem to be a lot less important to Millennials. The obvious case is sexual morality, where Millennials are almost totally over the debates that consumed our elders. Millennials* have consistently supported marriage equality more than other generations, and as of 2017 that Millennial support was at 75 percent, compared to 62 percent for the public as a whole.[20] Multiple polls find Millennials are less

---

* Born 1981 or later.

likely to be religious believers than older voters, a fact that makes us less interested in many of the religion-in-the-public-square debates that have raged for decades. We're also turned off by the drug war, with high levels of support for marijuana legalization among Millennials.

That doesn't mean we're libertines. Some studies have found that Millennials have sex for the first time later in life than previous generations did, have fewer partners, have less sex in general, cohabit with partners to whom we're not married but primarily as a way station toward marriage, and are more likely to stay faithful to our spouses once we do get hitched.[21] We may also be on track to get divorced less often than the Boomers did. But when one contrasts those quasi-Puritanical behaviors to a live-and-let-live attitude toward government policy on many of these fronts, one starts to get the impression we've decided that personal morality should be personal, and that this attitude transcends other party or ideological divisions among Millennials.[22]*

And it's not only the old social-policy political totems we're abandoning. We care a lot less about many of the economic-policy divides that excited the Boomers, too. The split has been particularly noticeable during the Trump administration, when so many of the economic debates consuming Boomers (and Gen Xers) in Washington feel so far removed from anything Millennials care about—such as trade. Trade policy dominated a lot of economic debates during the 1980s and '90s, and propelled a range of politicians onto presidential debate stages and cable-news chat shows, from Ross Perot to Pat Buchanan. In this regard, Donald Trump is an archetypal Boomer president: his fixation on the evils of foreign

---

* One exception is abortion—maybe. Unlike issues such as marriage equality, where Millennials by and large are coalescing around an open approach, abortion continues to divide Millennials in much the same way it divides older generations, up to a point. But in other ways, Millennial attitudes may be coalescing around a view that neither the pro-life nor the pro-choice crowds from the older generation will entirely like. Some polls find that although Millennials support allowing abortion earlier in a pregnancy, support for allowing late-term abortion is much lower.

competition—and his conviction that trade is a game other countries win while America loses—encapsulates a generation's worth of
Boomer angst about globalization.

That's out of step with Millennials, 48 percent of whom said in
a 2016 poll that they think free-trade agreements with other countries have been good for the United States, compared to 12 percent
who thought such agreements are bad for the country. That's more
enthusiasm for trade than the population as a whole, which thinks
trade deals are good only by a margin of 31 percent to 29 percent.[23]
Similarly, we feel a lot differently about immigration than our parents did. A *lot*. Three-fourths of Millennials* say they believe immigrants "strengthen the country" through hard work, versus 48
percent of Boomers. The same proportion of Millennials oppose
building a wall along America's border with Mexico, compared to
54 percent of Boomers who oppose a wall.[24]

The sum total of all these trends is that Millennial voters are up
for grabs, and that's one of the best things Millennials have going
for us right now. Although we're becoming a larger proportion of
the electorate by the day, realistically we're still some years away
from being in a position to fully take charge of the major parties,
let alone the government in general. While we await that day, by
rewarding policy success and failure while voting less predictably
along party lines, we can force both major parties to respond to our
needs and concerns—and to pay the price if they don't.

Right now this phenomenon is most obvious within the Democratic Party, which traditionally has taken younger voters for
granted to a greater extent than the Republicans. Millennials
flocked to Barack Obama in 2008 and 2012, partly because the op-
timistic vision of a bright economic future he presented resonated
and partly because he seemed like a hipper candidate who understood younger voters. And although Republicans won't like to hear
this, some elements of Obama's program did speak to Millennial
concerns. Such as Obamacare. We've seen how the Affordable Care

---

* Born after 1980.

Act is a fiscal time bomb for Millennials, but it did hold out a solution for a big problem Millennials continue to face: How can we get health insurance when we don't have steady jobs? Republicans never managed to offer a compelling answer to this question, although they could have found solutions consistent with their own free-market philosophy. They left the field to the Democrats.

Note, however, how other Democrats have struggled to maintain Obama-style levels of support from Millennials. In the 2016 presidential primary, Millennial voters (especially younger ones) flocked to Bernie Sanders. He's old, and wrong on a lot of issues, but like Millennials themselves he's only loosely affiliated with a party, and he seemed authentic. In the end he wasn't the Democratic nominee, however, and the politician who was—Hillary Clinton— struggled mightily and ultimately failed to win over Millennial voters in the same numbers Obama had. If she had, she'd be president now.[25] This doesn't precisely mean Millennial votes are the Republicans' for the taking. Instead, we seem to be more willing than previous generations to experiment with third parties. The Millennials who fled from Hillary Clinton in 2016 were more likely to end up voting for the Green Party or Libertarian candidates, especially in some of the swing states that ultimately cost Hillary the election, than they were to vote for Trump.

Another surprising consequence of our lack of party loyalty is that we might be more willing to challenge the leaders within parties in order to mold those parties to our political needs more quickly. Alexandria Ocasio-Cortez is the most famous example of this phenomenon, having ousted a veteran Democratic congressman who normally would have expected party loyalists to fall into line behind him. But she wasn't the only one—she wasn't even the only Millennial primary challenger in New York City. Millennials Adem Bunkeddeko and Suraj Patel also waged campaigns—ultimately unsuccessful—to displace long-serving Democratic representatives Yvette Clark and Carolyn Maloney in the 2018 primaries.[26] Bunkeddeko almost won.

What Millennials Want

All of that amounts to a long statement of what Millennials don't want from politics and politicians. What we do want is another matter.

At first glance, our wish list sounds pretty conventional. Right at the top, of course, is a working economy. In a poll of Millennials* released before the 2016 election, the economy was one of the top three concerns for 64 percent of respondents. We also want security—the threat of terrorism ranked second, with 39 percent of respondents listing it as a top-three worry. And notably, we also want a different kind of politics—31 percent of respondents wanted leaders who could "unite the country," and 23 percent wanted to reduce the role of money in politics.[27]† But probe deeper, and it becomes clearer that we have different ideas of how to measure economic success and failure—and are willing to explore new ways to get results.

In the Boomer era, economic debates typically focused on some combination of overall GDP growth, wage increases, and employment. But those arguments miss much of the point for Millennials—who may have jobs but not good ones that use all the expensive education and skills we've acquired; who might get a raise every once in a while but never enough of one to bring home-ownership into reach; and for whom quarterly GDP statistics can feel like just another bit of flimflam the politicians we don't entirely trust use to try to persuade us to distrust our own eyes when we notice something's going wrong.

---

* Born 1986–1998.

† That emphasis on unity might sound at odds with my argument that Millennials want more competition in politics, but I'm not sure it is. Americans of all ages typically tell pollsters they want a more cooperative government, but then vote very differently on election day. A cynic could interpret this as a voter's desire that everyone unite behind *her* preferred policies, but for Millennials this kind of result can also point to a general sense that the political system is stuck and not delivering partisan arguments about anything that matters to younger voters.

Instead, Millennials take a different approach. Inequality often ranks among Millennials' top concerns when we're asked what specifically discomfits us in the economy. Some of the data on inequality—especially of incomes and wealth—are so tortured as to be meaningless, which is one reason this debate tends to drive free-market political conservatives nuts. But we have to admit there's a kernel of truth in there—this book has laid out many areas in which the economy is misfiring for Millennials in ways that exacerbate economic divisions among us. The economy genuinely is not creating as many opportunities for as many people as it should, for wage growth, saving, homeownership, or other markers of personal economic and social advancement. Millennials may not always pick the best politicians with the best ideas for how to tackle this problem. That doesn't change the fact that the basic insight is correct: one symptom of economic dysfunction, no matter what the other data say, is that opportunities seem to be less evenly spread than they used to be.

Put in a broader way, one of the biggest things we seem to want is answers. We can tell the economy isn't working well for us, and that the kind of security we thought our parents had isn't available to us. Millennials want to know why that is and what we can do to fix it. I've offered my own version of that story. Boomer-style economic centrism has broken down for Millennials. It has left us with a distorted economy that struggles to create good jobs in many industries, that fails to invest enough in us, that's fundamentally unstable and prone to frequent crises. The thread running through all those failures is this: Boomers on both the Left and the Right spent most of their political careers trying to have it both ways. They wanted a government that would do more things—encourage more investment, finance more college, put more people in houses, offer better pensions. And they figured they could get the market to help. This approach was a boon for Democrats who had great faith in the government's ability to solve problems but worried American voters would shy away from too "radical" a left-wing program. But it also was a boon for Republicans, who wouldn't have to say "no" to constituents demanding services from the government but could still claim they were the party of free markets and economic opportunity. This book has highlighted many of the ways that model failed.

That's one take on some Millennials' curious embrace of older socialists as political leaders. This baffles conservatives like almost nothing else when it comes to younger voters. Millennials are supposed to be all about the new—new technologies, new career paths, new sexual mores, new culture. Yet some of us have adopted as political heroes old fogeys (not even young enough to be Baby Boomers in some cases, such as Bernie Sanders, who was born in 1941) espousing very old ideas about politics and economics. It seems downright bizarre. Millennials who are perpetually glued to our smartphones also are in thrall to a nineteenth-century economic philosophy.

But before there was Bernie Sanders in 2016, there was Ron Paul in 2012—and Paul, an aging and eccentric (to put it mildly) libertarian, also attracted Millennial support during his own quixotic primary run for the Republican presidential nomination.[28] Maybe Millennials are not exactly embracing socialism so much as desperately looking for explanations for what has gone wrong in our economic lives over the past decade. One criteria is that those explanations must come from outside the Boomer political mainstream that we think has failed us.

If they do nothing else, leaders like Bernie Sanders—or Alexandria Ocasio-Cortez—are able to spin a plausible-sounding yarn about what went wrong in the run-up to the Great Recession, why the economy hasn't fully recovered since, and why Millennials are getting such a bad deal. It's all about greed, they say, whether on the part of large companies or of mainstream politicians. That's deeply misleading, and following many of the solutions these politicians propose is a path to even worse outcomes for Millennials. But mainstream politicians, both Democrats and Republicans, have struggled to offer a better alternative to Millennials because, as we've seen throughout this book, they were all largely to blame for the conditions that created the 2007–2008 crisis and then exacerbated the Great Recession afterward.

So there is a certain logic to this Millennial political trend. That's because the main thing the political Left is doing right now is abandoning that middle-way economic and political model that a growing number of Millennials can tell broke down for us. A demand for more intense competition of ideas is emerging as a key part of Millennials' approach to our problems. The challenge for the political Right isn't to debunk socialism. It's to get the Right's own house in order, figuring out how and why Republican policy ideas failed before and after 2007–2008, and how conservatives should adjust if Millennial voters no longer find the political center compelling.

There's some evidence Millennials will reward conservative candidates who do this. A surprising story about young voters appeared in April 2018. A poll commissioned by the Reuters news service found that Millennials were drifting away from staunch support for Democrats. A reporter called a few respondents and discovered that Millennials were willing to give Republicans credit for some of the economic benefits of the late-2017 tax cut, especially higher take-home pay as a result.[29] It's further evidence that we're not doctrinaire, and that instead we're demanding—and respecting—results.

The Trump Exception

And then there's Donald Trump.

This book has focused disproportionately on the first eight years after the financial crisis, when Barack Obama was the president. He took office in the depth of the economic crisis, and also when Millennials as a cohort were entering, or had just recently entered, adulthood in large numbers. Obama also pursued an activist governing program with a lot of moving parts that affected Millennials significantly, often in unintended ways. It's inevitable that Obama will get either credit or blame for a lot of the trends that have shaped our economic fortunes. The crisis wasn't built on his watch—that honor belongs to George W. Bush and his other predecessors—but Obama was the first responder.

Now the Trump administration has shaped the last two years of the stolen decade—and will shape the first years of the next decade, which are determining whether Millennials will lose that one, too. And say what you will about him, there's no denying that his administration will be highly consequential for Millennials.

We don't like him very much. An Associated Press poll in March 2018 found Trump's approval rating at 33 percent among younger voters.[30]* That fits with other polling showing Millennials gave Trump the lowest approval rating of any generation after his first year in office—27 percent approval from Millennials, compared to 44 percent approval from Boomers. That contrasts to a 64 percent first-year approval rating for Obama among Millennials eight years earlier, whereas Trump's first-year rating among Boomers was only modestly lower than Obama's.[31]† The reasons for this are more interesting than most people seem to realize. There's certainly an element of aesthetics to it. Trump's behavior is off-putting, both personally and in office. His well-publicized comments demeaning women seem like exactly what a politician would say if he wanted to offend Millennials of all political stripes. His hostility to immigration and the perception—sometimes accurate, sometimes not— that he's not forceful enough in denouncing racism, offends the cohort that's the most diverse in American history. His whole character—his tendency to shirk business debts, his multiple marriages and affairs, the code of *omerta* he tries to impose on his staff—isn't what we want out of politics. In that AP poll, a whopping 72 percent of younger voters said Trump "doesn't reflect my personal values."[32]

The disillusionment with Trump is especially acute among some conservative Millennials, who grew up during the Bill Clinton sex scandals of the 1990s and were lectured by Republican elders about how "character counts." Conservative Millennial commentator Ben Shapiro has argued that after Boomer Republicans lost the character

---

* A mix of Millennials and Gen Z, born 1983–2003.

† Millennials born 1981–1996.

battle in their failed bid to impeach Clinton (and saw clean-cut candidates such as John McCain and Mitt Romney get dragged through the political mud despite their good characters), they concluded that they might as well vote for a candidate like Trump. But for Millennials, according to Shapiro, character still counts a great deal. "Young conservatives want to be able to tell their friends—all future voters, by the way—that they didn't stand by silently when a candidate of their party said he could grab women by their private parts," he wrote.[33]

Trump also has a major policy problem with Millennials that transcends the Republican-Democratic divide. He just seems so irrelevant. A theme that emerges again and again in media interviews of Millennial voters, such as the AP's report on its own 2018 poll, isn't so much that Millennials have specific policy disagreements with Trump as that they think he simply "doesn't care" about them.[34]

The debates and issues that obsess Trump, and that are distracting Washington now that he's in office, aren't our fights. On trade policy, for instance, Trump is relitigating ad nauseum (and potentially *ad recession*) the arguments about Japan, Western Europe, and China that consumed the Boomers in the 1980s and '90s. That doesn't mean anything to us, given our own broad support for trade.

The same story is repeating with immigration. Millennials are as divided as other Americans about how best to enforce America's immigration laws, with some preferring a very open system and others preferring stricter border enforcement. But overall, we're significantly less hostile to the idea of large-scale legal immigration than the Boomers have been. Not only is Trump's obsession with this issue—which is shared by a substantial portion of his Boomer base—off-putting, it seems downright mystifying. Millennials are a generation of immigrants, and we prize ethnic and cultural diversity. This is true even among self-identified Republican Millennials,* who are the only age cohort within the GOP among whom a majority (61 percent) say that America's openness to people from around the world "is essential to who we are as a nation."[35]

---

* Born 1981–1996.

Trump's and the Boomers' immigration obsession is even more out of touch than many Millennials probably realize, given that the major immigration problem in our future will be too *little* immigration. New arrivals already are the indispensable ingredient for American economic growth. Between 1990 and 2015, higher fertility among immigrant mothers meant that the total number of annual births declined only 4 percent, despite a 10 percent decrease in the numbers of births to women born in the United States.[36] Without immigration, the United States would be on track for the same kind of demographic and economic debacle facing Germany or Japan. And some economists are starting to wonder where all the immigrants we need will come from over the next few decades, particularly as economic growth continues apace and birth rates fall in many of the countries that have been the biggest sources of new immigration for America. It's a concern even at the low-skilled end of the immigration spectrum, and this suggests that the debate for Millennials won't be whether or not to build a wall.[37] It will be how to overhaul our work-visa rules so that we can continue attracting workers globally when those workers increasingly will feel they can enjoy good economic opportunities in their home countries, too.

The challenge, especially for the many Millennials who dislike Trump, is that despite all those problems, his policies—or more precisely, some ideas that he's been coaxed into supporting—do seem to be working for the economy.

The reality of the Trump era is that some indicators are definitely looking good for Millennials (and for Generation Z, which already is starting to hit the labor market for the first time). As I was writing this book in the summer of 2018, the unemployment rate briefly fell to a low of 3.8 percent, not seen since 2000, and has hovered around that level—and the unemployment rate for older Millennials, ages twenty-five to thirty-four, finally matches that low overall rate. The unemployment rates for younger cohorts of workers also have fallen, to 6.8 percent for twenty- to twenty-four-year-olds, and labor-force participation is trending upward for all age groups.*

---

* All data as of August 2018.

Superficially Trump seems to be pulling from the old Boomer playbook. The Trump administration and Republicans in Congress in late 2017 ushered through the largest tax reform since the Boomers were just becoming politically active in the 1980s, a repeat of the supply-side tax debates of the Reagan era. But in important ways this proved to be a surprisingly new style of tax reform. It's not just a tax cut as we saw in the George W. Bush era. It's a major overhaul. The top marginal rates on corporate and personal incomes have fallen—the corporate tax by a lot, the personal tax by a little. The punitive top 35 percent rate that applied to overseas corporate earnings when those cash hoards were repatriated has been eliminated in favor of a much lower tax rate intended to encourage companies to bring foreign earnings home for investment, or to pay out to workers or shareholders—both of which categories increasingly include Millennials along with members of other generations. The law also gives companies greater leeway to deduct the costs of real-world productive investments from their tax bills more quickly.* Crucially, though, the bill imposes relatively strict new limits on the ability of companies to deduct interest payments on their debts from their taxable income.

Most of the debate about that 2017 tax reform, from both the Left and the Right, has focused on its cost in terms of foregone revenue; the precise rates it sets for various taxpayers and on various kinds of economic activity; and most broadly of all whether it's just another "tax cut for the rich," or whether it's a massive economic stimulus. But that debate obscures the extent to which, whether by design or by accident, the reform legislation has finally taken a stab at fixing some of the problems that have dogged American tax policy and the economy for a generation or more. The Boomers have belatedly learned from some of their earlier mistakes.

The most important element is that the reform is narrowing the gap between low taxation on capital income and the much higher

---

* This happened under the provisions governing how companies can account for the depreciation of capital assets, and also goes under the common name of "full expensing" or "100 percent expensing" of business investment.

taxation that had previously applied to earnings from production in the real economy. As I've argued, bad distortions in incentives for different kinds of financial and productive investments are a major way in which Boomers failed to build an economy that would create a wider array of good job opportunities for Millennials especially. Fixing this is a necessary precondition for creating a functioning job market for Millennials, and finally the Boomers are trying. This is especially true in the case of provisions such as faster deductions for capital spending coupled with smaller deductions for interest expenses. Companies now have significantly less incentive to borrow heavily for short-term stock-price boosts and other machinations such as share buybacks, highly leveraged mergers and acquisitions activity, and other "investments" that we saw in earlier chapters diverted financial capital away from real investments that boost productivity. But they have more incentives to invest in boosting worker productivity (and ultimately wages) because the income companies earn will be taxed at lower rates.

Critics on the Left might have preferred that Washington close the loopholes that used to reward financial engineering over productive investment by increasing capital-gains rates or tightening other tax rules surrounding debt, but the 2017 plan is the better option because it tries to boost productive corporate investment without too heavily punishing the financial markets that are so crucial to funding those investments. And while that debate continues, there's some early evidence that the tax reform is paying off for workers, including Millennials. Hiring has ramped up in each month since the tax reform. And there's anecdotal evidence that at least some companies are using the cash to boost investment in training and skills for their workers. Disney, Boeing, and the Kroger supermarket chain have all announced new spending on employee training after the tax cut, which is the kind of productivity-boosting investment the economy needs.[38] Now we wait for a few more years to see how durable this positive jolt to investment, hiring, and the economy has been, or whether Boomers have managed instead to create another short-term sugar high that will burn off soon enough.

Other Trump-era policies have tried to even the scales between the costs of capital investment and the costs of labor—after cheap capital and expensive labor squeezed Millennials during the Obama years—although so far with harder-to-judge success. The most consequential of these efforts concerns deregulation, which if done right could open new outlets for genuine investment. And here Trump characteristically is claiming big successes—huuuge, even. The most commonly cited number is that he has axed twenty-two rules or regulations for each one new rule he has imposed.

That's based on the sixty-seven old regulations lifted in the first eight months of the Trump administration at the cost of only three new ones. However the Competitive Enterprise Institute, a right-leaning think tank, issues its own annual assessment of regulatory activity and concluded that the Trump administration in 2017 had added 53,678 pages to the *Federal Register*—a crude but popular estimate of new regulatory activity, since administration agencies must list proposed new rules (and their final versions) in that publication. That compared to an all-time high of 95,894 pages added to the *Register* in Obama's last year in office in 2016.[39] Even with a stated deregulation push under way, the *Federal Register* is still growing by tens of thousands of pages. And despite a pledge that every new rule would be accompanied by the lifting of two others, not every rule is created equal. Some deregulation has affected only niche industries, while the *new* rules coming on the books can apply much more widely.

It's a shame deregulation is so hard for Millennials to benchmark, because if it were to actually happen, deregulation would be the most important part of Trump's agenda from our perspective. Regulation has the power to shape the kinds of investments that get made, and the kinds of industries that are allowed to grow, in the post-Trump economy. Some of the Trump administration's highest-profile regulatory actions—such as reducing barriers to coal-fired power production in an effort to boost industrial employment, or scrapping the Obama-era proposal for an overtime pay rule that would make hiring more expensive—stand a good chance of benefiting at least some Millennials. But in this sense at least, Millennials will end up being very much like our parents: we'll continue to face difficult trade-offs between environmental concerns, which we consistently rank as a policy priority, and job creation.

The administration also is producing some attempts to address specific Millennial concerns, such as student debt. In early 2018, the Department of Education proposed a reform that would finally make it easier to discharge some student loans in bankruptcy court. As we saw in Chapter 3, this is currently all but impossible because a bankruptcy judge can only clear away student debt if the borrower can prove repaying would pose an "undue hardship"—a standard courts have interpreted so strictly no one meets it. The new proposal would revise the definition to cover more cases of genuine hardship. The administration also has tried to streamline some repayment programs. So far so good. More controversially, Education Secretary Betsy DeVos also has tried to make it harder for student borrowers to secure debt forgiveness from the government if they claim they were defrauded by their colleges, for instance with false claims about future job or earning prospects. Nor will measures narrowly focused on student debt address the bigger questions lurking behind Millennials' college crisis: Is a four-year degree really the best or only preparation for the modern job market, and what alternatives would better serve more young adults at lower cost? Any serious debate on those topics now will come too late to benefit Millennials directly, since we're all now past college age. But it's not too soon for us to think about our own children—and how we can draw on our own dreary college-financing experiences to inform education policy debates on our watch.

So right now the Millennial verdict on Trump's economic policies would have to be that some elements show some promise, but it's far too soon to say how well they'll all work. This suggests that rather than premature celebration or outright hostility, Millennials need to keep the pressure up on Washington. And that's especially the case because in several other critical areas, it's not clear the

Boomers—whether inside the Trump administration or outside—have fully learned the lessons of their own experience.

One obvious example is entitlements. Trump was elected on a promise to shake up Washington, but the two things he steadfastly refuses to shake are Social Security and Medicare. He promised when he announced he was running for president that he would "save Medicare, Medicaid, and Social Security without cuts."[40] Former Speaker of the House of Representatives Paul Ryan, a Republican Gen Xer, tried for years as a representative, committee chairman, vice presidential candidate, and then Speaker to persuade his colleagues to enact major entitlement reforms to put the old-age programs on a more sustainable path. Democrats were predictably resistant—even running television ads at one point suggesting Ryan wanted to push a grandmother in a wheelchair over a cliff. But equally disappointing, Ryan never got a majority of Republicans to go along either. Even many members of the Tea Party protest movement that began pulling the Republican Party further to the Right on economic matters starting in 2009 were ambivalent about entitlement reform, at best. The Boomer imperative to defend old-age entitlements is stronger than party loyalty or ideological consistency.

This is a major fiscal failure that threatens to hammer Millennials in the coming decades. Even after accounting for the revenue increases likely to result from the economic growth stimulated by tax reform, history shows the additional money won't be enough to cover the entitlement shortfall. Analysts and commentators argue about precisely how big a budget deficit the tax reform is likely to cause over the next decade, but the point is that no one is seriously arguing that there won't be a deficit of some size, absent significant spending restraint.

And in other important ways, Boomer orthodoxy still is very much in place. Consider a strange kerfuffle that erupted in July 2018, when Trump started opining on what monetary policies he'd like to see from Federal Reserve chair Jerome Powell (a Trump appointee, as it happens). "I'm not thrilled" about the Fed's determination to gradually raise interest rates, Trump said in a CNBC interview.[41] It was a rare intervention by a president in the Fed's deliberations, and clearly Trump was convinced that the economy would struggle to cope even with very modest rate increases. The president continued complaining about the Fed's rate decisions throughout the summer and in the fall.* This is vintage Boomer, as we've seen, given the faith Boomers of all political stripes have had in the Federal Reserve and interest rates to control the economy and spur economic growth. It highlights, in a way Trump almost certainly didn't intend, how little the Boomer understanding of and thinking on monetary policy has changed despite their own bad experiences.

It's also dangerous for Millennials. A theme in this book has been that the Boomers got monetary policy all wrong. They became very good at inflating economic bubbles with cheap money. But a lot of things they thought they knew about how to use interest rates to goose the economy are turning out to be dangerous errors. Those policies instead exacerbated economic instability and made it harder to create genuine economic growth and good jobs. And a problem is that a decade on from the financial crisis and Great Recession, central banks like the Federal Reserve still are dragging their heels on returning to normal, let alone rethinking what they did wrong before and during the last crisis.

Taking Back What's Ours

Fixing all of this is a tall order, and Millennials are barely starting. To do so, we're going to have to look past much of what our Boomer parents thought they knew about the economy, but didn't.

---

* And of course he *would* say something like this. A little-appreciated aspect of Trump as a policymaker is his business background in real estate—a relatively low-productivity industry that is always the first to benefit from cheap-money-induced booms and first to suffer from interest-rate increases. Indeed, it has never been obvious that Trump has any experience at all actually manufacturing anything, investing in R&D, or other productive activities. His expertise is primarily in branding. It's a contrast to the Republicans' previous businessman candidate, Mitt Romney, who had been involved in managing several manufacturing firms during his career at Bain Capital.

Too much of the political world, and academia, still reflects Boomer preoccupations, and probably will for a while. But at long last, Millennials are now in a position to start pointing to the specific problems we've suffered, especially over the past ten years, and to start shaping economic debates according to our own experiences and needs.

There are already signs that some of the critical innovation is happening in both the political and the policy realms. The past decade especially has seen a nascent movement start to question whether we're getting education right. Boomers made some tentative starts at trying to reform primary and secondary schools, whether by imposing national standards or experimenting with vouchers to give parents more options on the political Right, or contemplating public charter schools on the political Left. More intriguing, there's also growing discussion about how we can fix post–high school education to be more affordable and also more useful. Boomers at both ends of the political spectrum have proposed various ideas, from new apprenticeship systems that might resemble the German model of vocational training, to scrapping the four-year liberal arts bachelor's degree for many students and instead encouraging more people to study much shorter courses toward certification in specific skills.

As for health care, Boomers have taken so many stabs at reforming the system that it's starting to resemble an overused voodoo doll. Yet even under the Affordable Care Act, Boomers were never quite able to break free from an idea that employers should provide health insurance for most workers—even though that is manifestly unsuitable for an economy in which more people will be working more jobs over a lifetime, and in which more Millennials may feel the pull of striking out on their own as entrepreneurs. And on other pressing fiscal problems, such as entitlements, well, we Millennials are going to have an extraordinary mess to clean up. The Boomers have all but given up.

The most worrying trend for now is how little progress we seem to be making on understanding what has happened to the job market in recent years. Too many Millennials are falling into the Boomer habit of thinking that the solution to a problem like the gig economy is to regulate it into submission. Too few of us are thinking about what the job market is trying to tell us about what else has been happening in the economy—and particularly how the Boomers made bad decisions about investment and productivity growth.

Even here, though, there are signs that some of the pieces will be in place for a truly healthy debate about this when we finally are ready to engage. Trump's tax-and-deregulation agenda and its aftermath will create a natural experiment of sorts Millennials will be able to evaluate as we craft our own solutions. Meanwhile, a growing subset of monetary economists have spent the past decade and more trying to understand why investment has misfired so badly in our evolving economy, and whether different monetary policies might help. These economists, some of them Boomers, some younger, are asking whether much of what the Boomers assumed they knew about central banking is really correct—and, critically, whether central banks may inadvertently have worsened the economy in the aftermath of the 2007–2008 crisis and Great Recession. For instance, they ask whether we should be as afraid of consumer-price deflation as Boomer central bankers have been, and whether attempts to fix the crisis instead have distorted investment.* This work will pass most Millennials by—because most Millennials have less nerdy things to think about in their spare time—but this is important research that will shape how Millennial politicians think about these questions, and it opens the door to new debates in the coming decades.

One interesting question we Millennials will have to ask ourselves in a lot of these realms is what role we think technology can

---

* Important research from the Bank for International Settlements, an international clearinghouse for central banks, suggests that not all deflations are bad for overall economic growth, but large declines in asset prices *are* dangerous—and more likely to happen if central banks have encouraged large gains in asset prices while trying to stimulate inflation. (Claudio Borio, Magdalena Erdem, Andrew Filardo, and Boris Hofmann, "The Costs of Deflation: A Historical Perspective," Bank for International Settlements, *BIS Quarterly Review*, March 2015.)

or should play in solving these economic problems. A little-noticed trait of the Boomers is how tech-obsessed they've always been, and it's notable that so many Boomer solutions to so many problems involve harnessing a new technology. The desktop computing revolution was the Clinton administration's main plan for the economy and job creation in the late 1990s; online distance learning was the hot new innovation to make college more accessible and affordable for much of the 2000s; electronic medical records always show up as part of the fix in health care debates. It's a generation, after all, that was coming of age just as a man was landing on the moon for the first time. The stereotype of Millennials is that we're compulsive smartphoners, Googlers, iTuners, Facebookers, Instagrammers, YouTubers, and WhatsAppers. It's certainly true that we're far more comfortable with more technology than any previous generation (and Generation Z after us is even more so). But what we're about to find out is whether this has made Millennials more confident in technology's potential to solve economic problems—or more jaded.

And above all, Millennials have an opportunity to launch a fundamental rethink about how our economy—and our society—should balance the needs of different generations.

I've argued that Millennials got a bad deal from the Boomers, especially in the decade after the Great Recession. But that elides the question of what *fairness* would look like. The Boomers didn't necessarily owe us every creature comfort, yet they provided many of them anyway. As I noted in the Introduction, the paradox is that daily life for American Millennials is terrific in many regards. We live in greater safety, with more comforts and convenience, than any previous generation. We enjoy more freedom. For all our economic problems today, it's hard to think of an earlier era in which many of us would choose to live if given a one-way time machine.

But Boomers also—through thoughtlessness more than malice—exacted a cost for those benefits, and often a steep one. Millennials have come of age in an era when the job market has been distorted by Boomers' own old preoccupations, the education system has been shaped by what Boomers thought they knew (but didn't) about high-skilled work, the housing market has been deliberately fashioned to meet the needs of Boomer homeowners, and Boomers' state-funded retirement plans are going to press higher and higher taxes on younger generations.

And this has all happened as Boomers and Millennials alike embark on a new demographic and political reality. Our generations are going to have to coexist as adults, in roughly equal numbers, for much longer than has been the case for any previous pair of parent-child generations.

We're barely starting to grapple with what this will mean economically. The decision of some Boomers to stay in work longer inevitably will make it harder for Millennials to rise in the job market—if we don't find a way to stimulate job creation that works for both generations. As for the millions of other Boomers who retire as soon as they can, they'll exacerbate the fiscal strain on Millennial taxpayers, at the same time Boomer voters will still be able to obstruct reforms. Boomers are poised to accumulate more and more housing wealth, which they'll sell on (or bequeath) to Millennials much later in life. And the Boomers' relative longevity will impose its own political challenge, beyond the housing and entitlement questions we've examined. Millennials are going to have to wrest political and economic power and influence from the not-anywhere-close-to-cold-and-dead hands of our Boomer parents if we want our own chance to shape an economy that works for us.

Seen in this light, one of the hallmarks of generational fairness in coming decades will be whether Boomers really are prepared to recognize that they've made many mistakes—and that Millennials need to take a prominent role in finding solutions. The worst Boomer theft of all would be to deny us an opportunity to solve our own problems.

Hiding in Plain Sight

OF ALL THE FACTS IN THIS BOOK I BET THIS ONE IS THE MOST SURPRISING TO THE largest number of people: Millennials are older than you realize. In the spring of 2019, the oldest Millennials already are pushing forty. The youngest are either out of high school or even graduating from college, depending on where one draws the birth-year line. We're all adults now.

That secret is hiding in plain sight in most conversations about Millennials. Yet it seems likely that there are a large number of people who are Millennials in denial. Every time the topic of Millennials comes up in a conversation with a thirty-something, the first instinct is either surprise that he or she is in fact a Millennial or a vehement rejection of the label. At other times, we treat the term as a self-deprecating joke: "I'm cooking a recipe for dinner tonight that uses an avocado—how Millennial of me!" We older Millennials seem to associate the term more with youthfulness in general than with our own birth years—and yes, with certain snowflakey attitudes, too. Given all the marketing hype surrounding us, you'd be forgiven for assuming you don't fit in if you're not a social-media power user, an intrepid trekking vacationer, an avocado-toast-munching Brooklynite, or a vaguely trendy Silicon Valley nerd.

The truth is that we're a pretty diverse group—both superficially in terms of our kaleidoscopic mix of racial, ethnic, and immigrant backgrounds, and also in terms of our cultural tastes, career trajectories, and politics. But as we've seen throughout this book,

Millennials do share one common way of life no matter what kind of job we have, where we live, or for whom we vote: we all came of age in the shadow of the Great Recession. And this is where that surprising Millennial fact comes into play. We have less time to crawl out from under that cloud than many people think we do.

Those of us born in 1982 only have until 2049 before we retire—or realize we can't afford to. The thirty years until then might feel like a lifetime, but it's not. We'll have to navigate the coming three decades without much of a roadmap. Economists can tell us what happened to previous generations who came of age in recessions, but the recessions they've studied typically weren't as deep as the one that scarred our early careers. The economic recoveries weren't as slow. The underlying transformation in the labor market wasn't as dramatic. And the previous generations weren't so indebted, so house-poor, or so haunted by the prospect of substantial tax bills to come. In other words, previous generations hadn't had the deck rigged against them quite so thoroughly by their elders. Our futures are especially uncertain, and we know it in part because we can compare our own prospects to the lives our parents and grandparents enjoyed.

This isn't an entirely unprecedented challenge, but it is a pretty steep hill for us to climb. The generation that came of age during the Great Depression endured a protracted period of economic stagnation that prevented them from finding their economic feet. But that was followed by a period of jump-started economic growth that lasted for the second half of their working lives, in the 1950s and '60s. They had an opportunity to catch up. Where is the boom for Millennials going to come from?

We'll have to find the solution ourselves, and this book, I hope, has helped spark some ideas. No one on either the political Right or the Left has been able to give us a full and convincing explanation of how we got to where we are. And if we don't know that, we won't be able to do better. We're one of the smartest, most ambitious generations the world has ever known. It's time for us to take our fate in our own hands.

Acknowledgments

The successes in this book have many mothers and fathers, and I couldn't possibly list them all by name. The roll call stretches back to college and encompasses dozens upon dozens of professors, colleagues, op-ed contributors, sources, and friends who, over time and without realizing what they were doing, taught me how to think through a subject as complex as that of this book—and in some cases also patiently listened to me drone on ad nauseum about the problems of Millennials over the past year. I'm the only parent for the failures.

I've called the *Wall Street Journal* home for the past dozen years and across two continents and couldn't be luckier to do so. It's not easy to find time to take on a project of this sort when you work at a daily newspaper—or more precisely, it's not easy for your colleagues to help you make time. Editorial page editor Paul Gigot, Mary Kissel, Hugo Restall, Adrian Ho, Robert Messenger, Sohrab Ahmari, and Bret Stephens (some still at the *Journal*, others moved onto new adventures) all provided much-needed support at critical moments in the long process that has culminated in this book.

My fabulous agent, Zoë Pagnamenta, was quick to see the potential in my idea and tireless in her efforts to share it with the rest of the world. Most importantly, she shared it with Clive Priddle at PublicAffairs, who all along has understood the story I wanted to tell and how to help me tell it better. Authors customarily thank their editors, but readers owe a greater debt of gratitude to Clive, his colleagues Melissa Veronesi and Athena Bryan, and copyeditor Beth Wright than I do. They have spared this book's audience countless confusing sentences and infelicitous digressions, and thus have spared me a lot of embarrassment. Jaime Leifer's publicity efforts have spared me the indignity of writing a book no one reads.

Finally, my thanks to all the family and friends who have been such enthusiastic cheerleaders, with a special mention to my parents, Libby and Matthew; brother, David; sister, Hannah; and aunt, Leslie Lebl, all of whom read through many early drafts in whole or in part and offered constant encouragement. And most especially I want to thank my husband, Jax Chang, who didn't realize when we tied the knot that one day he'd find himself married to a book about Millennials. Without his steadfast practical and moral support, especially when I was most discouraged, this wouldn't be in your hands now.

Notes

INTRODUCTION: TAKING A BITE OUT OF THE BIG AVOCADO OF LIFE

1. *60 Minutes Australia*, May 15, 2017.

2. Linda Qiu and Daniel Victor, "Fact-Checking a Mogul's Claims About Avocado Toast, Millennials and Home Buying," *New York Times*, May 16, 2017.

3. Rhiannon Lucy Cosslett, "Stop Spending Money on Avocadoes? I'll Have a House Deposit by 2117," *Guardian* (London), May 16, 2017.

4. Jessica Roy, "Why You Can't Afford a House (Hint: It's Not the Avocado Toast)," *Los Angeles Times*, May 15, 2017.

5. Ben Chapman, "Property Tycoon Tells Millennials to Stop Buying Avocado Toast If They Ever Want to Buy a House," *Independent* (London), May 16, 2017.

6. Holly Johnson, "Yes, Avocado Toast Can Hurt Your Finances," *Indianapolis (Ind.) Star*, May 21, 2017.

7. Lawrie Holmes, "Tough Choices for First-Time Buyers to Help Save a Deposit," Strutt & Parker, November 10, 2017.

8. Mark Bridge, "Mushy Avocado and Prosecco Drought Are Millennials' Big Fears," *Times of London*, October 5, 2017.

9. Matthew Diebel, "Avocado Lattes May Be Just What Hipster Millennials Dreamed Of. Or Maybe Not," *USA Today*, May 22, 2017.

10. Florence Fabricant, "With New Avocado Bar, Brooklyn Really Has It All," *New York Times*, April 5, 2017.

11. Bruce Cannon Gibney, *A Generation of Sociopaths: How the Baby Boomers Betrayed America* (New York: Hachette, 2017).

12. Paul Taylor, *The Next America: Boomers, Millennials, and the Looming Generational Showdown* (New York: PublicAffairs, 2017), 22.

13. William Strauss and Neil Howe, *Generations: The History of America's Future, 1584–2069* (New York: William Morrow, 1991).

14. Ibid., 419.

15. Tim Fernholz, "The Pseudoscience That Prepared America for Steve Bannon's Apocalyptic Message," *Quartz*, May 27, 2017.

16. Richard Fry, "Millennials Projected to Overtake Baby Boomers as America's Largest Generation," Fact Tank (blog), Pew Research Center, March 1, 2018.

17. Ibid.

18. William H. Frey, "The Millennial Generation: A Demographic Bridge to America's Diverse Future," Metropolitan Policy Program, Brookings, January 2018, brookings.edu/research/millennials.

19. Council of Economic Advisors, "15 Economic Facts About Millennials," October 2014.

20. Frey, "The Millennial Generation."

21. Ibid.

22. Frank Nothaft, Molly Boesel, and Sam Khater, "Evaluating the Housing Market Since the Great Recession," CoreLogic Special Report, February 2018.

23. Ingrid Gould Ellen and Samuel Dastrup, "Housing and the Great Recession," Great Recession Brief, the Russell Sage Foundation and the Stanford Center on Poverty and Inequality, October 2012.

24. Federal Deposit Insurance Corporation, "Bank Failures in Brief: Bank Closing Summary, 2001–2018," July 18, 2018.

25. US Bureau of Economic Analysis, Real Gross Domestic Product, retrieved from Federal Reserve Bank of St. Louis, fred.stlouisfed.org/series/GDPC1, accessed September 12, 2018.

26. Judiciary Data and Analysis Office, "Just the Facts: Consumer Bankruptcy Filings, 2006–2017," Administrative Office of the US Courts, March 7, 2018, and data from the Administrative Office of the US Courts.

27. US Bureau of Labor Statistics, Civilian Unemployment Rate, retrieved from Federal Reserve Bank of St. Louis, fred.stlouisfed.org/series/UNRATENSA, accessed September 12, 2018.

28. US Bureau of Economic Analysis, Real Gross Domestic Product.

29. Ibid.

30. US Bureau of Labor Statistics, Civilian Unemployment Rate.

31. Kevin L. Kliesen, "The 2001 Recession: How Was It Different and What Developments May Have Caused It?" *Federal Reserve Bank of St. Louis Review* 85, no. 5 (September–October 2003); US Bureau of Labor Statistics, Civilian Unemployment Rate.

32. YiLi Chen and Paul Morris, "Is U.S. Manufacturing Really Declining?" On the Economy (blog), Federal Reserve Bank of St. Louis, April 11, 2017.

33. Ibid.

34. Concord Coalition, "Baby Boomers Now a Majority in U.S. House of Representatives," press release, November 3, 1998.

35. Data from the Roper Center for Public Opinion Research, Cornell University.

CHAPTER 1: THE YOUNG AND THE WORKLESS

1. Alison Green, Ask a Manager (blog), June 28, 2016, askamanager.org /2016/06/i-was-fired-from-my-internship-for-writing-a-proposal-for-a-more -flexible-dress-code.html.

2. Ibid.

3. Rebecca Koenig, "The 10 Best Jobs for Millennials," *U.S. News & World Report*, October 25, 2017, money.usnews.com/money/careers/articles /the-10-best-jobs-for-millennials.

4. Derek Miller, "The Most Popular Jobs for Millennials," SmartAsset.com, May 18, 2018, smartasset.com/retirement/popular-jobs-for-millennials.

5. Bureau of Labor Statistics, Table 11b: Employed Persons by Occupation and Age, in *Current Population Survey*, Annual Averages 2017; author's own calculations.

6. Deloitte Global, *Deloitte Millennial Survey*, 2018.

7. Bruce Tulgan, *Not Everyone Gets a Trophy: How to Manage Millennials*, rev. and updated ed. (Hoboken, NJ: Wiley, 2016).

8. US Bureau of Labor Statistics, data from Federal Reserve Bank of St. Louis, May 29, 2018.

9. ManpowerGroup, "Millennial Careers: 2020 Vision," 2016.

10. Neil Howe, "The Unhappy Rise of the Millennial Intern," *Forbes*, April 22, 2014.

11. US Bureau of Labor Statistics, Civilian Unemployment Rate, data retrieved from Federal Reserve Bank of St. Louis, May 30, 2018.

12. National Employment Law Project (NELP), "The Good Jobs Deficit: A Closer Look at Recent Job Loss and Job Growth Trends Using Occupational Data," Data Brief, July 2011.

13. Harry Holzer, "Job Market Polarization and U.S. Worker Skills: A Tale of Two Middles," Brookings, April 2015.

14. See, for instance, David H. Autor, Frank Levy, and Richard J. Murnane, "The Skill Content of Recent Technological Change: An Empirical Exploration," *Quarterly Journal of Economics* 118, no. 4 (November 2003).

15. Nir Jaimovich and Henry E. Siu, "The Trend Is the Cycle: Job Polarization and Jobless Recoveries," National Bureau of Economic Research Working Paper No. 18334, August 2012.

16. Ibid.

17. Imani Moise, "For the Elderly Who Are Lonely, Robots Offer Companionship," *Wall Street Journal*, May 28, 2018; David H. Autor and David Dorn, "The Growth of Low-Skill Service Jobs and the Polarization of the U.S. Labor Market," *American Economic Review* 103, no. 5 (August 2013).

18. Rachel E. Dwyer, "The Care Economy? Gender, Economic Restructuring, and Job Polarization in the U.S. Labor Market," *American Sociological Review* 78, no. 3 (June 2013).

19. Jaimovich and Siu, "The Trend Is the Cycle."

20. David Autor and David Dorn, "This Job Is 'Getting Old': Measuring Changes in Job Opportunities Using Occupational Age Structure," *American Economic Review* 99, no. 2 (2009).

21. Ibid.

22. Jeffrey D. Sachs and Laurence J. Kotlikoff, "Smart Machines and Long-Term Misery," National Bureau of Economic Research Working Paper No. 18629, 2012.

23. Author's own calculations from Current Population Survey (CPS) Annual Social and Economic (ASEC) Supplement, Table PINC-01.

24. Brad J. Hershbein and Lisa B. Kahn, "Do Recessions Accelerate Routine-Biased Technological Change? Evidence From Vacancy Postings," W. E. Upjohn Institute Working Paper 16-254, 2016.

25. US Bureau of Labor Statistics, Quits: Total Nonfarm, retrieved from Federal Reserve Bank of St. Louis, fred.stlouisfed.org/series/JTSQUL, June 10, 2018.

26. Eliza Forsythe, "Young Workers Left Behind: Hiring and the Great Recession," Upjohn Institute Employment Research 22, no. 1 (January 2015).

27. Jiaosheng He, Derek Messacar, and Yuri Ostrovsky, "The Relationship Between Firm Size and Age of Workforce: A Cross-Industry Analysis for Canada," *Analytical Studies: Methods and References*, Statistics Canada, November 2017.

28. Giuseppe Moscarini and Fabian Postel-Vinay, "Did the Job Ladder Fail After the Great Recession?" *Journal of Labor Economics* 34, no. 1 pt. 2 (2016).

29. Lisa B. Kahn, "The Long-Term Labor Market Consequences of Graduating From College in a Bad Economy," *Labour Economics* 17, no. 2 (April 2010).

30. Philip Oreopoulos, Till von Wachter, and Andrew Heisz, "The Short- and Long-Term Career Effects of Graduating in a Recession," *American Economic Journal: Applied Economics* 4, no. 1 (2012).

31. Richard Florida, "Preface to the Original Edition," in *The Rise of the Creative Class, Revisited* (New York: Basic Books, 2012).

32. Erik Brynjolfsson and Andrew McAfee, *The Second Machine Age: Work, Progress, and Prosperity in a Time of Brilliant Technologies* (New York: Norton, 2014).

33. Tyler Cowen, *Average Is Over: Powering America Beyond the Age of the Great Stagnation* (New York: Plume, 2013).

34. Paul Beaudry, David A. Green, and Benjamin M. Sand, "The Great Reversal in the Demand for Skill and Cognitive Tasks," National Bureau of Economic Research Working Paper No. 18901, March 2013.

35. Joseph G. Altonji, Lisa B. Kahn, and Jamin D. Speer, "Cashier or Consultant? Labor Market Entry Conditions, Field of Study, and Career Success," *Journal of Labor Economics* 43, no. 1, pt. 2 (2016).

36. Paul Beaudry, David A. Green, and Benjamin M. Sand, "The Declining Fortunes of the Young Since 2000," *American Economic Review* 104, no. 5 (May 2014).

37. Federal Reserve Board Division of Consumer and Community Affairs, "In the Shadow of the Great Recession: Experiences and Perspectives of Young Workers," November 2014.

CHAPTER 2: NOT OUR PARENTS' JOB MARKET

1. Author's own calculations, from University of Groningen and University of California, Davis, Share of Labour Compensation in GDP at Current National Prices for United States, retrieved from Federal Reserve Bank of St. Louis, fred .stlouisfed.org/series/LABSHPUSA156NRUG, accessed June 9, 2018.

2. Bureau of Labor Statistics data as quoted in Louis Uchitelle, *The Disposable American: Layoffs and Their Consequences* (New York: Knopf, 2006), 5.

3. US Bureau of Labor Statistics, Civilian Labor Force Participation Rate, retrieved from Federal Reserve Bank of St. Louis, fred.stlouisfed.org/series /CIVPART, accessed June 9, 2018.

4. US Bureau of Economic Analysis, Hours Worked by Full-Time and Part-Time Employees, retrieved from Federal Reserve Bank of St. Louis, fred.stlouis fed.org/series/B4701C0A222NBEA, accessed June 9, 2018.

5. University of Groningen and University of California, Davis, Share of Labour Compensation in GDP at Current National Prices for United States.

6. Author's own calculations, from US Bureau of Labor Statistics, Nonfarm Business Sector: Real Output Per Person, retrieved from Federal Reserve Bank of St. Louis, fred.stlouisfed.org/series/PRS85006162, accessed June 7, 2018.

7. Author's own calculations, from US Bureau of Economic Analysis, Real Gross Private Domestic Investment: Fixed Investment: Nonresidential, retrieved from Federal Reserve Bank of St. Louis, fred.stlouisfed.org/series/A008RL1A 225NBEA, accessed June 7, 2018.

8. Holman W. Jenkins Jr., "What Labor Could Learn from NFL Refs," *Wall Street Journal*, September 29, 2012.

9. US Bureau of Economic Analysis, Shares of Gross Domestic Product: Personal Consumption Expenditures, retrieved from Federal Reserve Bank of St. Louis, fred.stlouisfed.org/series/DPCERE1Q156NBEA, accessed September 23, 2018.

10. Author's own calculations, from US Bureau of Labor Statistics, Nonfarm Business Sector: Real Output Per Person.

11. Lester Thurow, *Head to Head: The Coming Economic Battle Among Japan, Europe, and America* (New York: William Morrow, 1992), 186–188.

12. Author's own calculations, from US Bureau of Economic Analysis, Real Gross Private Domestic Investment: Fixed Investment: Nonresidential.

13. Jude Wanniski, *The Way the World Works* (New York: Touchstone, 1978), 217.

14. See, for instance, Martin Feldstein, "American Economic Policy in the 1980s: A Personal View," in *American Economic Policy in the 1980s*, edited by Martin Feldstein (Chicago: University of Chicago Press, 1994), 15.

15. For one of the most comprehensive analyses to date in this growing field, see John W. Dawson and John J. Seater, "Federal Regulation and Aggregate Economic Growth," *Journal of Economic Growth* 18, no. 2 (June 2013).

16. Ibid.

17. Paul L. Joskow and Roger G. Noll, "Deregulation and Regulatory Reform During the 1980s," in Feldstein, ed., *American Economic Policy in the 1980s*, 368.

18. Author's own calculations, from US Bureau of Labor Statistics, Nonfarm Business Sector: Real Output Per Person.

19. US Bureau of Economic Analysis, Shares of Gross Domestic Product: Personal Consumption Expenditures.

20. Author's own calculations, from US Bureau of Economic Analysis, Real Gross Private Domestic Investment: Fixed Investment: Nonresidential.

21. US Bureau of Economic Analysis, Private Fixed Investment in Information Processing Equipment and Software, retrieved from Federal Reserve Bank of St. Louis, fred.stlouisfed.org/series/A679RC1Q027SBEA, accessed June 7, 2018.

22. US Bureau of Labor Statistics, Civilian Labor Force Participation Rate, retrieved from Federal Reserve Bank of St. Louis, fred.stlouisfed.org/series /CIVPART, accessed June 7, 2018.

23. University of Groningen and University of California, Davis, Share of Labour Compensation in GDP at Current National Prices for United States.

24. Pamela Samuelson and Hal R. Varian, "The 'New Economy' and Information Technology Policy," in *American Economic Policy in the 1990s*, edited by Jeffrey A. Frankel and Peter R. Orszag (Cambridge, MA: MIT Press, 2002), 377–381.

25. US Bureau of Economic Analysis, Shares of Gross Domestic Product: Personal Consumption Expenditures.

26. Author's own calculations, from US Bureau of Economic Analysis, Real Gross Private Domestic Investment: Fixed Investment: Nonresidential.

27. Author's own calculations, from US Bureau of Labor Statistics, Nonfarm Business Sector: Real Output Per Person.

28. Board of Governors of the Federal Reserve System (US), Households and Nonprofit Organizations, Home Mortgages, Liability, Level, retrieved from Federal Reserve Bank of St. Louis, fred.stlouisfed.org/series/HHMSDODNS, accessed June 9, 2018.

29. US Treasury, "Citizen's Report: Office of Financial Stability—Troubled Asset Relief Program, Fiscal 2017," November 2017.

30. Data in this paragraph from US Bureau of Economic Analysis, Private Nonresidential Fixed Investment.

31. Adrian Blundell-Wignall and Caroline Roulet, "Long-Term Investment, the Cost of Capital and the Dividend and Buyback Puzzle," *OECD Journal: Financial Market Trends* 1 (2013).

32. Indraneel Chakraborty, Itay Goldstein, and Andrew MacKinlay, "Monetary Stimulus and Bank Lending," paper presented at the Finance Down Under 2017 conference at the University of Melbourne, Australia.

33. US Bureau of Labor Statistics, Nonfarm Business Sector: Real Output Per Person.

34. Author's calculations, from University of Groningen and University of California, Davis, Share of Labour Compensation in GDP at Current National Prices for United States.

35. See, for instance, Loukas Karabarbounis and Brent Neiman, "The Global Decline in the Labor Share," *Quarterly Journal of Economics* 129, no. 1 (2014): 61–103.

36. Daron Acemoglu, "Labor- and Capital-Augmenting Technical Change," *Journal of the European Economic Association* 1, no. 1 (March 2003).

37. Daron Acemoglu and Pascual Restrepo, "The Race Between Machine and Man: Implications of Technology for Growth, Factor Shares and Employment," National Bureau of Economic Research Working Paper No. 22252, 2017.

38. US Bureau of Labor Statistics, Private Non-Farm Business Sector: Capital Intensity, retrieved from Federal Reserve Bank of St. Louis, fred.stlouisfed.org /series/MPU4910082, accessed June 9, 2018.

39. US Bureau of Economic Analysis, Hours Worked by Full-Time and Part-Time Employees.

40. Barack Obama, Acceptance Speech at the Democratic National Convention, 2008, National Public Radio, npr.org/templates/story/story.php?storyId =94087570, accessed June 10, 2018.

41. Data presented in Michael D. Giandrea and Shawn A. Sprague, "Estimating the U.S. Labor Share," *Monthly Labor Review*, US Bureau of Labor Statistics, February 2017.

42. Alex Blumberg and Adam Davidson, "Accidents of History Created U.S. Health System," National Public Radio, October 22, 2009, npr.org/templates /story/story.php?storyId=114045132.

43. Will Kimball and Lawrence Mishel, "Nearly One-Third of Salaried Workers Will Be Guaranteed Overtime Under the New Rule, but That Falls Short of the Half Covered in the Mid-1970s," Economic Snapshot, June 1, 2016, epi.org/publication /nearly-one-third-of-salaried-workers-will-be-guaranteed-overtime-under-the -new-rule-but-that-falls-short-of-the-half-covered-in-the-mid-1970s.

44. Acemoglu and Restrepo, "The Race Between Machine and Man."

45. Josh Zumbrun and Anna Louie Sussman, "Proof of a 'Gig Economy' Revolution Is Hard to Find," Wall Street Journal, July 26, 2015.

46. Prudential Insurance Company of America, "Gig Economy Impact by Generation," 2018.

47. Eli Dourado and Christopher Koopman, "Evaluating the Growth of the 1099 Work Force," Mercatus on Policy series, Mercatus Center, George Mason University, 2015.

48. Patrick Gillespie, "Intuit: Gig Economy Is 34 Percent of US Workforce," CNN Money, May 24, 2017, money.cnn.com/2017/05/24/news/economy/gig -economy-intuit/index.html.

CHAPTER 3: HUMAN-CAPITAL PUNISHMENT

1. Fidelity Brokerage Services, "2016 Fidelity Investments Millennial Money Study," October 13, 2016.

2. Bank of America, "Better Money Habits Millennial Report," January 2018.

3. Ibid.

4. Merrill Lynch, "Merrill Edge Report," Fall 2017.

5. Alicia H. Munnell and Wenliang Hu, "Will Millennials Be Ready for Retirement?" Center for Retirement Research at Boston College: Issue in Brief 18-2, January 2018.

6. Carlo De Bassa Scheresberg, Annamaria Lusardi, and Paul J. Yakoboski, "College-Educated Millennials: An Overview of Their Personal Finances," TIAA-CREF Institute, February 2014.

7. William R. Emmons, Ana Hernandez Kent, and Lowell R. Ricketts, "A Lost Generation? Long-Lasting Wealth Impacts of the Great Recession on Young Families," Federal Reserve Bank of St. Louis: The Demographics of Wealth, 2018 Series, May 2018.

8. US Bureau of Labor Statistics, "National Compensation Survey," 2017, bls .gov/ncs/ebs/benefits/2017/ownership/civilian/table02a.htm.

9. Board of Governors of the Federal Reserve System, "Survey of Consumer Finances, 2016," 2017.

10. Munnell and Hu, "Will Millennials Be Ready for Retirement?"

11. Jennifer Erin Brown, "Millennials and Retirement: Already Falling Short," report published by the National Institute on Retirement Security, 2018.

12. Fidelity Brokerage Services, "2016 Fidelity Investments Millennial Money Study."

13. De Bassa Scheresberg, Lusardi, and Yakoboski, "College-Educated Millennials."

14. Ulrike Malmendier and Leslie Sheng Shen, "Scarred Consumption," National Bureau of Economic Research Working Paper No. 24696, June 2018.

15. Frank Newport, "Young, Old in U.S. Plan on Relying More on Social Security," Gallup, May 25, 2017.

16. Federal Reserve Bank of New York, "Household Debt and Credit, Q1," May 17, 2018.

17. Consumer Financial Protection Bureau, "Snapshot of Older Consumers and Student Loan Debt," Report by the Office for Older Americans and the Office for Students and Young Consumers, 2017.

18. Raji Chakrabarti, Andrew Haughwout, Donghoon Lee, Joelle Scally, and Wilbert van der Klaauw, "Press Briefing on Household Debt, with Focus on Student Debt," Federal Reserve Bank of New York, April 3, 2017.

19. Ibid.

20. Sandy Baum, Jennifer Ma, Matea Pender, and Meredith Welch, *Trends in Student Aid 2017* (New York: The College Board, 2017).

21. Sandy Baum, *Student Debt: Rhetoric and Realities of Higher Education Financing* (New York: Palgrave Pivot, 2016), 8.

22. Jason N. Houle, "A Generation Indebted: Young Adult Debt Across Three Cohorts," *Social Problems* 61, no. 3 (August 2014).

23. Jennifer Ma, Sandy Baum, Matea Pender, and Meredith Welch, *Trends in College Pricing 2017* (New York: The College Board, 2017).

24. Elyssa Kirkham, "Study: Here's How Much College Credits Actually Cost," StudentLoanHero.com, January 24, 2018.

25. National Center for Education Statistics, "Table 302.10: Recent High-School Completers and Their Enrollment in College, by Sex and Level of Institution: 1960 through 2016," Digest of Education Statistics, 2018.

26. National Center for Education Statistics, "Table 104.20: Percentage of Persons 25 to 29 Years Old with Selected Levels of Educational Attainment, by Race/Ethnicity and Sex: Selected Years, 1920 Through 2017," Digest of Education Statistics, 2018.

27. Baum, *Student Debt*, 39.

28. Ibid., 40.

29. Philip Oreopoulos and Uros Petronijevic, "Making College Worth It: A Review of the Returns to Higher Education," *Future of Children* 23, no. 1 (Spring 2013).

30. Anthony P. Carnevale, Ban Cheah, and Andrew R. Hanson, "The Economic Value of College Majors," Georgetown University Center on Education and Workforce, 2015.

31. Ibid.

32. Joseph G. Altonji, Erica Blom, and Costas Meghir, "Heterogeneity in Human Capital Investment: High School Curriculum, College Major, and Careers," *Annual Review of Economics* 4 (2012).

33. Joe Pinsker, "Rich Kids Study English," *Atlantic*, July 6, 2015.

34. Kevin Kiley, "White House's New Scorecard Oversimplifies Institutions, Liberal Arts Advocates Say," *Inside Higher Ed*, February 14, 2013.

35. Beth Akers and Matthew M. Chingos, *Game of Loans: The Rhetoric and Reality of Student Debt* (Princeton, NJ: Princeton University Press, 2016), 106.

36. Ethan Dornhelm, "FICO Research: Student Loan Explosion Hurts Other Borrowing," FICO Blog, October 20, 2016, fico.com/en/blogs/collections-recovery /fico-research-student-loans-explode-and-suppress-other-borrowing.

37. TransUnion, "Generational Differences in Credit," TransUnion (blog), May 4, 2016, transunion.com/blog/credit-advice/generational-differences-credit.

38. Rajashri Chakrabarti, Nicole Gorton, and Wilbert van der Klaauw, "Diplomas to Doorsteps: Education, Student Debt, and Homeownership," Liberty Street Economics (blog), Federal Reserve Bank of New York, April 3, 2017, libertystreeteconomics.newyorkfed.org/2017/04/diplomas-to-doorsteps -education-student-debt-and-homeownership.html.

39. Jason N. Houle, "Disparities in Debt: Parents' Socioeconomic Resources and Young Adult Student Loan Debt," *Sociology of Education* 87, no. 1 (January 2014).

40. Sara Goldrick-Rab, Robert Kelchen, and Jason N. Houle, "The Color of Student Debt: Implications of Federal Loan Program Reforms for Black Students and Historically Black Colleges and Universities," Working Paper, Wisconsin HOPE Lab, University of Wisconsin–Madison, 2014.

41. Sara Goldrick-Rab, *Paying the Price: College Costs, Financial Aid, and the Betrayal of the American Dream* (Chicago: University of Chicago Press, 2016), 90–91.

42. Akers and Chingos, *Game of Loans*, 46–48.

43. Barack Obama, "Address to a Joint Session of Congress," February 24, 2009, washingtonpost.com/wp-srv/politics/documents/obama_address_022409.html.

44. Barack Obama, "State of the Union Address," January 27, 2010, obamawhite house.archives.gov/the-press-office/remarks-president-state-union-address.

45. Barack Obama, "Remarks by the President on College Affordability— Buffalo, N.Y.," August 22, 2013, obamawhitehouse.archives.gov/the-press-office /2013/08/22/remarks-president-college-affordability-buffalo-ny.

46. US Department of Education, "Strengthening the Student Loan System to Better Protect All Borrowers," October 1, 2015, www2.ed.gov/documents/ press-releases/strengthening-student-loan-system.pdf.

47. Val Srinivas and Urval Goradia, "The Future of Wealth in the United States: Mapping Trends in Generational Wealth," Deloitte, 2015.

48. Elizabeth Arias, Melonie Heron, and Jiaquan Xu, "United States Life Tables, 2014," *National Vital Statistics Reports* 66, no. 4 (2017).

49. Dana E. King, Eric Matheson, Svetlana Chirina, Anoop Shankar, and Jordan Broman-Fulks, "The Status of Baby Boomers' Health in the United States: The Healthiest Generation?" *JAMA Internal Medicine* 173, no. 5 (2013).

50. Fidelity, "A Couple Retiring in 2018 Would Need an Estimated $280,000 to Cover Health Care Costs in Retirement, Fidelity Analysis Shows," 2018, fidelity.com/about-fidelity/employer-services/a-couple-retiring-in-2018-would -need-estimated-280000.

51. PwC, "Employee Financial Wellness Survey," 2013, pwc.com/us/en/private -company-services/publications/assets/pwc-2018-employee-wellness-survey.pdf.

52. Fidelity, "Family and Finance Study," 2016, fidelity.com/bin-public/060_ www_fidelity_com/documents/Family-Finance-Study-Executive-Summary.pdf.

53. PwC, "Employee Financial Wellness Survey," 2018, pwc.com/us/en /private-company-services/publications/assets/pwc-2018-employee-wellness -survey.pdf.

CHAPTER 4: *MILLENNIUS DOMESTICUS*

1. HSBC, "Beyond the Bricks: The Meaning of Home," Global Factsheet, 2017.

2. Melody Hahm, "Why Millennials Are Obsessed with HGTV," *Yahoo Finance*, November 13, 2017, uk.finance.yahoo.com/news/millennials-obsessed -hgtv-205022165.html.

3. Richard Fry, "For First Time in Modern Era, Living with Parents Edges Out Other Living Arrangements for 18- to 34-Year-Olds," Pew Research Center, May 2016.

4. Drew DeSilver, "Increase in Living with Parents Driven by Those Aged 25– 34, Non-College Grads," Fact Tank (blog), Pew Research Center, June 8, 2016, pewresearch.org/fact-tank/2016/06/08/increase-in-living-with-parents-driven-by -those-ages-25-34-non-college-grads.

5. Richard Fry, "It's Becoming More Common for Young Adults to Live at Home—and for Longer Stretches," Fact Tank (blog), Pew Research Center, May 5, 2017, pewresearch.org/fact-tank/2017/05/05/its-becoming-more-common -for-young-adults-to-live-at-home-and-for-longer-stretches.

6. D'Vera Cohn and Jeffrey S. Passel, "A Record 64 Million Americans Live in Multigenerational Households," Fact Tank (blog), Pew Research Center, April 5, 2018, pewresearch.org/fact-tank/2018/04/05/a-record-64-million-americans -live-in-multigenerational-households.

7. National Alliance for Caregiving and AARP Public Policy Institute, *Caregiving in the U.S. 2015*, June 2015.

8. Fry, "For First Time in Modern Era, Living with Parents Edges Out Other Living Arrangements."

9. Jonathan Vespa, "The Changing Economics and Demographics of Young Adulthood, 1975–2016," US Census Bureau, Current Population Reports, April 2017.

10. Steven Ruggles, "The Decline of Generational Coresidence in the United States, 1850–2000," *American Sociological Review* 72, no. 6 (December 2007).

11. Florentina Sarac, "Millennials Spend About $93,000 on Rent by the Time They Hit 30," RentCafé Blog, March 27, 2018, rentcafe.com/blog /apartment-search-2/money/millennials-spend-93000-on-rent-by-the-time -they-hit-30.

12. Jung Choi, Jun Zhu, Laurie Goodman, Bhargavi Ganes, and Sarah Strochak, "Millennial Homeownership: Why Is It So Low, and How Can We Increase It?" Research Report, Urban Institute, July 2018.

13. Ibid.

14. Ibid.

15. Ibid.

16. Paul Davidson, "From Their Parents' Basements to Dream Homes: Millennials Are Skipping Starter Houses," *USA Today*, May 8, 2018.

17. Ralph McLaughlin, "House Arrest: How Low Inventory Is Slowing Home Buying," Trulia Research, March 21, 2016, trulia.com/research/inventory -price-watch-q116; Cheryl Young, "The American Starter Home: Expensive, Small, Broken Down, and Hard to Find," Truly Research, March 21, 2018, trulia .com/research/inventory-q118.

18. Patrick Simmons, "Many Starter Homes Have Shifted from Owner-Occupancy to Rentals," Fannie Mae Economic and Strategic Research Group: Housing Insights, October 17, 2018.

19. Jordan Rappaport, "The Large Unmet Demand for Housing," Federal Reserve Bank of Kansas City: Main Street Views, April 12, 2017.

20. Choi, Zhu, Goodman, Ganes, and Strochak, "Millennial Homeownership."

21. Edward L. Glaeser, Joseph Gyourko, and Raven E. Saks, "Why Have Housing Prices Gone Up?" National Bureau of Economic Research Working Paper No. 11129, February 2005.

22. Author's own calculations from data presented in Christopher Mazur and Ellen Wilson, "Housing Characteristics: 2010," 2010 Census Briefs, US Census Bureau, October 2011.

23. Matthew Chambers, Carlos Garriga, and Donald E. Schlagenhauf, "Did Housing Policies Cause the Postwar Boom in Homeownership?" National Bureau of Economic Research Working Paper No. 18821, February 2013.

24. Richard K. Green and Susan M. Wachter, "The American Mortgage in Historical and International Perspective," *Journal of Economic Perspectives* 19, no. 4 (Fall 2005).

25. US Census Bureau, Housing and Household Economic Statistics Division, October 31, 2011, census.gov/hhes/www/housing/census/historic/owner.html.

26. Matthew Chambers, Carlos Garriga, and Don E. Schlagenhauf, "The Postwar Conquest of the Homeownership Dream," Federal Reserve Bank of St. Louis Working Paper No. 2016-007A, April 12, 2016.

27. Green and Wachter, "The American Mortgage in Historical and International Perspective."

28. Emmanuel Saez and Gabriel Zucman, "Wealth Inequality in the United States Since 1913: Evidence from Capitalized Income Tax Data," *Quarterly Journal of Economics* 131, no. 2 (May 2016).

29. "Table 14. Quarterly Homeownership Rates for the U.S. and Regions: 1964 to Present," Housing Vacancies and Homeownership (CPS/HVS): Historical Tables, US Census Bureau, accessed November 19, 2018.

30. Edward J. Pinto, "Government Housing Policies in the Lead-Up to the Financial Crisis: A Forensic Study," Submission to the Financial Crisis Inquiry Commission, November 4, 2010.

31. William J. Clinton, "Remarks on the National Homeownership Strategy," June 5, 1995.

32. US Department of Housing and Urban Development, "The National Homeownership Strategy: Partners in the American Dream," May 1995.

33. Pinto, "Government Housing Policies in the Lead-Up to the Financial Crisis."

34. Peter J. Wallison, Dissenting Statement to the Financial Crisis Inquiry Commission, January 2011.

35. Freddie Mac, 30-Year Fixed Rate Mortgage Average in the United States, retrieved from Federal Reserve Bank of St. Louis, fred.stlouisfed.org/series/MORTGAGE30US, July 30, 2018.

36. US Census Bureau, Homeownership Rate for the United States, retrieved from Federal Reserve Bank of St. Louis, fred.stlouisfed.org/series/USHOWN, July 31, 2018.

37. Board of Governors of the Federal Reserve System (US), Households, Owners' Equity in Real Estate as a Percentage of Household Real Estate, Level, retrieved from Federal Reserve Bank of St. Louis, fred.stlouisfed.org/series/HOEREPHRE, July 30, 2018.

38. Linda Cavanaugh, "Home Equity Lines of Credit—Who Uses This Source of Credit?" US Census Bureau, Census 2000 Brief, September 2007.

39. Freddie Mac Office of the Chief Economist, "Cash-Out Refinance Report," 2013.

40. Author's calculations, from US Bureau of Economic Analysis, Private Nonresidential Fixed Investment, retrieved from Federal Reserve Bank of St. Louis, fred.stlouisfed.org/series/PNFI, August 8, 2018, and US Bureau of Economic Analysis, Private Residential Fixed Investment, retrieved from Federal Reserve Bank of St. Louis, fred.stlouisfed.org/series/PRFI, August 8, 2018.

41. Board of Governors of the Federal Reserve System (US), Delinquency Rate on Single-Family Residential Mortgages, Booked in Domestic Offices, All Commercial Banks, retrieved from Federal Reserve Bank of St. Louis, fred.stlouis fed.org/series/DRSFRMACBS, August 1, 2018.

42. HSBC, "HSBC Trading Update—US Mortgage Services," February 7, 2007.

43. The timeline of programs and their description in this and subsequent paragraphs comes from Katie Jones, "Preserving Homeownership: Foreclosure Prevention Initiatives," Congressional Research Service Report No. R40210, May 14, 2015.

44. George W. Bush, "Remarks at a Roundtable on Housing Counseling," July 1, 2008, georgewbush-whitehouse.archives.gov/news/releases/2008/07/20080701-6.html.

45. Barack Obama, "Remarks by the President on the Home Mortgage Crisis," February 18, 2009, obamawhitehouse.archives.gov/the-press-office/remarks-president-mortgage-crisis.

46. Ben S. Bernanke, "Deflation: Making Sure 'It' Doesn't Happen Here," Speech to the National Economists Club, November 21, 2002.

47. Board of Governors of the Federal Reserve System, "Federal Reserve Announces It Will Initiate a Program to Purchase the Direct Obligations of Housing-Related Government-Sponsored Enterprises and Mortgage-Backed Securities Backed by Fannie Mae, Freddie Mac, and Ginnie Mae," press release, November 25, 2008.

48. Marco Di Maggio, Amir Kermani, and Christopher Palmer, "How Quantitative Easing Works: Evidence on the Refinancing Channel," National Bureau of Economic Research Working Paper No. 22638, September 2016.

49. Dong Beom Choi, Hyun-Soo Choi, and Jung-Eun Kim, "QE Frictions: Could Banks Have Favored Refinancing over New Purchase Borrowing?" Liberty Street Economics (blog), Federal Reserve Bank of New York, March 29, 2017, libertystreeteconomics.newyorkfed.org/2017/03/qe-frictions-could-banks-have-favored-refinancing-over-new-purchase-borrowing.html.

50. S&P Dow Jones Indices LLC, S&P/Case-Shiller 20-City Composite Home Price Index, retrieved from Federal Reserve Bank of St. Louis, fred.stlouisfed.org/series/SPCS20RSA, August 12, 2018.

51. National Association of Realtors, "Home Buyer and Seller Generational Trends: 2018," March 2018.

52. Michele Lerner, "A New Low Down-Payment Option for First-Time Home Buyers," *Washington Post*, May 16, 2018.

53. Jennifer Brown and David A. Matsa, "Locked In by Leverage: Job Search During the Housing Crisis," National Bureau of Economic Research Working Paper No. 22929, December 2016.

54. Martin Beraja, Andreas Fuster, Erik Hurst, and Joseph Vavra, "Regional Heterogeneity and the Refinancing Channel of Monetary Policy," Federal Reserve Bank of New York Staff Report No. 731, March 2018 (rev.).

55. Geoff Smith, Sarah Duda, and Tina Fassett, "The Impact of Lock-In Effects on Housing Turnover and Implications for a Housing Recovery," Research Brief, Institute for Housing Studies, DePaul University, February 2014.

56. Conor Dougherty, "Real Estate's New Normal: Homeowners Staying Put," *New York Times*, May 14, 2017.

57. John Hendren, "Obama: Wall Street 'Arrogance and Greed' Won't Be Tolerated," ABC News, January 31, 2009, abcnews.go.com/Politics/CEOProfiles/story?id=6778419.

58. Urban Institute Housing Finance Policy Center, "Housing Finance at a Glance: A Monthly Chartbook," July 2018.

59. Urban Institute Housing Finance Policy Center, "Housing Credit Availability Index, Q1 2018," July 12, 2018.

CHAPTER 5: THE SATURDAY-MORNING BANK HEIST

1. Congressional Budget Office, "The Federal Budget in 2017: An Infographic," March 5, 2018.

2. Office of Management and Budget, "Historical Tables" series, 2018.

3. Congressional Budget Office, "Historical Data on Federal Debt Held by the Public," July 2010.

4. Jacob E. Cooke, "Introduction," in *The Reports of Alexander Hamilton*, edited by Jacob E. Cooke (New York: Harper Torchbooks, 1964), xiii.

5. Alexander Hamilton, "Report Relative to a Provision for the Support of Public Credit," January 9, 1790, reprinted in Cooke, ed., *The Reports of Alexander Hamilton*.

6. Congressional Budget Office, "Historical Data on Federal Debt Held by the Public," July 2010.

7. Office of Management and Budget, "Historical Tables" series.

8. Federal Reserve Bank of St. Louis and US Office of Management and Budget, Gross Federal Debt as Percent of Gross Domestic Product, retrieved from Federal Reserve Bank of St. Louis, fred.stlouisfed.org/series/GFDGDPA188S, August 11, 2018.

9. Author calculations from US Bureau of Economic Analysis, Government Current Expenditures: Federal: National Defense, retrieved from Federal Reserve Bank of St. Louis, fred.stlouisfed.org/series/G160461A027NBEA, August 11, 2018; and US Bureau of Economic Analysis, Gross Domestic Product, retrieved from Federal Reserve Bank of St. Louis, fred.stlouisfed.org/series/GDPA, August 11, 2018.

10. Author calculations from US Bureau of Economic Analysis, Government Current Expenditures: Federal: National Defense, retrieved from Federal Reserve Bank of St. Louis, fred.stlouisfed.org/series/G160461A027NBEA, August 11, 2018; and US Bureau of Economic Analysis, Gross Domestic Product, retrieved from Federal Reserve Bank of St. Louis, fred.stlouisfed.org/series/GDPA, August 11, 2018.

11. Max Ehrenfreund, "How Welfare Reform Changed American Poverty, in 9 Charts," Wonkblog, *Washington Post*, August 22, 2016, washingtonpost.com /news/wonk/wp/2016/08/22/the-enduring-legacy-of-welfare-reform-20-years -later.

12. Neta C. Crawford, "United States Budgetary Costs of Post-9/11 Wars Through FY2018," Costs of War: Watson Institute for International and Public Affairs, Brown University, November 2017.

13. Author calculations from US Bureau of Economic Analysis, Government Current Expenditures: Federal: National Defense, retrieved from Federal Reserve Bank of St. Louis, fred.stlouisfed.org/series/G160461A027NBEA, August 11, 2018; and US Bureau of Economic Analysis, Gross Domestic Product, retrieved from Federal Reserve Bank of St. Louis, fred.stlouisfed.org/series/GDPA, August 11, 2018.

14. Jeffrey Frankel, "Over-Optimism in Forecasts by Official Budget Agencies and Its Implications," *Oxford Review of Economic Policy* 27, no. 4 (Winter 2011).

15. William Easterly, "The Role of Growth Slowdowns and Forecast Errors in Public Debt Crises," in *Fiscal Policy After the Financial Crisis*, edited by Alberto Alesina and Francesco Giavazzi (Chicago: University of Chicago Press, 2013).

16. Robert M. McNab, Mark Rider, and Kent D. Wall, "Are Errors in Official U.S. Budget Receipts Forecasts Just Noise?" Andrew Young School of Policy Studies, Working Paper No. 07-22, April 2007.

17. C. Eugene Steuerle and Caleb Quakenbush, "Social Security and Medicare Lifetime Benefits and Taxes: 2017 Update," Urban Institute Research Report, June 2018.

18. Congressional Budget Office, "The 2017 Long-Term Budget Outlook," March 2017.

19. Congressional Budget Office, "The Budget and Economic Outlook: 2018–2028," April 2018.

20. C. Eugene Steuerle, *Dead Men Ruling: How to Restore Fiscal Freedom and Rescue Our Future* (New York: Century Foundation Press, 2014).

21. Board of Trustees, Federal Old-Age and Survivors Insurance and Federal Disability Insurance Trust Funds, "The 2018 Annual Report of the Board of Trustees of the Federal Old-Age and Survivors Insurance and Federal Disability Insurance Trust Funds," June 5, 2018.

22. Boards of Trustees, Federal Hospital Insurance and Federal Supplementary Medical Insurance Trust Funds, "2018 Annual Report of the Boards of Trustees of the Federal Hospital Insurance and Federal Supplementary Medical Insurance Trust Funds," June 5, 2018.

23. Ibid.

24. Pew Charitable Trusts, "The State Pension Funding Gap: 2016," Brief, April 2018.

25. Ibid.

26. Thurston Powers, Elliot Young, Bob Williams, and Erica York, "Unaffordable and Unaccountable 2017," Report from the American Legislative Exchange Council, December 13, 2017.

27. Board of Trustees, "2018 Annual Report."

28. Ibid.

29. Ibid.

30. Ibid.

31. Federal Reserve Bank of St. Louis and US Office of Management and Budget, Federal Surplus or Deficit as Percent of Gross Domestic Product, retrieved from Federal Reserve Bank of St. Louis, fred.stlouisfed.org/series/FYFS GDA188S, August 14, 2018; and US Office of Management and Budget, Federal Surplus or Deficit, retrieved from Federal Reserve Bank of St. Louis, fred.stlouis fed.org/series/FYFSD, August 14, 2018.

32. US Department of the Treasury, Fiscal Service, Federal Debt: Total Public Debt, retrieved from Federal Reserve Bank of St. Louis, fred.stlouisfed.org /series/GFDEBTN, August 14, 2018.

33. Federal Reserve Bank of St. Louis and US Office of Management and Budget, Federal Debt: Total Public Debt as Percent of Gross Domestic Product, retrieved from Federal Reserve Bank of St. Louis, fred.stlouisfed.org/series/GFD EGDQ188S, August 13, 2018.

34. Congressional Budget Office, "Estimated Impact of the American Recovery and Reinvestment Act on Employment and Economic Output in 2014," February 2015.

35. Casey B. Mulligan, *The Redistribution Recession: How Labor Market Distortions Contracted the Economy* (New York: Oxford University Press, 2012), 266.

36. Ibid., 264.

37. Congressional Budget Office, "H.R.4872, Reconciliation Act of 2010 (Final Health Care Legislation)," Letter to Speaker of the House of Representatives Nancy Pelosi, March 20, 2010.

38. Alan J. Auerbach, Jagadeesh Gkohale, and Laurence J. Kotlikoff, "Generational Accounts: A Meaningful Alternative to Deficit Accounting," in *Tax Policy and the Economy, Volume 5*, edited by David Bradford (Cambridge, MA: MIT Press, 1991).

39. Jagadeesh Gokhale and Laurence J. Kotlikoff, "Is War Between Generations Inevitable?" National Center for Policy Analysis Policy Report No. 246, November 2001.

40. Laurence J. Kotlikoff and Scott Burns, *The Clash of Generations: Saving Ourselves, Our Kids, and Our Economy* (New York: MIT Press, 2012), 30–31.

41. See, for instance, Kathleen Romig, "Increasing Payroll Taxes Would Strengthen Social Security," Center for Budget and Policy Priorities Policy Futures Brief, September 27, 2016; and Karen E. Smith, "How Can We Make Social Security Solvent?" Urban Wire (blog), Urban Institute, October 16, 2015.

42. Congressional Budget Office, "The 2017 Long-Term Budget Outlook," March 2017.

43. Alan Cole and Scott Greenberg, "Details and Analysis of Senator Bernie Sanders's Tax Plan," Tax Foundation Fiscal Fact Report No. 498, January 2016.

44. OECD, "Revenue Statistics: Comparative Tables," OECD Tax Statistics (database), 2018, doi.org/10.1787/data-00262-en.

45. Keith Brainard and Alex Brown, "Significant Reforms to State Retirement Systems," National Association of State Retirement Administrators Spotlight brief, June 2016.

46. Susan Tompor, "Even 5 Years Later, Retirees Still Feel the Effects of Detroit's Bankruptcy," *Detroit Free Press*, July 18, 2018.

47. Catherine Candisky, "Ohio Public Employees Pension System Oks Benefit Cuts," *Columbus (OH) Dispatch*, October 19, 2017.

48. Catherine Candisky, "Legislation to Cut OPERS Benefits Dies," *Columbus (OH) Dispatch*, March 23, 2018.

CHAPTER 6: THEIR PRESENT, OUR FUTURE

1. Adam Corlett, "As Time Goes By: Shifting Income and Inequality Between and Within Generations," Resolution Foundation: Intergenerational Commission Report, February 2017.

2. Eurostat, "Statistics on Young People Neither in Employment nor in Education or Training," July 2018.

3. Eurostat, "Tertiary Educational Attainment by Sex," 2018.

4. Angana Banerji, Huidan Lin, and Sergejs Saksonovs, "Youth Unemployment in Advanced Europe: Okun's Law and Beyond," International Monetary Fund Working Paper No. WP/15/5, January 2015.

5. Ibid.

6. Organization for Economic Cooperation and Development, "Minimum Relative to Average Wages for Full-Time Workers," OECD.Stat, 2018.

7. Organization for Economic Cooperation and Development, *Economic Policy Reforms 2012: Going for Growth*, 2012.

8. Eurostat, "Temporary Employees as Percentage of the Total Number of Employees, by Sex, Age and Country of Birth," August 3, 2018.

9. Giuseppe Bertola, Francine D. Blau, and Lawrence M. Kahn, "Market Institutions and Demographic Employment Patterns," *Journal of Population Economics* 20, no. 4 (October 2007).

10. Michael Savage, "Millennial Housing Crisis Engulfs Britain," *Guardian* (London), April 28, 2018.

11. Chris York, "Millennial Couples Making 'Heart-Breaking' Family Decisions Because of Housing Market," *Huffington Post*, February 14, 2018.

12. Katie Morley and Christopher Hope, "Tories Fear Middle-Class Millennials Priced Out of Housing Market Could Sink Party at Next Election," *Daily Telegraph* (London), February 16, 2018.

13. Fahmida Rahman and David Tomlinson, "Cross Countries: International Comparisons of Intergenerational Trends," Resolution Foundation: Intergenerational Commission Report, February 2018.

14. Jonathan Cribb, Andrew Hood, and Jack Hoyle, "The Decline of Homeownership Among Young Adults," Institute for Fiscal Studies Briefing Note No. BN224, February 16, 2018.

15. Stephen Clarke, "The Future Fiscal Cost of 'Generation Rent,'" Resolution Foundation (blog), April 17, 2018.

16. Shelter, "Generation Pause: 60 Percent of Under 45s Left Behind by Housing Crisis," press release, June 6, 2016.

17. Jenny Pennington, Dalia Ben-Galim, and Graeme Cooke, "No Place to Call Home: The Social Impacts of Housing Undersupply on Young People," Institute for Public Policy Research, December 2012.

18. Corlett, "As Time Goes By."

19. Clarke, "The Future Fiscal Cost of 'Generation Rent.'"

20. Author's calculations from Eurostat, Real Gross Domestic Product for United Kingdom, retrieved from Federal Reserve Bank of St. Louis, fred.stlouisfed.org/series/CLVMNACSCAB1GQUK, August 22, 2018; and US Bureau of Economic Analysis, Real Gross Domestic Product, retrieved from Federal Reserve Bank of St. Louis, fred.stlouisfed.org/series/GDPC1, August 22, 2018.

21. Fahmida Rahman and David Tomlinson, *Cross Countries: International Comparisons of Intergenerational Trends*, Resolution Foundation: Intergenerational Commission Report, February 2018.

22. UK Office of National Statistics, "A Century of Home Ownership and Renting in England and Wales," 2011 Census Analysis, April 19, 2013, webarchive.nationalarchives.gov.uk/20160105160709/ons.gov.uk/ons/rel/census/2011-census-analysis/a-century-of-home-ownership-and-renting-in-england-and-wales/short-story-on-housing.html.

23. Wendy Wilson and Cassie Barton, "Tackling the Under-Supply of Housing in England," House of Commons Library Briefing Paper No. 07671, August 8, 2018.

24. Cribb, Hood, and Hoyle, "The Decline of Homeownership Among Young Adults."

25. Home Builders Federation, "New Home Planning 'Permissions' Up—But System Remains a Constraint," press release, January 3, 2017.

26. Rowena Crawford, "Retired People Look Set to Bequeath Rather Than Use Most of Their Wealth," Institute for Fiscal Studies press release, June 11, 2018; Resolution Foundation, "21st Century Britain Has Seen a 30 Per Cent Increase in Second Home Ownership," press release, August 19, 2017.

27. Ibid.

28. Chihiro Udagawa and Paul Sanderson, "The Impacts of Family Support on Access to Homeownership for Young People in the UK," Social Mobility Commission, March 2017.

29. OECD, "Revenue Statistics 2017: Germany," briefing note, 2018.

30. Ibid.

31. OCED, "Taxing Wages 2018: Germany," briefing note, 2018; and OECD, "Taxing Wages 2018: United States," briefing note, 2018.

32. Tom Fairless, "Germany's Coffers Are Overflowing, But No One Is Talking About Tax Cuts," *Wall Street Journal*, February 17, 2018.

33. Bernd Hayo, Florian Neumeier, and Matthias Uhl, "Topics in Fiscal Policy: Evidence from a Representative Survey of the German Population," Joint Discussion Paper Series in Economics No. 10-2014, February 2014.

34. Author calculations from Statistisches Bundesamt (Destatis), "13th Coordinated Population Project: Continued Trend Based on Higher Population," 2015; and Jeff Desjardins, "Germany Will Hit a Significant Demographic Milestone Over the Next Year," Agenda (blog), World Economic Forum, January 18, 2018.

35. Martin Greive, Gregor Waschinski, and Jean-Michel Hauteville, "Aging Population on Course to Wipe Out Germany's Finances Within 30 Years," *Handelsblatt Global*, June 1, 2018.

36. Martin Werding, "Simulations for the 4th Sustainability Report," Study Commissioned by the German Federal Ministry of Finance, January 2016.

37. Ibid.

38. Manpower Group, "Millennial Careers: 2020 Vision," survey results, 2016.

39. Keiko Ujikane, "In Japan, World's Gloomiest Millennials See a Future of Struggle," Bloomberg, reprinted in *Japan Times*, November 24, 2016.

40. Andrew Gordon, "New and Enduring Dual Structures of Employment in Japan: The Rise of Non-Regular Labor, 1980s–2010s," *Social Science Japan Journal* 20, no. 1 (February 2017).

41. Alana Semuels, "The Mystery of Why Japanese People Are Having So Few Babies," *Atlantic*, July 20, 2017.

42. Georg D. Blind and Stefania Lottanti von Mandach, "Decades Not Lost, But Won: Increased Employment, Higher Wages, and More Equal Opportunities in the Japanese Labour Market," *Social Science Japan Journal* 18, no. 1 (January 2015).

43. Chie Aoyagi and Giovanni Ganelli, "The Path to Higher Growth: Does Revamping Japan's Dual Labor Market Matter?" International Monetary Fund Working Paper WP/13/202, October 2013.

44. Gordon, "New and Enduring Dual Structures of Employment in Japan."

45. As quoted in Aoyagi and Ganelli, "The Path to Higher Growth."

46. Ministry of Finance of Japan, Central Government Debt as of June 30, 2018, data released August 10, 2018.

47. International Monetary Fund, General Government Gross Debt for Japan, retrieved from Federal Reserve Bank of St. Louis, fred.stlouisfed.org /series/GGGDTAJPA188N, September 1, 2018.

48. Martin Fackler, "Japan's Big-Works Stimulus Is Lesson," *New York Times*, February 5, 2009.

49. Emiko Jozuka and Will Ripley, "Why Are Almost Half of Japan's Millennials Still Virgins?" CNN, September 20, 2016.

50. Keiko Ujikane, "In Japan, World's Gloomiest Millennials See a Future of Struggle," Bloomberg, reprinted in *Japan Times*, November 24, 2016.

CHAPTER 7: MILLENNIALS IN CHARGE

1. Gideon Resnick, "Alexandria Ocasio-Cortez Is Risking Her Reputation Before She Gets to Congress," *Daily Beast*, August 15, 2018.

2. Jennifer E. Manning, "Membership of the 111th Congress: A Profile," Congressional Research Service, November 19, 2010.

3. Randy James, "The First Gen Y Congressman," *Time*, January 8, 2009.

4. Jennifer E. Manning, "Membership of the 113th Congress: A Profile," Congressional Research Service, November 24, 2014.

5. Dave Merrill and Yvette Romero, "Millennials Can't Crack Congress," *Bloomberg*, November 10, 2016.

6. Jennifer E. Manning, "Membership of the 115th Congress: A Profile," Congressional Research Service, July 11, 2018.

7. Luke Rosiak, "Congressional Staffers, Public Shortchanged by High Turnover, Low Pay," *Washington Times*, June 6, 2012.

8. Richard Fry, "Younger Generations Make Up a Majority of the Electorate, But May Not Be a Majority of Voters This November," Fact Tank (blog), Pew Research Center, June 14, 2018.

9. "Young People Dramatically Increase Their Turnout to 31%, Shape 2018 Midterm Elections," The Center for Information and Research on Civil Learning and Engagements, Tufts University, November 7, 2018.

10. Kristen Soltis Anderson, "Conservatives Have a Millennial Problem," *Weekly Standard*, May 11, 2018.

11. Victims of Communism Memorial Foundation and YouGov, "Third Annual Report on US Attitudes Toward Socialism," 2018, victimsofcommunism .org/2018-annual-report.

12. Reason Foundation, "Millennials: The Politically Unclaimed Generation," Reason-Rupe Spring 2014 Millennial Survey, July 10, 2014.

13. Ibid.

14. Jean M. Twenge, Nathan Honeycutt, Radmila Prislin, and Ryne A. Sherman, "More Polarized but More Independent: Political Party Identification and Ideological Self-Categorization Among U.S. Adults, College Students, and Late Adolescents, 1970-2015," *Personality and Social Psychology Bulletin* 42, no. 10 (September 7, 2016).

15. William A. Galston and Clara Hendrickson, "How Millennials Voted This Election," Fixgov (blog), Brookings, November 21, 2016, brookings.edu/blog /fixgov/2016/11/21/how-millennials-voted.

16. Ibid.

17. Ibid.

18. Henry Olsen, "Republicans' Millennial Problem Isn't What You Think," *City Journal*, May 28, 2018.

19. Galston and Hendrickson, "How Millennials Voted This Election."

20. Pew Research Center, "Changing Attitudes on Gay Marriage," fact sheet, June 26, 2017.

21. Tara Bahrampour, "'There Isn't Really Anything Magical About It': Why More Millennials Are Avoiding Sex," *Washington Post*, August 2, 2016; Shana Lebowitz, "9 Ways Millennials Are Approaching Marriage Differently from Their Parents," *Business Insider*, November 19, 2017.

22. Ben Shapiro, "How Conservatives Can Win Back Young Americans," *Weekly Standard*, May 9, 2018.

23. Peter Moore, "Support for Free Trade Highest Among Millennials," YouGov polling, May 10, 2016.

24. Bradley Jones, "Americans' Views of Immigrants Marked by Widening Partisan, Generational Divides," Fact Tank (blog), Pew Research Center, April 15, 2016.

25. Aaron Blake, "Yes, You Can Blame Millennials for Hillary Clinton's Loss," The Fix (blog), *Washington Post*, December 2, 2016.

26. Mike Vilensky, "The Millennials Shaking Up New York Politics," *Wall Street Journal*, February 14, 2018.

27. Harvard Kennedy School, Institute of Politics, "Harvard Youth Poll Unveils Millennial Agenda for Next President," July 18, 2016.

28. Henry Blodget, "Hey, America, Half of Young Voters Just Voted for Ron Paul—Half!" *Business Insider*, January 12, 2012.

29. Chris Kahn, "Democrats Lose Ground with Millennials," Reuters, April 30, 2018.

30. Steve Peoples and Emily Swanson, "Young People Run from Trump," Associated Press, March 30, 2018.

31. Pew Research Center, "The Generation Gap in American Politics," March 1, 2018.

32. Peoples and Swanson, "Young People Run from Trump."

33. Shapiro, "How Conservatives Can Win Back Young Americans."

34. Peoples and Swanson, "Young People Run from Trump."

35. Pew Research Center, "The Generation Gap in American Politics."

36. Gretchen Livingston, "Over the Past 25 Years, Immigrant Moms Bolstered Births in 48 States," FactTank (blog), Pew Research Center, August 29, 2017.

37. Gordon Hanson, Chen Liu, and Craig McIntosh, "Along the Watchtower: The Rise and Fall of U.S. Low-Skilled Immigration," *Brookings Papers on Economic Activity*, March 2017.

38. For Disney: Yuri Vanetik, "Tax Reform Is Already Benefitting Californians," *Orange County Register*, May 20, 2018; for Kroger: Joe Taschler, "Kroger to Use Tax Cut to Enhance Benefits, Wages," *Milwaukee Journal Sentinel*, April 17, 2018; for Boeing: Boeing, company press release, June 4, 2018, boeing .mediaroom.com/2018-06-04-Boeing-announces-details-of-100-million-employee -education-investment.

39. Clyde Wayne Crews Jr., "Ten Thousand Commandments: An Annual Snapshot of the Federal Regulatory State," Competitive Enterprise Institute, April 19, 2018.

40. Donald J. Trump, Speech announcing candidacy for the presidency, *Time*, June 16, 2015.

41. Jeff Cox, "Trump Lays Into the Federal Reserve, Says He's 'Not Thrilled' About Interest Rate Hikes," CNBC.com, July 19, 2018.

Index

Joseph C. Sternberg is a member of the editorial board of the *Wall Street Journal*, where he writes the Political Economics column. He joined the *Journal* in 2006 as an editorial writer in Hong Kong, where he also edited the Business Asia column. Born in 1982, he lives in London.